# SIGNATURE COCKTAILS

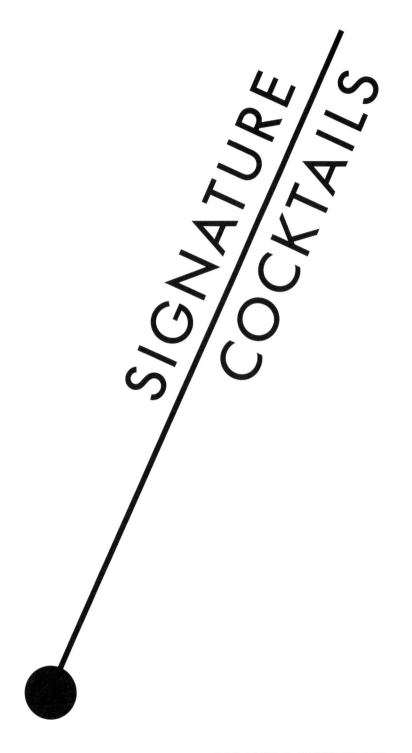

# SIGNATURE COCKTAILS

AMANDA SCHUSTER

YEAR ☉

ORIGIN ⊳

INVENTOR ⚇

PREMISES ⌂

ALCOHOL TYPE ⬦

GLASSWARE ⅄

# FOREWORD

Creating a cocktail that will stand the test of time is the prerogative of mixologists. This goes beyond the mere action of designing a beautiful and acclaimed recipe. It involves marking the memory of guests to the extent of claiming a place in cocktail lore. This collection of 200 signature recipes is testament to how liquid creations have integrated into the lifestyle and eventually the history of humankind throughout the centuries, to become icons encompassing place, culture, feeling, and experience.

So, where does the process of creating a signature start and end? It begins at the intersection where inspiration meets knowledge and technicality. Inspiration can be a vague, all-encompassing term, though. The sort of inspiration that prompts the creation of something remarkable is rare. It is powerful, meaningful, and relates strongly to culturally relevant venues, events, people, and flavours. Plus, it elicits that indefinable emotional connection between the creator and the source of inspiration. It requires the correct expert tools, just as good photography stems from the skills and tools of the photographer, who is able to capture that ephemeral moment in time. Last, but not least, it needs a narrative that can speak to the recipient. No signature piece of work has ever been truly understood if the person receiving it does not have the necessary set of codes to interpret and appreciate it—in this sense, many misunderstood works in the history of art are emblematic in showing us the importance of finding the appropriate set of communication tools to convey the meaning in a masterpiece.

When all of the above-mentioned boxes are ticked, one has the ingredients for a signature cocktail. In this book, you will have the pleasure of discovering, and hopefully preparing, many of them. From Jerry Thomas's Blue Blazer, through to more contemporary creations such as Dick Bradsell's Espresso Martini, passing through best-sellers such as the Negroni, and even wonderful signatures of the current vibrant cocktail era we're experiencing—a period in which I am flattered to find the Connaught Martini, the epitome of a personalized drinking experience.

This ensemble of liquid recipes and stories by cocktail writer Amanda Schuster is not just one of the most comprehensive, but also one of the most compelling because at the heart of this book you won't just find beautiful cocktails; you will get a taste of how a signature mix of liquid ingredients has traveled from one bar and bartender to another, from one country to another, as a simple quest for pleasure or status. These drinks have also become reasons to travel, to visit a venue, and meet a bartender. They are the icon of a destination, prompting a set of expectations, feelings, and memories in those who have experienced them. Over centuries, these cocktails, and the human connections and stories that lie behind them, have also reflected evolving tastes and trends.

In true Phaidon style, this book is a globe-trotting journey through art served in liquid form. It is the art of hospitality, which connects humankind over the pleasure of a glass, and represents the reason why we, and I, love bartending.

*Salute!*

Agostino Perrone

Director of Mixology
The Connaught Hotel, London

# INTRODUCTION

A signature cocktail is a bespoke drink that expresses the nature of the time, person, venue, city, or country for which it was created. One can order a Martini just about anywhere in the world that serves cocktails. However, sipping a Martini in London at Dukes or the Connaught hotel bars are experiences unto themselves. These two distinct and iconic Martinis are prepared with thrillingly unique methods and presentations that characterize those settings. Their marks are on them. It's not just a Martini. It's a Dukes Martini. A Connaught Martini. That's a signature.

A signature can be originated by a bar or bartender—such as the Bellini, created by Giuseppe Cipriani as the house aperitif at Harry's Bar, Venice, and named for Renaissance artist Giovanni Bellini following his grand exhibition in the city in 1948. Or the Espresso Martini by Dick Bradsell at Soho Brasserie, London, the result of a now-legendary request from a certain supermodel.

It might be a recipe that already existed, but the go-to is a perfected version. Dr. Funk is based on a recipe by Dr. Bernard Funk, physician to author Robert Louis Stevenson, who concocted it to help Stevenson cope with the intense heat and humidity of Samoa, and which was then reinvented and popularized in the 1950s, with the addition of rum, at Hollywood's famous Don the Beachcomber's tiki bar.

Maybe the signature represents a place or public figure—think Ian Fleming and the Vesper, which makes its first literary appearance in 1953's *Casino Royale*. Or New Orleans bartender Abigail Gullo's Her Name Is Rio, created as an homage to the band Duran Duran, and served with an edible print on rice paper in the style of their iconic album.

Sometimes it's a recipe born in one city and raised in another, such as the Irish Coffee created at Foyne's Airport in Shannon, Ireland, in the 1940s to wake bleary-eyed travelers arriving from the USA, which was adopted by the Buena Vista Café in San Francisco (before taking over the world); while the Gimlet becomes destination-worthy thanks to Kazuo Uyeda's hard shake technique for Tender Bar in Ginza, Japan.

There are national signatures—Ti' Punch of Martinique (born in Guadeloupe), the Pisco Sour of Peru, or the Siam Sunray of Thailand— as well as playful twists on an existing theme. The Grasshopper Gibson at Hanky Panky, Mexico City, is served with dried grasshoppers and Parmesan, to replicate a traditional Oaxacan snack; and Liz Furlong's Leche de Tigre Martini is made with a clarified mix of sea bass, chili, and peppers (among other things), reminiscent of a Costa Rican white fish ceviche.

And there are dozens of modern classics— Leslie Cofresi's Lavender Mule at La Factoría in Puerto Rico is an elegant take on the Moscow Mule; Anu Apte's Saffron Sandalwood Sour at Rob Roy in Seattle uses flavors of Eastern Indian cuisine in a twist on a gin sour; and Sam Ross at Milk & Honey in New York rearranged the architecture of the Gold Rush and New York Sour to create the Penicillin— to name just a few.

Occasionally a signature marks a moment in time, and we are proud to introduce the Phaidon 100, created by Agostino Perrone in 2023 to celebrate the 100th anniversary of Phaidon Press, the newest cocktail to appear in the book, and its first ever outing in print.

*Signature Cocktails* is both a cultural history and glorious celebration of 200 of the most unique and iconic cocktails from all corners of the globe, brought together for the first time and spanning almost 600 years. Each original recipe is given, alongside a brand-new image of its contemporary interpretation. A glossary provides details of the glassware and terms used throughout, as well as instructions covering the basic recipe components of many of the cocktails in the book—simple and rich syrups, and oleos.

Why did so many cocktails of the past find new life decades later? And do we even need variations on proven formulas like Negronis? In the world of cocktails, there's always room for exploration, ways to adapt flavor combinations, and more ingredients and gadgets within reach than ever before. People and places want to be known for certain drinks, to leave their mark, and more importantly, people want to drink them.

And while it is still possible to visit the Long Bar at Raffles for a Singapore Sling (order both versions), or beat the heat with a Daiquiri at La Floridita in Havana, having the signature punch at Philadelphia's Fish House Club, the Line Cocktail at Café Line in Tokyo, or a Bird of Paradise Fizz at the Strangers Club in Panama would be impossible without a time machine. However, with this book, we can learn their stories, revisit them in spirit, and re-create our own versions.

So grab your tools, friends. A whole world of signatures awaits.

# SIGNATURE COCKTAILS

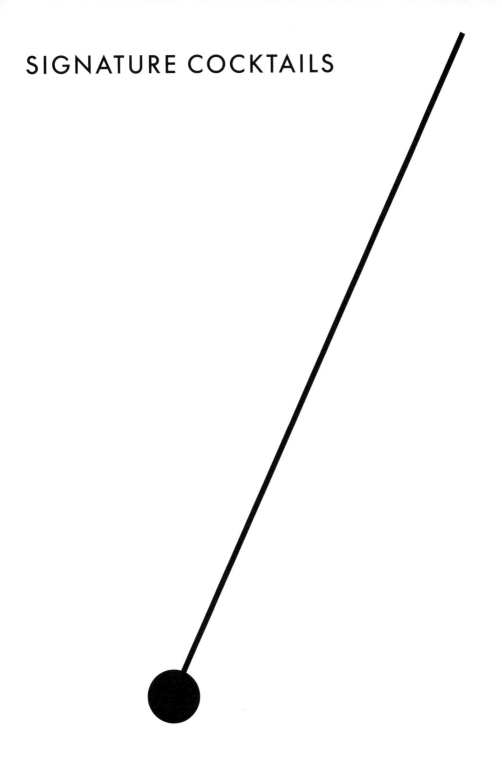

# ATHOLL BROSE

🕐 1475
⚑ HIGHLANDS, SCOTLAND
⚘ EARL OF ATHOLL

⌂ N/A
⚗ SCOTCH
🍸 COUPE OR SMALL ROCKS

Atholl Brose is a Scottish signature associated with Hogmanay—New Year's Eve—as well as other winter celebrations. Also enjoyed in other locales, it's a creamy concoction made from oats and whisky, and named for John Stewart, 1st Earl of Atholl of the Highlands.

Local legend has it that he used a boozy brose (porridge made from oats or other grain and water) as a sort of culinary-based weapon in 1475 to thwart an attack from Iain McDonald, the Earl of Ross, as he was leading a rebellion against King James II. Atholl was given intel that Ross's spies had discovered the well from which he drew his drinking water. This knowledge is said to have inspired him to fill the well with an enticing mixture of honey, oatmeal, and ample amounts of whisky, thus rendering Ross and his posse inebriated beyond all reasonable function when they drank of it. They were then captured and Atholl emerged the hero.

Obviously, Atholl's efforts would have required epic amounts of oats, honey, and whisky—however, there are recipes from roving bon-vivant Charles H. Baker in *The Gentleman's Companion: Being an Exotic Drinking Book* (1939) that provide instructions for far more sensible portions. (No need to serve an entire well's worth just for the sake of authenticity.)

It is advised to begin the process a day ahead for a more harmonious brose-sipping experience. As for the whisky, celebrate Atholl's Highland victory with an unpeated single malt Scotch from the Highlands region, such as GlenDronach, Glenfiddich, Aberfeldy, Deanston, Dalmore, Tomatin, etc.

- 2 oz (60 ml) unpeated Highland single malt Scotch (or blended, unpeated Scotch)
- 1½ oz (45 ml) Traditional Brose Mix
- 1½ oz (45 ml) Honey Syrup (page 86)
- 1 oz (30 ml) heavy (double) cream

- Garnish: grated nutmeg or cinnamon (optional)

Combine all ingredients in a cocktail shaker with ice and shake for at least 20 seconds. Strain into a coupe or small rocks glass and garnish with grated nutmeg or cinnamon, if desired.

## For the Traditional Brose Mix

- 12 oz (360 ml) water
- ½ cup (100 g) steel cut (pinhead) oats

Boil the water in a saucepan. Stir in the oats, then remove from the heat and let sit overnight. Strain and reserve the liquid (which is now brose), and discard the oats.

# FISH HOUSE PUNCH

🕒 1730s
⚐ PHILADELPHIA, USA
👤 UNKNOWN

⌂ COLONY CLUB
🍶 RUM
🍸 PUNCH

Ask a real cocktail nerd for their favorite punch recipe to serve to a crowd, and chances are they'll name the Fish House Punch.

It's one of those recipes that resurfaced during the cocktail renaissance, although it dates much farther back than most of the others. One of its biggest fans is historian David Wondrich, who serves it at July 4 gatherings, and has even said it should be taught as part of the mandatory American history curriculum. A sweetened mix of lemon, rum, and fruit brandies, it was the signature serve at the Colony Club in Schuylkill, Pennsylvania, just outside of Philadelphia, which opened in 1732. Its upper-class members, many considered important figures in the American Revolution, referred to it as their "fish house."

Notably, the drink was not created by a club steward. According to Wondrich, the members of the club each had their own task in bringing the venue's banquets to life. They wore wide-brimmed straw hats and large white aprons with fishes on them as they prepared food and mixed the punch. The recipe was likely developed some time in the 1790s, when punches with more than one spirit were *de rigueur*.

Although no official recipe was revealed at the time, it wasn't exactly a secret with club members. Recipes began to show up in print by the 1850s, including in Jerry Thomas' *How To Mix Drinks, or the Bon-Vivant's Companion* published in 1862, and have undergone multiple tweaks and ingredient substitutions over the centuries.

Note: freeze water in a small bowl or bundt pan (tin) to create a large block of ice the day before serving. This is the best way to keep the prepared punch cool and not dilute it too much as it sits. Additionally, plan to begin making the punch a couple of hours before serving, even the morning (or night!) before.

Serves 18 to 20

- 1 cup (200 g) sugar
- 4 lemons, peeled, with peels set aside
- 32 oz (950 ml) hot water (some prefer using brewed black tea for extra flavor)
- 8 oz (240 ml) lemon juice
- 32 oz (950 ml) dark rum, preferably a mildly estery style such as those from Jamaica
- 16 oz (480 ml) cognac or good grape brandy
- 4 oz (about 120 ml) peach brandy

- Garnish: grated nutmeg and at least 2 lemons, sliced

Create an ole-saccharum in a large bowl by thoroughly mixing the sugar with the lemon peels (best done with clean hands) and letting it sit for at least 30 minutes (a couple of hours is best) to release the lemon oils. Dissolve the sugar in the same bowl with the hot water. Do not discard the peels. Add the lemon juice and spirits and mix. Grate nutmeg over, add ice, and arrange lemon slices over the top.

# BOOTHBY

- ◷ 1800s
- ⚐ SAN FRANCISCO, USA
- ⚇ WILLIAM T. BOOTHBY
- ⌂ PALACE HOTEL
- ⬥ WHISKEY
- ⏝ COUPE

A good bartender makes decent drinks and maintains a tidy, well-run bar, all while keeping customers' glasses full. A great bartender is a bit of a hot shot, a sweet talker who has stratospheric ambitions to charm a crowd while making terrific drinks that people come back for.

In the late 1890s, William T. Boothby, aka "Cocktail Bill" Boothby, was the most famous bartender on the US West Coast, with a storied pedigree in the business of aiming to please. A San Francisco native (his parents were Forty-Niners), by the time he wiped his first glass, he'd been a vaudeville dancer, real estate agent, tailor, the nineteenth-century equivalent of a pharmaceutical rep selling legal medications, and had run a restaurant/bakery with his mother.

After writing *Cocktail Boothby's American Bartender* and *The World's Drinks and How to Mix Them*, he briefly worked in the local state legislature. Thus, boasting the official title The Honorable William T. Boothby, he became the head bartender at what was then considered one of the rebuilt city's best bars, the Palace Hotel.

This is where he had the idea to take one of the most beloved of stiff drinks, the Manhattan, and put it in gladrags by adding Champagne. Naturally, he named his swanky creation after the chic, charismatic figure he clearly loved most: himself.

Oddly, the recipe isn't in any of Cocktail Bill's books, but it's the drink he's most known for. The bubbles make it festive enough to mix up for New Year's Eve, but it deserves to be sipped at any of life's celebrations, big or small. Just keep in mind that not unlike the man it's named for, having more than one could bowl you over with its charms.

- 2 oz (60 ml) rye whiskey
- 1 oz (30 ml) sweet vermouth
- 2 dashes orange bitters
- 2 dashes aromatic bitters
- 1 oz (30 ml) chilled Brut Champagne or other dry sparkling wine

- Garnish: cocktail cherry

In a mixing glass, stir all ingredients except the bubbly with ice until well chilled. Strain into a chilled coupe glass. Top with bubbly and add a cherry to the bottom of the glass.

# CLOVER CLUB

🕐 1800s
⚑ PHILADELPHIA, USA
🙎 UNKNOWN

⌂ CLOVER CLUB, BELLEVUE-
STRATFORD HOTEL
🍶 GIN
🍸 COUPE

The Clover Club is one of, if not *the*, only cocktail to be the namesake signature of two major institutions. It originated in the late 1800s in the luxe gentlemen's club of the same name within Philadelphia's Bellevue-Stratford hotel. Its members were mostly writers and various intellectuals who were known to hold roasts there, and, ironically, this fancy-pants group of males did so with a frothy pink drink made with egg white gin, lemon juice, dry vermouth, and raspberries.

Essentially a Daisy cocktail with extra cushioning, the Clover Club was the Cosmo of its day, eventually a hit among members of both sexes of high society. By the turn of the twentieth century, it was served in high-end hotel bars, such as New York City's Waldorf-Astoria and the Plaza. However, by the 1930s, like so many cocktails of the era, it fell between the velvet sofa cracks of time.

In 2008, the Clover Club inspired the name of one of the first major cocktail bars in South Brooklyn. It was opened by three women—Julie Reiner, Susan Federoff, and Christine Williams—as a sort of in-joke, because the original was known to be such an exclusive, yet bawdy gentlemen's club. But the similarity doesn't stop at the name. The Cobble Hill venue, although open to every thirsty (and hungry) customer, also displays exquisite wood paneling, high ceilings, and cozy flourishes, such as a working fireplace.

The fruity, yet not-too-sweet classic is a crowd-pleaser for both gin afficionados and gin newbies alike. A few recipes over the years have called for the use of store-bought syrups and even grenadine for the raspberry component, but using fresh raspberry syrup captures the tartness of the fruit along with the sweetness. Pro tip: using raspberry jam also works beautifully in a pinch, though it's recommended to try the syrup, if possible.

- 1½ oz (45 ml) dry gin
- ½ oz (15 ml) dry vermouth
- ½ oz (15 ml) fresh lemon juice
- ½ oz (15 ml) Raspberry Syrup (or use 1 heaping barspoon raspberry jam)
- ½ oz (15 ml) egg white (about half of a whole egg)

- Garnish: 1 to 3 fresh raspberries

Combine all ingredients in a cocktail shaker and dry shake (without ice) for about 20 seconds. Add ice and shake until well chilled. Strain into a coupe glass. Garnish with berries threaded on a cocktail pick laid across the rim of the glass.

### For the Raspberry Syrup

- 1 cup (200 g) granulated sugar
- 5 oz (150 g) fresh raspberries

Add the sugar and 1 cup (250 ml) water to a medium saucepan and cook over medium heat until the sugar dissolves, about 5 minutes. Add the raspberries and reduce the heat to low, cooking the berries until they break down, about 5 minutes. (It's OK to use a spoon or spatula to press them into the liquid to help them along.) Allow to cool, then strain into a sealed container. The syrup will keep in the refrigerator for up to 10 days.

# QUOIT CLUB PUNCH

⏲ 1800s  
⚐ RICHMOND (VIRGINIA), USA  
👤 JASPER CROUCH  

⌂ QUOIT CLUB  
🍶 BRANDY  
🍸 PUNCH  

....................................................................................................

The Quoit Club was founded in 1788 in Richmond, Virginia as a members-only social club that hosted two main outdoor lawn activities: throwing heavy objects and drinking punch, often at the same time. The club, and its house punch, are named for quoits, weighty metal ring-shaped objects that are hurled toward a post a few feet away, similar to horseshoes before that was also popularized as sport. The weekend barbecues at the club surrounding this game were attended by Virginia high society, and Jasper Crouch, "a free person of color," was the club's caterer. He is credited with inventing the recipe for the Quoit Club Punch and heralded as one of the first southern Black chefs and bartenders with a recorded following.

Like the Fish House Punch from Philadelphia (page 16), the recipe for Quoit Club Punch is oft interpreted but never exact, though it always includes oleo saccharum, Madeira (the Portuguese fortified wine that was particularly favored among Colonial-era politicians and aristocrats), brandy, rum, and the juice from the oleo lemons — no other non-boozy liquid.

In the contemporary era, Richmond's Jasper Bar, named for Jasper Crouch, gave the Quoit Club Punch a new audience by making it their signature, although the club itself is still in operation. The punch has also made the rounds as an official Virginia state drink.

....................................................................................................

Note: begin preparation several hours ahead. It is recommended to freeze a small bowl of water to use as a large ice cube.

Serves 18 to 20

• 2 x 25 oz (750 ml) bottles grape brandy (VSOP cognac or similar)
• 16 oz (480 ml) strong rum (such as Smith & Cross)
• 8 oz (240 ml) dry to medium-dry Madeira
• Oleo Saccharum
• 16 oz (480 ml) fresh lemon juice (use the lemons from the oleo)

Make the oleo several hours or the day before serving and reserve the juice. Just before serving, mix the juice, prepared oleo (including the peels), and all other ingredients in a punch bowl. Add the large ice cube, or if not available, smaller cubes. Ladle into punch glasses.

For the Oleo Saccharum

• 12 whole lemons
• 2 cups (400 g) turbinado sugar

Peel the lemons and set the fruit aside for juicing. Thoroughly mix the lemon peels and sugar in a bowl, making sure the peels are completely coated. Let sit for at least 3 hours (best if longer, or even overnight) until the sugar has dissolved.

....................................................................................................

# PIMM'S CUP

- 🕐 1823
- ⚑ LONDON, UK
- 👤 JAMES PIMM
- ⌂ PIMM'S OYSTER BAR
- 🍸 PIMM'S CUP
- 🍸 HIGHBALL OR PINT

When outside temperatures rise and thirsts call for quenching with something a little more interesting than the workaday gin and tonic, a Pimm's Cup is in order.

The cocktail and the liqueur it's made from are named for nineteenth-century London restaurateur James Pimm. The 2009 book *Spirituous Journey: A History of Drink* mentions that Pimm began serving a light, tall highball/Collins-esque tonic in place of the typical stout or spirit punch to accompany platters of fresh oysters. By the 1850s, the base mixture from Pimm's Oyster Bar (which saw a few different locations throughout the city over the years) was eventually bottled and marketed.

Through the centuries, six Pimm's expressions were commercialized with a different base spirit. The most successful has been the gin-based No. 1 Cup, which is akin to a sling, made with fruit flavorings (mostly citrus), liqueurs, herbs, spices, and sugar.

The basic recipe is simple, but like the Bloody Mary (page 88) or Sherry Cobbler, the garnishes and flavorings used in modern Pimm's Cup presentations vary wildly, depending on the interpretative fancies of the bartender mixing it.

In summertime at London's Lido Café in Hyde Park, Pimm's Cups are often served by the pitcher. Across the pond, they're one of the most-ordered cocktails at the storied Napoleon House in New Orleans. While at the now-closed Ward III in New York City, Pimm's were spiced up with ginger beer instead of ginger ale, sometimes with the addition of Amaro Montenegro. The Copper Grouse in Manchester, Vermont even mixes theirs with mezcal.

Here's the basic recipe from which to launch your Pimm's whims.

- 2 oz (60 ml) Pimm's Cup liqueur (pick your number, but you'll mostly find No. 1 available)
- ½ oz (15 ml) fresh lemon juice
- Ginger ale, to top

- Garnishes: mint sprig, 1 or 2 lemon slices, orange slice, 1-inch (2.5 cm) slice of cucumber, 1 strawberry, sliced*

Add the Pimm's and lemon juice to a highball or pint glass and stir to combine. Add ice cubes, then top with ginger ale. Arrange the garnishes in the glass.

*Some venues opt to muddle the strawberry slices in the glass before adding the Pimm's and lemon, then add more strawberry for garnish. It's never a bad idea.

# TI' PUNCH

⊕ 1840s  ⌂ UNKNOWN
ᑭ MARIE-GALANTE, GUADELOUPE  ᓂ RHUM AGRICOLE
ᗅ UNKNOWN  ᗡ ROCKS

........................................................................

Ti' Punch is the most popular drink in the West Indies, its Creole name a play on the French *"petit punch."* It is said to have originated on Marie-Galante in the Guadeloupe archipelago in the 1840s to celebrate the abolition of slavery. Its key ingredient is rhum agricole, the national spirit of Martinique (although it is also made elsewhere), where more Ti' Punch is served than anywhere else in the world.

In Martinique, Ti' Punch is neither an aperitif nor a digestif—it's consumed any time of day, and with any part of a meal, everywhere both private and public. There are only three ingredients: unaged rhum agricole, sugar or cane syrup, and a wheel or wedge of fresh lime (though most prefer a "coin" of lime, where one side is peel and the other with varying amounts of pulp still attached to it), mixed with a *bois lélé*, a five-pronged stirrer made from a local plant of the same name.

Rhum agricole, produced exclusively from fresh sugar cane juice, is the pride of Martinique, and there, Ti' Punch is often served with the bottle on the table to showcase the work of local distillers and celebrate the spirit in all its grassy, slightly musky glory. Some maintain the rhum must not be diluted, therefore it is traditionally served without ice. However, for the sake of refreshment, ice does come into play in some serves, particularly in other locales.

Bars around the world with good rum selections have also adopted the Ti' Punch. Naturally, variations abound—as highballs, with added flavors, frozen, etc. However, the best way to get to know it is the classic preparation. Use granulated sugar if a layer of sweetness at the bottom of the glass is preferred; use syrup if a more streamlined texture is called for.

........................................................................

- 1 lime coin with pulp still attached
- 1 tsp (some prefer as much as a tbsp or more) cane sugar or cane syrup, to taste
- 2 oz (60 ml) white rhum agricole (such as Rhum Clémont Blanc)

- Garnish: additional lime coin (optional)

Squeeze the lime coin into a rocks glass. Add the sugar or syrup and press the lime into the sweetener until dissolved using a *bois lélé*, muddler, or spoon. Add the rhum agricole (and ice if using) and stir to mix. Garnish with an additional lime coin, if desired.

........................................................................

# SMOKING BISHOP

| | |
|---|---|
| 🕐 1843 | ⌂ N/A |
| ⚑ UK | 🝪 RED WINE; PORT |
| 👤 (POP. BY) CHARLES DICKENS | 🍸 HEATPROOF GLASS MUG |

The Smoking Bishop is a centuries-old warm mulled wine or punch (aka wassail)-type beverage made with port and roasted Seville oranges that was popularized in nineteenth-century Victorian England during the winter holiday season. The writer Charles Dickens, though not quite the Hemingway-esque drink connoisseur of his time, was known to enjoy a good tipple, and the Smoking Bishop features in his 1843 classic, *A Christmas Carol*.

Toward the end of the book, Scrooge says to his bedraggled employee Bob Cratchit, "I'll raise your salary and endeavor to assist your struggling family and we will discuss your affairs this very afternoon, over a Christmas bowl of Smoking Bishop, Bob!"

This sweet-spiced hot punch is all about communal celebrations and good cheer. That Scrooge had come around and offered to share a Smoking Bishop with Cratchit is significant in that he is not only displaying his newfound generosity by buying a round, but he also wants to enjoy it with him as a neighborly gesture in the true spirit of Christmas. Offering to share in a Smoking Bishop was Victorian speak for "let's live a little."

Smoking Bishop's ingredients harken to a time when port-style fortified wine flowed heavily in Great Britain, since the country owned most of the fortified wine-making estates in Portugal and, through shipping commerce, had steady access to citrus from there and Spain. That specific variety of orange may be tough to come by now, particularly during December, as it's more in season in the earlier months of the year. In the *New York Times*, writer Rosie Schaap suggests using five navel oranges and one lemon as a substitute to capture the slight bitterness of Sevilles.

---

Note: start making this a day ahead.

Serves 10 to 12

- 6 Seville oranges (or 5 navel and 1 lemon), rinsed well and dried
- 30 whole cloves
- ½ cup (100 g) Demerara sugar
- 25 oz (750 ml) fruity-style red wine
- 25 oz (750 ml) ruby-style port
- 2 cinnamon sticks
- Whole spices, such as cardamom, star anise, etc. (optional)

- Garnish: grated nutmeg (optional) and orange peel

Preheat an oven to 325°F (165°C). Stud the whole citrus with cloves so that each one has an equal amount studded throughout. Roast in the oven for an hour, then transfer to a glass or ceramic bowl. Add the sugar and red wine to the bowl. Cover and let stand at room temperature for at least 12 hours, or up to 24 hours.

Cut the fruits in half and juice them through a strainer (sieve) back into the same bowl with the wine and sugar. Mix, then strain into a heavy medium saucepan and discard the solids. Add the port, cinnamon, and, if desired, other whole spices (a few pieces of cardamom, star anise, etc.) to the pot. Heat on low until vapors rise (that's the "smoking" bit), but don't allow to come to a full boil. Remove the solid spices, grate a few scrapes of nutmeg over the top, if using, and either transfer to a heatproof bowl to serve or ladle directly from the pot into heatproof glass mugs or punch cups. Serve warm and garnish with an orange peel in each cup.

# BLUE BLAZER

🕐 1850s
⚑ NEW YORK CITY, USA
🅐 JERRY THOMAS

⌂ OCCIDENTAL HOTEL
◊ WHISKY
🍸 HEATPROOF GLASS MUG

A Blue Blazer is a Scotch hot toddy that is prepared as the liquid is passed back and forth between two mugs while set aflame. Although its origin is up for debate, this pyrotechnic spectacle is closely linked to nineteenth-century New York City bartender Jerry Thomas—the most widely circulated illustration of him even depicts him gracefully making one in a long arc—who was the first to write down a recipe, which appeared in his 1862 book *How To Mix Drinks*.

And if Thomas isn't the originator (there is evidence he once took credit), he could at least be attributed with perfecting the quintessential Blue Blazer specs and technique from a version he either first witnessed during his time serving in the US Navy, or much later at the St. Nicholas Hotel while he was working nearby at the Occidental.

Drink historian David Wondrich notes that by the 1880s this style of flair bartending was already passé and, by the 1930s, so were the high-proof single malt Scotch whiskies that were inherently flammable. However, the late twentieth- and early twenty-first-century obsession with antiquated techniques, as well as the prevalence of cask strength whiskies, have, well, reignited appreciation for this sort of bar theater.

The original Blue Blazer recipe calls for Scotch, though as the cocktail and the technique of passing a flaming liquid between mugs have become synonymous, modern interpretations often swap out the Scotch for other whiskies and base spirits—rum, gin, tequila, mezcal, brandy, other liqueurs, etc. It's been noted, particularly by modern cocktail revivalist Dale DeGroff, that if not using a high-strength spirit, preheating it prior to setting the whole drink ablaze should do the trick.

Note: it is important to clear the prep area of anything flammable before proceeding, and, as an added precaution, have a damp towel and perhaps even a fire extinguisher at hand. Use flameproof mugs with ample handles.

Serves 2

- 4 oz (120 ml) high-proof
  (50% ABV or over) Scotch whisky
- 2 barspoons Demerara or raw sugar
- 3 oz (90 ml) boiling water,
  plus extra to heat mugs

- Garnish: 2 lemon twists

Preheat two glass toddy mugs, or other non-ceramic, heatproof mugs, with boiling water, then discard before proceeding. Add the whisky, sugar, and 3 oz (90 ml) boiling water to one of the mugs, then carefully light the liquid within. Pass the flaming liquid between the mugs (Thomas was known for his ability to perform this task in a long, perfect, blazing arc, but it's more than acceptable at first to just get it between the mugs over a much shorter distance) at least four or five times. Divide the liquid evenly between the mugs and, if necessary, extinguish the liquid using the bottom of the opposite mug. Garnish each mug with a lemon twist.

# PISCO PUNCH

| | | | |
|---|---|---|---|
| ◔ | 1850s | ⌂ | BANK EXCHANGE SALOON |
| ⚑ | SAN FRANCISCO, USA | ◊ | PISCO |
| 🜨 | DUNCAN NICOL | ⅄ | COUPE OR ROCKS |

If a cocktail can be a mascot, Pisco Punch is San Francisco's. For almost as long as there has been Pisco, the grape brandy from Chile and Peru, there has been punch. However, the version most associated with the city, which by the 1850s had become a sort of West Coast host to the spirit thanks to immigrant miners, belongs to Duncan "Pisco John" Nicol, a Scotsman who ran the Bank Exchange Saloon from 1893 until Prohibition. *The Oxford Companion to Spirits & Cocktails* mentions that those who consumed even one cup of his potent formula were quoted as claiming it would inspire the urge to "make a gnat fight an elephant." Gary Kamiya states in a December 27, 2019 article for the *San Francisco Chronicle* that author Rudyard Kipling once said, "I have a theory it [Pisco Punch] is compounded of cherub's wings, the glory of a tropical dawn, the red clouds of sunset, and fragments of lost epics by dead masters."

Nicol apparently took his personal formula to the grave, although some sources, such as his personal friend Emile J. Peterson, have published recipes claiming to have been passed on at Nicol's deathbed. However, apparently none have quite captured the specific buzz experienced at the hands of Nicol. Further investigation suggests some of the tonics and syrups could have contained cocaine, which was not well regulated at the time, and was even in the original Coca-Cola formula. Hence the secret.

Regardless, Pisco Punch, albeit less heady, and probably much safer to drink these days, is still a big part of San Francisco bar culture, served throughout the city, including at the Comstock Saloon. Although as with any good punch, each bar serves its own tweak.

---

- 2 oz (60 ml) Pisco Punch Mix
- ¾ oz (22 ml) fresh lemon or lime juice
- 1½ oz (45 ml) water (ideally distilled)

- Garnish: pineapple chunk

Stir all ingredients with cracked ice. Strain into a large, chilled coupe or into a rocks glass over fresh ice. Garnish with the pineapple chunk on the rim of the glass.

For the Pisco Punch Mix

- 2½ cups (500 g) sugar
- 8¼ oz (250 ml) water (distilled preferred)
- 1 pineapple, cut into rings
- 25 oz (750 ml) Peruvian Pisco

Heat the sugar and water in a saucepan until the sugar is dissolved. Cut the pineapple rings into 6 to 8 wedges each and add to the syrup, letting it sit overnight. Strain and discard the chunks and refrigerate the syrup to cool. Combine the Pisco and a generous cup (250 ml) of the syrup and place in an airtight container with a lid. Keeps for about a week in the refrigerator.

# SOYER-AU-CHAMPAGNE

| | |
|---|---|
| ⏲ 1851 | ⌂ SOYER'S UNIVERSAL SYMPOSIUM OF ALL NATIONS |
| ⚑ LONDON, UK | |
| ⚥ ALEXIS BENOÎT SOYER | 🍾 CHAMPAGNE |
| | 🍸 COUPE OR MARTINI |

Soyer-au-Champagne is an ice cream soda for adults. Imagine a root beer float, but with vanilla ice cream frothing in a decadently potent mix of Champagne, maraschino liqueur, orange curaçao, and brandy instead of the soda pop. This fanciful concoction was conceived by Alexis Benoît Soyer, London's most famous chef of the mid-1850s. According to drink historians Anistatia Miller and Jared Brown in *Spirituous Journey: A History of Drink Book Two*, the French gourmet was so in demand that he made £1,000 a year (that's around £1.2 million in 2022) running the kitchen at the Reform Club.

In 1851, Soyer opened Soyer's Universal Symposium of All Nations on the site of what is now the Royal Albert Hall. It was a complex of different culinary vignettes with separate themes, including a Chinese boudoir, an Italian grotto, and even a dungeon (one can only imagine what was served in that room, and how it was delivered). Soyer-au-Champagne was on the drinks menu, which also included Mint Juleps, Brandy Smashes, and Nectar Cobblers (also his own creation), but it wasn't a runaway hit at the time. According to Miller and Brown, it wasn't until the 1880s, a couple of decades following Soyer's death, that his Champagne float became a sensation among the upper classes and was reportedly a favorite treat of Queen Victoria. In the UK and parts of Europe, it is now associated with the Christmas holidays.

Although it may be rare to find year-round these days, Soyer-au-Champagne is still one of the signature offerings at St Pancras Hotel in London, where the bubbly delight has been served since the nineteenth century.

- 1 scoop (ideally French) vanilla ice cream
- ½ oz (15 ml) cognac
- ½ oz (15 ml) orange curaçao liqueur
- ½ oz (15 ml) maraschino liqueur
- Brut Champagne or other dry sparkling wine, to top

- Garnish: orange slice and/or cocktail cherry

Scoop the ice cream into a large coupe or Martini glass. Add the other liqueurs to the glass and top with the bubbly. Garnish with an orange slice and/or cocktail cherry.

# BLACK VELVET

| | | | |
|---|---|---|---|
| ⊕ | 1861 | ⌂ | BROOKS'S CLUB |
| ⚑ | LONDON, UK | ◊ | GUINNESS STOUT; CHAMPAGNE |
| ⚥ | UNKNOWN | ⏣ | PINT |

........................................................................................................

The UK was in a state of shock when Prince Albert, husband of Queen Victoria, died in his bed at Windsor Castle on December 14, 1861 of what was reported as typhoid fever. At this point, it could be argued that no other royal passing had had quite the same impact on British society as that of the Prince at age forty-two. The entire country, including public services, went into a prolonged state of mourning.

At the time, Brooks's Club on St. James's Street, London was a gentlemen-only establishment—and the sort that was not just for *any* man of British society either. They reportedly stated that the royal death was so devastating that "even the Champagne should be in mourning, dressed all in black." To mark the occasion, an unnamed steward (a source at the still-existing club states there is no record of his name, but that he might as well be called "George," since there is a long line of stewards with that name) added Guinness Extra Stout to Champagne.

"George" was not the first to add stout-style beer to bubbly—other concoctions, such as the Menschenfreund ("Philanthropist"), popular with German students in the 1830s, precede it. However, the Black Velvet is the version that specifically calls for Guinness as the stout ingredient.

While it is still considered a mourning drink, it is also considered a morning drink. Bars and pubs around the world tend to serve it most often at midday, and it is also seen on many a brunch menu. Many swear by it as a hangover cure as well.

"An even balance of rich, frothy stout and light, fizzy Champagne—this is a happy marriage," say drinks historians Anistatia Miller and Jared Brown in their 1990 book *Champagne Cocktails*.

........................................................................................................

Add about 6 oz (180 ml) Guinness Stout to a pint glass, preferably a chilled one (this will be just over half the way up the glass if merely eyeballing it). Then top the rest with chilled Champagne. No need to stir.

........................................................................................................

# BAMBOO

🕒 1870s
▷ YOKOHAMA, JAPAN
𝗔 LOUIS EPPINGER

⌂ GRAND HOTEL
◊ SHERRY
🍸 NICK & NORA

The Bamboo cocktail was born in San Francisco, but its star rose in Japan. It was created in the 1870s by Bay Area bartender Louis Eppinger when he tended bar on Halleck Street, traveled with him briefly to Portland, Oregon, and then famously became a fixture on the menu at the Grand Hotel in Yokohama, Japan, where he managed the bar from 1890 until his death in 1908. It's been a staple all over Japan and is a go-to low-ABV recipe in modern mixology around the world.

According to spirits historian David Wondrich, Bamboo is the second cocktail on record to use sherry split with vermouth and dashes of bitters (the first is Adonis [page 46], distinguished with its use of sweet vermouth while Bamboo uses dry). In recent times, sherry as a cocktail ingredient has become somewhat of a secret handshake, signifying a certain level of sophistication. However, in the late 1800s, the use of sherry was simply a bar hack, used

to replace the higher ABV wallop of spirits, such as whiskey, gin, or brandy, but also likely because it packed good flavor while holding a shelf life.

Bamboo first appears in William T. "Cocktail Bill" Boothby's 1934 book *World Drinks and How to Mix Them*, but that recipe does not specify which sherry to use, and simply calls for "French vermouth," orange bitters, and 2 drops of simply "bitters," though one assumes that would mean an aromatic such as Angostura. Most modern serves use dry or medium-dry sherry styles (Palo Cortado, Manzanilla, Fino, dry Oloroso, Amontillado), and in slightly higher proportions, modified with dry vermouth. Updated recipes sometimes add further flair, as did bartender and consultant Natasha David at now-closed low-ABV-focused New York City bar Nitecap, where the frozen Bamboozicle (page 302) was a crowd favorite.

Eppinger's recipe

- 1½ oz (45 ml) sherry
- 1½ oz (45 ml) French vermouth
- 2 dashes orange bitters
- 2 drops bitters

- Garnish: lemon or orange twist, green olive (optional)

Stir all ingredients with ice until well-chilled. Strain into a Nick & Nora glass. Twist the citrus peel over the drink and place in the glass. Thread a green olive (if using) on a cocktail pick, and balance on the rim of the glass.

# CRITERION MILK PUNCH

🕐 1870s
⚑ LONDON, UK
👤 LEO ENGEL

⌂ CRITERION
🍶 BRANDY; RUM
🍸 PUNCH

The Criterion Milk Punch was created by bartender Leo Engel when he was hired to come up with an opening menu for the American Bar (aka Long Bar) at The Criterion, London in 1874. This was a year after the impressive five-story eatery complex was cofounded by Australian restaurateurs Felix William Spiers and Christopher Pond in the heart of Piccadilly Circus. According to *The Oxford Companion to Spirits & Cocktails*, the American Bar was the first "fully-realized" American bar, meaning a bar serving mixed or what were known as "American-style" drinks, in London.

But because the average Londoner was not yet used to ice cold serves, this clarified milk punch became the signature darling of the bar and sold more than anything else on the menu. Apparently, the Brits could always relate to a good punch.

The Criterion's punch recipe using clarified milk has served as a template for many other punches in London and elsewhere around the world. Because of its labor-intensive (but worth it!) steps, and because punches in general fell out of fashion, Criterion Milk Punch had dropped out of rotation by the mid- to late twentieth century. However, it was revived in London in 2006 by bar consultant Nick Strangeway, when he opened Hawksmoor Spitalfields and then Mark's Bar at HIX in Soho. It has since been adapted and riffed on by numerous bars in the US and UK. The Connaught Bar in London notably still uses it as the basis for their house milk punches.

Engel's recipe

Put the following ingredients into a very clean pitcher: The juice of three lemons, the rind of two lemons; one pound of powdered [icing] sugar; one pine-apple, peeled, sliced, and pounded; six cloves, twenty coriander seeds; one small stick of cinnamon; one pint of brandy; one pint of rum; one gill of arrack; one cup of strong green tea; one quart of boiling water; the boiling water to be added last. Cork this down to prevent evaporation, and allow these ingredients to steep for at least six hours, then add a quart of hot milk and the juice of two lemons. Mix and filter through a jelly bag, and when the punch has passed bright, bottle it and cork it tightly.

# AMERICANO

🕘 1880s               ⌂ CAMPARI BAR
⚑ MILAN, ITALY      ◊ CAMPARI; VERMOUTH
A GASPARE CAMPARI    Y HIGHBALL

Think of an Americano as the "little red dress" of bittersweet aperitivo cocktails. It can be dressed up with other "jewels" (spirits), but on its own is still elegant in its sleek simplicity. It is a combination of Italian aperitivo, a digestive bitter liqueur with a tawny-orange hue, red Italian vermouth, and seltzer or club soda, served in a tall glass over ice with an orange or lemon twist.

The Americano rose to popularity in Milan in the late 1880s as an offshoot of the Torino Milano, a combination of Turin's local vermouth and Campari from Milan served at the Campari bar and, eventually, other cafés. American tourists preferred a highball serve to tone down the bitters, but the Italians soon caught on to its refreshment. The Americano is considered the first known thread between traditional Italian aperitivo drinking culture and American bartending.

The Americano was famously the canvas upon which the ever-popular Negroni was created. Legend has it that in 1918, weary of bubbles and thirsty for something more high octane, Count Camillo Negroni returned to Milan from North America and requested bartender Fosco Scarselli at Bar Casoni make him an Americano, but hold the soda, booze it up with gin. And thus, the Americano mothered the Negroni.

The Americano continued to be popular throughout Italy and abroad, particularly through the Swinging Sixties. While it faded from fashion for some time, and was more recently upstaged by the Negroni, the Americano is still valued for its chic straight-forwardness and adaptability, particularly when showcasing a new swath of aperitivo and/or bitter liqueur brands and vermouths now available in the marketplace, either as a traditional serve or in more intricate spritz interpretations. Many bars around the world even serve house Americanos on tap.

• 1½ oz (45 ml) red vermouth
  (Italian for authenticity)
• 1½ oz (45 ml) Campari or other
  Italian-style aperitivo
• Soda water, to top

• Garnish: orange wedge

Combine the vermouth and aperitivo in a tall or double rocks glass and stir. Add ice, top with soda water, and stir again. Garnish with an orange wedge.

# RICKEY

🕐 1880s
⚑ WASHINGTON, D.C., USA
👤 GEORGE A. WILLIAMSON

⌂ SHOOMAKER'S BAR
🍶 GIN
🍸 HIGHBALL

"Only a few years ago . . . I was Col. Rickey, of Missouri, the friend of senators, judges and statesmen and something of an authority on political matters and political movements . . . But am I ever spoken of for those reasons? I fear not. No, I am known to fame as the author of the 'rickey,' and I have to be satisfied with that." These are the words of Col. Joseph Rickey, which appeared in an article titled "Not Proud of His Honors" in *The Wellsboro Gazette*, July 26, 1901.

He's speaking of his namesake cocktail, the Rickey highball, which most of us consume made with gin or bourbon and lime juice. Drink consultant Derek Brown says the Rickey legacy can be traced to the 1880s at Shoomaker's bar in Washington, D.C., likely when Col. Joe Rickey stopped in with his friends Representative William Hatch and

Fred Mussey to visit bartender George A. Williamson. Rickey was feeling a little delicate after the previous night's shenanigans, and, spying a bowl of limes on the bar, Hatch suggested adding some lime juice to their bourbon highballs. It henceforth became known as the "Joe Rickey" drink.

Over time, the "Joe" part was dropped, as well as the bourbon, and the gin Rickey took its place as the default preparation, spawning numerous variations as well as pop cultural appearances, with F. Scott Fitzgerald's *The Great Gatsby* being its most famous cameo of the era.

According to Brown, in 2011, the Rickey was named Washington, D.C.'s "official native cocktail," with July known locally as an official Rickey Month that includes Rickey-themed cocktail competitions.

• 1¾ oz (50 ml) dry gin or bourbon
• 3½ oz (100 ml) sparkling water or soda water
• 2 lime wedges

Add the gin and sparkling water or soda water to a highball glass filled with ice. Squeeze the lime wedges into the drink, drop them in, and give it all a quick stir.

Note: the typical instructions call for the juice of half a lime. However, this measurement can be problematic, depending on the size and species of the lime. *SIP: 100 Gin Cocktails With Only 3 Ingredients*, published by Sipsmith Gin, suggests using the more reliable measurement of the juice of two lime wedges instead.

# ADONIS

🕐 1884/85
⚑ NEW YORK CITY, USA
👤 JOSEPH F. MCKONE

⌂ HOFFMAN HOUSE
🍶 SHERRY
🍸 NICK & NORA

The Adonis has the distinction of being the first popular low-ABV, sherry-based cocktail in recorded history. It's named for a wildly successful musical that first opened in Chicago in the early 1880s; the tribute was invented a couple of years later by Joseph F. McKone, head bartender at Madison Square's Hoffman House hotel in New York City, to celebrate the 500th Broadway performance of what was the *Hamilton* of its day.

This cocktail, so closely associated with theater, was invented in what was itself a showstopper of a bar, which, according to cocktail historian David Wondrich in *The Oxford Companion to Spirits & Cocktails*, included paintings by famous artists, such as J. M. W. Turner, and a nymph-tastic centerpiece by William-Adolphe Bouguereau, as well as an authentic Napoleonic tapestry. The grandiose bar would not survive the 1890s, but the cocktail lived on as a signature at the Waldorf-Astoria hotel, which is sometimes incorrectly cited as its origin. The recipe appears in the 1935 *Old Waldorf-Astoria Bar Book*, as well as the 2016 update by then beverage manager Frank Caiafa.

Think of Adonis as the older and more *zaftig* of the two most famous sherry-and-vermouth aperitifs of its day—the other being the Bamboo, invented a couple of years later, made with vermouth blanc. While they both call for a drier style of sherry, the use of sweet vermouth in the Adonis adds more body and heft, as well as spice notes. As a popular go-to, low-ABV cocktail option, as with the Bamboo, modern recipes for the Adonis often call for a higher ratio of sherry to vermouth than the original recipe. Aside from its popularity in modern cocktail bars, it has enjoyed new life in wine bars, served alongside tapas and cheese boards.

• 1½ oz (45 ml) dry sherry (use Manzanilla, Fino, Palo Cortado, or dry Oloroso)
• 1½ oz (45 ml) sweet vermouth
• 2 dashes orange bitters

• Garnish: orange twist

Stir all ingredients in a mixing glass with ice until well chilled. Strain into a Nick & Nora glass. Express the oils from a piece of orange peel into the drink, skin side down, then twist and place in the glass.

# RAMOS GIN FIZZ

| | | | |
|---|---|---|---|
| 🕐 | 1888 | ⌂ | IMPERIAL CABINET SALOON |
| ⚑ | NEW ORLEANS, USA | ◊ | GIN |
| ⚲ | HENRY CHARLES RAMOS | ⍦ | HIGHBALL |

One of the top signature cocktails associated with the city of New Orleans, Louisiana is undoubtedly the Ramos Gin Fizz. People love to sip this aromatic, pillowy delight as much as busy bartenders hate having to make it.

The cocktail is named for Henry Charles Ramos, head bartender of Pat Moran's Imperial Cabinet Saloon from 1887 until Prohibition. Although he may not be the creator of the ingredients part of the recipe, what he *can* take credit for, according to *The Oxford Companion to Spirits & Cocktails*, is the precise and rather strenuous technique of preparing what is essentially a combination of two other popular cocktails of that era—the Silver Fizz (aka New Orleans Fizz) and the Cream Lemonade—shaking the daylights out of it for several minutes (Ramos reportedly shook for 12 minutes), then adding club soda. The result

should form a billowy cloud of egg white foam over a creamy, fizzy sour with a subtle florescence from the orange blossom water.

These days, certain bartenders around town, such as Chris McMillian at Revel, pride themselves on shaking Ramos Gin Fizzes from scratch (he even uses a timer). Other venues, such as Court of Two Sisters, use a special dedicated soda jerk gadget (think boozy egg cream) to prep theirs. A Tales of the Cocktail convention event in the mid-2010s even showcased groups of bartenders taking turns shaking them relay style, a popular method back in the early 1900s when some bars hired "shaker boys" for the task.

Below is a tried-and-true recipe for making a Ramos Gin Fizz. A yummy treat is the reward for a vigorous upper body workout.

- ½ oz (15 ml) fresh lemon juice
- ½ oz (15 ml) fresh lime juice
- ⅓ oz (10 g) powdered (icing) sugar
- 1½ oz (45 ml) dry or Old Tom-style gin (the latter would have been used in the early 1900s)
- ½ oz (15 ml) egg white
- 3 or 4 drops orange blossom water
- 1 oz (30 ml) heavy (double) cream
- 1 oz (30 ml) soda water, chilled

Add all ingredients except the cream and soda water to a shaker filled with ice pellets and shake for a good 15 seconds. Add the cream and shake again for at least 30 seconds, longer for a bigger head of foam. Strain into a chilled highball glass over the soda water and watch the froth work its magic.

# ALABAZAM

| | | | |
|---|---|---|---|
| ⊕ | 1890s | ⌂ | BRIDGE EXCHANGE |
| ⊳ | NEW YORK CITY, USA | ◊ | BRANDY |
| ⅄ | LEO ENGEL/WILLIAM SCHMIDT | ⅄ | HIGHBALL OR DOUBLE ROCKS |

Like many of the earliest cocktail recipes, Alabazam began its life in one iteration, but became a star thanks to another bartender's interpretive tweaks. In this instance, Leo Engel published a bitters-heavy brandy sour recipe called Alabazam in his 1878 book *American and Other Drinks*. However, by the time William Schmidt featured the cocktail in 1892's *The Flowing Bowl: When and What to Drink*, Alabazam was the refreshing sour highball still served around the world today.

Schmidt, who traveled to the US from Heide, Germany, was hands down the most popular bartender in New York City during the 1890s and early 1900s. As he worked behind the bar at George Hillen's Bridge Exchange near the Brooklyn Bridge, he became known for his artful showmanship, delicious drinks, and witty banter, and could perform all three of these talents simultaneously and seamlessly.

Journalists in local and national publications loved writing about him and, by the time he opened his bar on Park Row in 1889, he was known as "The Only William."

*The Flowing Bowl* is one of the rare examples of an early cocktail book featuring mostly original recipes, or at least personal reworkings of ones, such as Alabazam. Schmidt's variation is true to its bones as a brandy sour, but the addition of fizz and just a couple of dashes of orange bitters, as opposed to a major dousing of Angostura, makes it less stodgy than Engel's version.

Schmidt's recipe wears like a good T-shirt, being easy to dress up or down, hence why one can find several video demonstrations online, most notably in 2022 on TikTok by Cincinnati, Ohio-based cocktail maven Molly Wellmann.

- 2 oz (60 ml) Cognac VSOP or aged American brandy
- 1 oz (30 ml) orange liqueur (preferably brandy-based, such as Grand Marnier)
- 1 oz (30 ml) fresh lemon juice
- ½ oz (15 ml) rich syrup
- 1 or 2 dashes orange bitters
- Soda water, club soda, or seltzer, to top

- Garnish: orange twist or orange slice (optional)

Shake all ingredients except the soda water, club soda, or seltzer in a shaker with ice until well chilled. Strain over fresh ice (either large cubes or crushed) into a tall or double rocks glass. Top with fizz and add the garnish, if using.

# QUEEN'S PARK SWIZZLE

🕐 1890s
⚑ PORT OF SPAIN, TRINIDAD
🧍 UNKNOWN

⌂ QUEEN'S PARK HOTEL
🍸 RUM
🍸 HIGHBALL

........................................................................................

There's nothing like a great hotel bar. However, these days it's become the exception, when it used to be the rule, to find one that's simultaneously elegant, comfortable, and serves above-average drinks. Hotel bars had a golden age, and some say Trinidad's Queen's Park Hotel was one of the grandest of them all.

Before the modern era of all-inclusive resorts and hasty cruise stops, in the 1920s the Port of Spain in Trinidad was a bustling center of trade and upscale vacationing. The Queen's Park Savannah neighborhood was its dazzling, vibrant leisure center, a festive destination for eating, drinking, and dancing the night away. And the Queen's Park Hotel was the star of this tropical retreat, where everyone who was anyone, as they say, made a point of staying.

The Queen's Park Swizzle is a tall, boozy rum concoction that Trader Vic famously touted in 1946 as "the most delightful form of anesthesia given out today." Although the hotel is long gone, this spectacular Prohibition-era cocktail has survived the ages.

This tall, colorful refresher is not nearly as complicated to prepare as it looks, though it takes time to come together. One just needs a tall glass, the booze, a good swizzle stick, and a willingness to take a few moments to unwind and hang loose.

........................................................................................

• 8 to 12 fresh mint leaves
• 1 oz (30 ml) lime juice
• 1 oz (30 ml) Demerara syrup
• 2 oz (60 ml) aged rum
• 8 dashes Angostura bitters

In a highball glass, muddle the fresh mint leaves in the lime juice and syrup. Fill the glass with crushed ice. Pour the rum over the crushed ice and, using both hands, work the swizzle stick back and forth in the drink until the glass is ice cold and frosted. Add more crushed ice, then top with the bitters.

# DAIQUIRI

- ⏲ 1898
- ⚐ CUBA
- ⚭ JENNINGS S. COX, JR.
- ⌂ N/A
- ⚬ RUM
- ⍬ COUPE

One would assume the original Daiquiri was invented by a skillful *cantinero* in one of the grand bars of Havana, Cuba. However, its origins are far more laid back. In fact, the most famous rum drink of all time, an essential beverage that launched thousands of signatures, was not invented in a bar at all, or by a bartender. Its creator is Jennings S. Cox, Jr., a mining engineer from New York who casually threw it together for Francesco Domenico Pagliuchi, a fellow engineer, commander of the Liberating Army of Cuba, and war correspondent for *Harper's Monthly*.

In 2017's *Spirit of the Cane*, drink historians Anistatia Miller and Jared Brown record how, in 1898, at the end of Cuba's War of Independence, Pagliuchi invited himself for drinks with Jennings at the El Cobre copper mines. Decades later, Pagliuchi reported that, ". . . in the sideboard of the mine's dining room, there was not gin, nor vermouth; there was only Bacardí*, lemons, sugar, and ice" which were shaken together. Jennings said the drink was called a "Rum Sour," but since whiskey sours were then so popular, Pagliuchi suggested the drink be named for the region of its invention: ". . . why not call it 'Daiquiri'?"

The name stuck, but the recipe was tweaked and riffed on many times over the years. What is considered a traditional Daiquiri is the recipe food and travel writer Charles H. Baker published in 1939's *The Gentleman's Companion* using white rum, lime juice (not lemon), and sugar. This simple drink has been added to, subtracted from, multiplied, and divided countless times, and inspired the iconic No. 4 recipe, El Floridita, whizzed in thousands of blenders. Most modern cocktail purists will use it as a, well, barometer of sorts: a well-made Daiquiri will almost certainly indicate a good bar, or at least bartender.

Original Cuban Daiquiri
(based on Charles H. Baker's recipe)

- 1½ oz (45 ml) white rum (*Havana Club 3 Year would be the most authentic to the original Bacardí formula made in Cuba)
- 2 tsp sugar
- 1 oz (30 ml) fresh lime juice

- Garnish: lime wheel (optional)

Shake all ingredients with finely cracked ice until well chilled and frothy. Strain into a coupe glass. Garnish with a lime wheel, if desired.

# COMMODORE

🕐 1899
⚑ CINCINNATI, USA
👤 PHILIP O. GROSS

⌂ HONING HOTEL
🍾 BOURBON
🍸 COUPE

The Commodore is the late nineteenth-century version of what would happen if a Margarita and a Daiquiri had a surrogate love child with a Martini and made it out of American whiskey. According to cocktail writer Robert Simonson in his Substack newsletter *The Mix*, what was originally a mixture of bourbon, orange curaçao, sugar, and lime garnished with an olive and a dash of rum, was invented in the late 1880s or early 1890s by Philip O. Gross while he was behind the bar at the Honing Hotel in Cincinnati, Ohio. Named for naval hero Commodore George Dewey, it was the winner of a cocktail competition against a reported 9,000 (yes, that's the actual figure) other national bartenders.

Years later, Gross would bestow the name Commodore on a local concert hall he was managing. The cocktail was featured in two titles by Harry MacElhone—1922's *ABC of*

*Mixing Cocktails* and 1927's *Barflies and Cocktails*—as well as Harry Craddock's *The Savoy Cocktail Book* in 1930. It became so popular that it was even the official toast for the Silver Jubilee of King George V in 1935.

But despite its fame in the US and UK, the Commodore fell out of circulation during the 1940s and 50s. It wasn't until the early twenty-first century that Molly Wellmann, then owner and head bartender of Japp's cocktail bar, made it a personal mission to revive what had been a local signature and put it on her menu. Her version nixes the curaçao, adds gum syrup instead of the sugar, and uses a healthy measure of blackstrap rum. Simonson notes that both MacElhone and Craddock nix the rum *and* curaçao but use orange bitters for that touch of citric brightness instead. Wellmann's version has become the preferred serve.

• 1½ oz (45 ml) bourbon
• ½ oz (15 ml) lime juice
• ½ oz (15 ml) gum syrup or simple syrup
• 1 oz (30 ml) blackstrap-style rum

Shake the bourbon, lime juice, and syrup with ice until well chilled. Strain into a chilled cocktail glass. Carefully top with the blackstrap rum.

# JACK ROSE

🕐 1899
⚑ NEW YORK CITY, USA
ჿ FRANK HAAS

⌂ EBERLIN'S
◊ APPLEJACK
Y COUPE

The Jack Rose is one of the most polarizing classics from the early twentieth century—people either love or hate it. But those who love it, really love it.

There is some debate over who it's named for—it has been attributed to notorious gambler "Bald Jack" Rose, as well as Jersey City bartender and wrestling enthusiast Frank "Jack Rose," among many other theories. What we do know is that in 1899, it was reported that bartender Frank Haas was making a dusty rose-hued drink he called the Jack Rose for the business folk who flocked to Fred Eberlin's bar in downtown New York City. In 1913, he finally shared the recipe, which was essentially an apple brandy-based riff on the Whisky Daisy: applejack, raspberry syrup, lemon, and orange juice.

From the 1910s onward, the cocktail made the rounds and was eventually reinvented. The surviving streamlined version uses only one kind of citrus, typically lemon but sometimes lime, and grenadine instead of raspberry syrup. In 1917, Tom Bullock, the first Black bartender to write a cocktail book in the US, included the simplified recipe in what is likely its first published form in *The Ideal Bartender*.

This sleeper hit of a drink even got its own literary cameo. In a passage in Ernest Hemingway's 1926 novel *The Sun Also Rises*, the narrator orders a Jack Rose at a bar.

As with many pre-Prohibition cocktails, the Jack Rose seemed lost to history. However, in the early 2000s, the cocktail become a sort of obsession with a new generation of bar folk and aficionados, particularly Jackson Cannon, head bartender at Eastern Standard in Boston and a founding member of the Jack Rose Society, whose mission has been to preserve and defend the legacy of once-forgotten, oft-disparaged cocktails such as the Jack Rose. Cannon makes notable tweaks by increasing the amount of applejack, swapping the ratio of grenadine to citrus, and adding a couple of dashes of Peychaud's bitters for structure.

1910s recipe

- 1½ oz (45 ml) applejack
- ¾ oz (22 ml) fresh lemon or lime juice
- ½ oz (15 ml) high-quality grenadine, homemade or store-bought

- Garnish: lemon peel

Shake all ingredients with ice until well chilled. Strain into a cocktail glass and garnish with lemon peel.

Cannon's recipe

- 2 oz (60 ml) applejack
- ¾ oz (22 ml) grenadine
- ½ oz (15 ml) fresh lemon juice
  2 to 3 dashes Peychaud's bitters

- Garnish: lemon peel (expressed and discarded)

Shake all ingredients with ice until well chilled. Strain into a cocktail glass. Express the oils from the peel over the drink, skin side down, then discard.

# TURF CLUB

&#128336; C.1900

&#9707; UNKNOWN

&#9654; NEW YORK CITY, USA

&#9728; GIN

&#9776; HARRY JOHNSON

&#7468; COUPE OR MARTINI

Cocktailians love a Turf Cocktail, aka Turf Club, for its "deep cuts" status in the classic canon. It's a cool one to name-check, because the drink pre-dates the dry Martini by some decades, although, made from gin, French vermouth, absinthe, maraschino, and orange bitters, it certainly shares DNA. It was invented sometime in the late 1800s, although the variation most consumed now was perfected by German-born New York City bar man Harry Johnson, likely developed while he worked at Delmonico's steak house in lower Manhattan, or perhaps at his swank, albeit sadly short-lived Bowery lounge Little Jumbo. However, it was not one of the drinks listed on the iconic pyramid sign.

Nonetheless, it's one of the drinks most associated with Johnson. The stirred and boozy concoction was originally prepared with Old Tom-style gin, but he had clearly been tinkering with the recipe behind the bar for some time to brighten it up and, by 1900, it was published in his *New and Improved Bartender's Manual* calling for Plymouth gin in a 50/50 measurement with the vermouth. It's one of the first cocktails to mix herbal and woodsy-tasting ingredients together to coax the aromatics out of dry gin.

The Turf Club is one of the last of the oldies to make a comeback, but as of this writing, several modern bars and restaurants have added it to their menus, such as the revamped Gage & Tollner in Brooklyn. It's what people order when they want a stiff cocktail that's like a Martini but are looking to try something new—well, at least new to *them*. Perhaps the old-world flavors themselves add some nostalgic intrigue that seems to match the ornate, vintage-style wallpaper.

- 1½ oz (45 ml) Plymouth gin (or another dry gin)
- 1½ oz (45 ml) vermouth blanc
- ¼ oz (7 ml) maraschino liqueur
- 1 dash orange bitters
- 1 dash absinthe

- Garnish: lemon twist and cocktail cherry

Stir all ingredients with ice (cracked is best) until well chilled. Strain into a chilled coupe or Martini glass. Express the oils of the lemon twist over the drink and discard. Garnish with the cherry.

# BIZZY IZZY

- 1910s
- ST. LOUIS (MISSOURI), USA
- TOM BULLOCK
- ST. LOUIS CLUB
- BOURBON; SHERRY
- HIGHBALL

Nothing beats a refreshing highball in the height of summer. A simple combination of base spirit and soda water typically does the trick. However, order a highball from someone who is truly the master of their craft, and it becomes even more delicious and refreshing.

Such was the case for Tom Bullock, who was the first Black "star-tender" and the first to write his own cocktail manual, 1917's *The Ideal Bartender*. He wrote it during his nearly three decades at the St. Louis Club at the start of the twentieth century and into Prohibition. There, he served the likes of then Colonel Teddy Roosevelt, who famously almost lost a libel case that questioned his claims of sobriety, because a 1913 editorial in the *St. Louis Post-Dispatch* adulated so effusively over the deliciousness of Bullock's Mint Juleps. There was no way Roosevelt tasted only part of one and left the rest, it argued. "Have we found the living superman at last?"

As terrific as Bullock's Julep must have been, in modern times, Bizzy Izzy is considered his signature. It's named for Izzy Mark, a character popularized by vaudeville performer George Sidney in the 1910s. It's a simple drink made phenomenal by the sum of its parts—lemon juice, pineapple syrup, sherry, and rye or bourbon topped with soda water.

The scrumptious warm weather pick-me-up is still served from Brooklyn to Belgium, plus everywhere outside and in between.

Bullock's original recipe

- 2 dashes lemon juice
- 2 tsp pineapple syrup
- ½ jigger sherry wine
- ½ jigger rye or bourbon whiskey
- Soda water, to top

Drop "one piece of ice"* into a highball glass. Add the remaining ingredients and top with soda water.

*"One piece of ice" would have referred to a long, rectangular block cut to fit the glass.

Bartender Al Sotack's interpretation, with sweetener added along with juice instead of pineapple syrup, a staple on the menu at Jupiter Disco in Brooklyn, NY.

- 1 oz (30 ml) rye whiskey
- 1 oz (30 ml) Amontillado sherry
- 1 oz (30 ml) pineapple juice
- ¾ oz (45 ml) lemon juice
- ¾ oz (45 ml) simple syrup
- 1 dash Angostura bitters
- Soda water, to top

- Garnish: lemon wheel

Combine all ingredients, except the soda water, in a mixing tin and shake with ice. Strain into a Collins glass over ice. Garnish with a lemon wheel.

# PEGU CLUB

🕐 1910s
⚐ RANGOON, BURMA
👤 UNKNOWN

⌂ PEGU CLUB
🍸 GIN
🍸 COUPE

The original Pegu Club in what was then known as Rangoon, Burma (now Yangon, Myanmar), was not a glitzy cocktail lounge, but one of several private British officers' clubs in the then colonized territories throughout Asia. Granted, it was still a place in which to socialize and enjoy mixed drinks, and the house cocktail was a sharp combination of gin, bitters, lime juice, and orange curaçao.

The precise attribution for the recipe is lost to history, but the Pegu Club cocktail was served there since at least the early 1900s, possibly earlier, and the recipe first appeared in print in the 1927 edition of *Barflies and Cocktails* by Harry MacElhone. The drink gained international recognition when Harry Craddock borrowed MacElhone's recipe for the 1930 *Savoy Cocktail Book* and added a few "modern" tweaks, such as Rose's lime juice.

The fresh version, however, was still favored in some establishments throughout London and elsewhere.

In 2005, Audrey Saunders opened a modern upper-floor cocktail den in New York City's SoHo district called the Pegu Club, which featured certain design elements inspired by the original colonial nineteenth-century club, such as the ornate woodwork and Asian artwork, but was open to anyone willing to climb the stairs to quench their thirst. Among the staples that never left the menu until the bar's closing in 2020 was Saunders' version of the Pegu Club, which reinstated the fresh lime juice and reconfigured the other ingredients, also with the addition of orange bitters. This recipe is now considered the industry standard, and Pegu Club cocktails can still be ordered in many bars around the world.

- 2 oz (60 ml) dry gin
- ¾ oz (22 ml) fresh lime juice
- ¾ oz (22 ml) orange curaçao
- 1 dash Angostura bitters
- 1 dash orange bitters

Shake all ingredients with ice until well chilled. Strain into a coupe glass.

# MOJITO (LA CONCHA)

🕐 1910
⚑ HAVANA, CUBA
👤 ROGELIO

⌂ LA CONCHA BAR,
HOTEL BALNEARIO
🍶 RUM
🍸 HURRICANE OR ROCKS

It is not widely known, but there are two versions of the Mojito that originated in Havana, Cuba in the early twentieth century. La Concha is the "deep cut" recipe. In fact, the most recognizable muddled mint variation is a mutation of this earlier version of the Mojito, which was the signature cocktail of La Concha Bar in Hotel Balneario, and itself derived from another local drink, the Draquecito.

This somewhat complicated Mojito evolution might sound as dizzying as the aftermath of drinking five of any of them, but drink historians Anistatia Miller and Jared Brown map it out in 2017's *Spirit of the Cane*. Draquecito was a popular concoction made with local aguardiente and sugar. It is documented that in 1910 at La Concha, a bar man named Rogelio made a derivation called "Mojito Batido" out of white rum, ice, lemon juice, unrefined sugar, and Angostura bitters topped with soda water.

Nary a mint sprig or muddler in sight. Not even a lime. Yet.

In the 1910s and 1920s, La Concha Mojitos were so popular on Mariano Beach that the bar often ran out of lemons, hence a pomelo substitute. It's been documented that because pomelos were more costly than lemons, the pomelo version was considered the hoity-toity variation.

The mint Mojito from Sloppy Joe's became the default serve by the 1930s, with recipes calling for the addition of mint muddled with lime and sugar. However, if you want to really impress your friends (or simply prepare a less sweet and slightly more structured Mojito), serve La Concha Mojito and tell them this was the popular way to make them before the muddled mint version was considered cool.

- 1½ oz (45 ml) white rum
- ¾ oz (22 ml) fresh pomelo juice (or lemon)
- 1 tsp unrefined sugar
- 2 dashes Angostura bitters
- Soda water, to top

Build all ingredients except the soda water in a hurricane or rocks glass. Add ice. Top with soda and stir.

# EL PRESIDENTE

| | | | |
|---|---|---|---|
| ⊕ | 1915 | ⌂ | HOTEL INGLATERRA |
| ⚑ | HAVANA, CUBA | ⬗ | RUM |
| ⚇ | JOHN B. ESCALANTE | ⏝ | COUPE |

El Presidente is an anomaly of the classic Cuban cocktail canon, because it eschews tropical ingredients. As the name suggests, it was invented to fete presidents and foreign dignitaries visiting the country during the 1910s to early 1950s. The first print mention of the drink is in the 1915 *Manual del Cantinero* and credited to bartender John B. Escalante. At the time, he was serving at Hotel Inglaterra in Havana, where then president Marió García Menocal y Deop would have likely been received.

The most popular and enduring variation is attributed to bartender Eddie Woelke, an American who escaped Prohibition and originally landed at Havana's Sevilla-Biltmore hotel, then Gran Casino Nacional by 1924. At the time, the famous cantinero Constante Ribalaigua Vert was also known for regularly serving El Presidente at El Floridita, although garnished with a cherry to match the grenadine in the recipe.

Drink historians Jared Brown and Anistatia Miller discovered that the recipe had been tweaked by the time President Gerard Machado came into office in May of 1925, with a Presidente Machado variation. Both the original and the variation are printed in *El Arte de Hacer un Cocktail y Algo Mas*, first published in 1927 by Compañia Cervecera International SA. Machado was so enamored of the drink that he famously served it to President Calvin Coolidge, who visited during Prohibition.

Woelke returned to New York in 1933, where he continued to prepare the drink at the bar at Hotel Weylin, where it was popularized in the United States and beyond.

The original 1915 recipe was simply half and half gold rum to French vermouth Chambéry with a dash of grenadine. However, the most common modern preparation is based on the Presidente Machado, yet is simply referred to as El Presidente.

- 1½ oz (45 ml) gold or dark rum
- ¾ oz (22 ml) vermouth blanc
- ½ oz (15 ml) orange curaçao
- 1 barspoon grenadine

- Garnish: orange peel (expressed and discarded); cocktail cherry (optional) as a nod to Ribalaigua Vert

Stir the ingredients in a cocktail glass with ice until well chilled. Strain into a chilled cocktail glass. Express the oils from a piece of orange peel into the drink, skin side down, then discard. Add the cherry, if using.

# SINGAPORE SLING

🕐 1915       ⌂ RAFFLES HOTEL
⚑ SINGAPORE       ◊ GIN
👤 NGIAM TONG BOON       ⏱ HURRICANE OR HIGHBALL

..............................................................................................

The Singapore Sling is perhaps the most baffling cocktail in the entire canon. To some, the name conjures thoughts of big pink umbrella drinks; to others, something resembling more of an aromatic highball. The short story is that it's both, each born at the Long Bar in the Raffles Hotel in Singapore, although the more tropical variation was popularized decades later.

According to gin historian Keli Rivers, the word "sling" is derived from the German word *schlingen*, "to swallow," and confusingly describes a number of 1800s cocktails, either hot or cold, made with sugar and water. By the early 1900s, there is recorded history of a gin and bitters highball called a Straits Sling served in Asia. Drinks historian Jared Brown cites an article in a 1913 *Straits Times Singapore* column that mentions that a "really decent sling" was had at the Singapore Cricket Club made of "one Cherry Brandy, one Dom [Benedictine], one Gin, one Lime Juice, some Ice and water, a few dashes of bitters."

In 1915, head bartender at Raffles Long Bar, Ngiam Tong Boon, perfected his recipe based on that drink—gin, cherry brandy (historically most likely Cherry Heering), Bénédictine, lime juice, bitters, soda water—now known as the Singapore Sling.

Raffles closed in the 1940s during World War II, reopening under different names for a couple of decades before rebranding as Raffles in the mid-1970s. Perhaps riding the foam of the very last waves of the tiki era, somehow the Singapore Sling widened its lapels and changed from what for decades had been the house signature to an iteration with pineapple juice and grenadine, the reflection of its mirror ball cast on menus around the globe.

The second version, which is now the Long Bar's default recipe, is considered a not-so-guilty pleasure by modern cocktailians in the know (who will probably swear by the original anyway). Here are both versions.

..............................................................................................

Original Singapore Sling (Singapore Gin Sling)

- 1½ oz (45 ml) dry gin
- ½ oz (15 ml) cherry brandy
- ¼ oz (7 ml) Bénédictine D.O.M. liqueur
- ½ oz (15 ml) lime juice
- 1 dash each Angostura and orange bitters
- Generous splash of soda water

- Garnish: lime wheel and cocktail cherry

Shake everything except the soda water with ice until well chilled. Strain into a highball glass over fresh and ice top with soda water. Garnish with a lime wheel and cocktail cherry.

1970s Singapore Sling

- 1½ oz (45 ml) dry gin
- ¾ oz (22 ml) cherry brandy
- ¼ oz (7 ml) each Bénédictine D.O.M. liqueur, Cointreau, and grenadine
- 2 oz (60 ml) pineapple juice
- ¾ oz (22 ml) lime juice
- 1 dash Angostura bitters
- Soda water, to top

- Garnish: pineapple slice and cherry

Shake everything but the soda water with ice until well chilled and frothy. Strain into a hurricane glass over ice and top with soda water. Garnish and serve with a straw.

..............................................................................................

# THE LAST WORD

- ⏱ 1915/16
- ⚑ DETROIT, USA
- ⚕ UNKNOWN
- ⌂ DETROIT ATHLETIC CLUB
- ◊ GIN
- ♉ COUPE OR COCKTAIL

Though it dates to the pre-Prohibition era, by the end of the twentieth century, The Last Word cocktail almost had a literal meaning.

The drink can originally be traced to the Detroit Athletic Club, where, according to a November 2014 article by Sylvia Rector in the *Detroit Free Press*, it was found on a menu from 1916 by club historian Ken Voyles. In the 1920s, the drink was introduced to New York City society by vaudevillian Frank Fogarty, who was such a promoter of it that he is sometimes incorrectly credited with inventing it to mask low-grade bathtub gin.

Decades after its mid-twentieth century disappearance, The Last Word found new entry points into the global cocktail conversation, thanks to bartender Murray Stenson at Seattle's Zig Zag Café, who in 2004 discovered it while perusing a 1951 copy of *Bottoms Up* by Waldorf-Astoria hotel publicist Ted Saucier.

A major part of The Last Word's modern allure is the inclusion of green Chartreuse, an aromatic liqueur made in France by Carthusian monks, keepers of its secret recipe of herbs and botanicals. Coinciding with The Last Word's popularity in the early 2000s was a similarly cultish fascination with the liqueur, including new collectors of rare, numbered bottlings of both the green and yellow varieties.

In the years following Stenson's discovery, The Last Word has not only found its way onto countless menus around the world, it has also spawned many riffs on the theme—sometimes made with bubbles, or with different base spirits and/or liqueurs, using different fruit juices, serving it hot—not to mention all the cheeky name variations, such as Oh, My Word!, The Last Laugh, Not Another Word, Word Up, etc.

It's all about the proportions. Here is the basic recipe to start with.

- ¾ oz (45 ml) dry gin
- ¾ oz (45 ml) fresh lime juice
- ¾ oz (45 ml) maraschino liqueur
- ¾ oz (45 ml) green Chartreuse liqueur

Shake all ingredients with ice until well chilled. Strain into a chilled coupe or cocktail glass.

# AVIATION

| | | | |
|---|---|---|---|
| ⏱ | 1916 | ⌂ | HOTEL WALLICK |
| ⚑ | NEW YORK CITY, USA | ◊ | GIN |
| 👤 | HUGO ENSSLIN | 🍸 | COUPE OR COCKTAIL |

The Aviation is admittedly a peculiar little purple number. Born in the 1910s, then lost to time, it's enjoyed a long haul in the modern cocktail renaissance largely thanks to Eric Seed, whose import company Haus Alpenz recommercialized crème de violette liqueur—the defining ingredient, which lends both its florality and its striking hue—in 2007, specifically to facilitate the preparation of the sweet-tart flavored cocktail again after decades of obscurity.

The most popular pre-Prohibition recipe—made with gin, lemon juice, maraschino liqueur, and crème de violette—was first published in 1916 by Hugo Ensslin, head bartender at the Hotel Wallick in New York City, in his book *Recipes For Mixed Drinks*.

Unlike most Pre-Prohibition concoctions touted by cocktailians, one can't exactly say that Aviation was one of those drinks everyone loved that then disappeared because of the laws of the land. Truth is, it really wasn't much of a sensation, although versions of the recipe were featured in 1930 by Harry Craddock in *The Savoy Cocktail Book* and by Patrick Gavin Duffy in 1934 in *The Official Mixer's Manual*.

The Aviation might have been forgotten entirely had writer Paul Harrington not mentioned it in his online column for *Wired* magazine in the late 1990s, and in a book he co-wrote with Laura Moorhead in 1998, *Cocktail: The Drinks Bible for the 21st Century*. From here, one can say, the Seed was planted (pun intended).

With its old-but-new-again cache, the Aviation became one of the defining cocktails of the twenty-first-century cocktail scene. While it has been circumnavigated through multiple variations and hundreds of house signatures around the world—not to mention competing purple floral liqueurs—and, one could even argue, inspired the popular American gin brand of the same name, purists are divided on their go-to recipe template. Some insist on Ensslin's recipe, while others go with Craddock's subtle tweaking, which calls for less of the violette.

Ensslin's recipe

- 2 oz (60 ml) dry gin
- ¼ oz (7 ml) maraschino liqueur
- ½ oz (15 ml) fresh lemon juice
- ¼ oz (7 ml) crème de violette

- Garnish: cocktail cherry

Shake all ingredients with ice until well chilled. Strain into a chilled coupe or cocktail glass. Add a cherry to the bottom of the glass.

Craddock's recipe

- 1¾ oz (50 ml) dry gin
- ½ oz (15 ml) fresh lemon juice
- ¼ oz (7 ml) maraschino liqueur
- 1 tsp (5 ml) crème de violette

Prepare as opposite, with optional cherry garnish.

# PISCO SOUR

🕐 1916
⚐ LIMA, PERU
👤 VICTOR MORRIS

⌂ MORRIS BAR
🍶 PISCO
🍸 COUPE

The Pisco Sour, consisting of pisco (Peruvian or Chilean grape brandy, typically unaged), lemon or lime juice, simple syrup, egg white, and bitters, is the national drink of Peru. Unlike many such cocktails of this period, it does have traceable origins. The original recipe is credited to American-born bartender Victor Morris, who moved to Peru in the early twentieth century with intentions to work on the railroads, but somehow got sidetracked into opening his own namesake bar in Lima instead. He ran the Morris Bar from 1916 to 1929. According to pisco historian Guillermo L. Toro-Lima, Morris published his recipe in a 1924 Lima cookbook that contained no egg white or bitters and was based on the whiskey sour.

The egg white came into play some time in the late 1920s and was likely originated on the Peruvian luxury hotel circuit by a Morris protégé. The egg white version became the default recipe in the 1950s, often gussied up with artful swirls of bitters atop the fluffy white clouds in the glass. Toro-Lima suggests it was restaurateur Joe Baum who popularized the Pisco Sour in New York City in 1960, when he featured it on the opening menu of La Fonda del Sol as the "Pisco Sawyer," and a few years later when Braniff Airways served it on its South American-bound flights.

In 2007, sometime after modern cocktailians globally embraced the Pisco Sour and helped expand its appreciation, the National Institute of Culture of Peru officially declared the first Saturday in February as World Pisco Sour Day. This day not only celebrates the cocktail but boosts the reputation of Peruvian pisco, spotlighting its quality and complexities. The festival naturally includes its own cocktail competition with classics and twists.

- 2 oz (60 ml) pisco
- ¾ oz (22 ml) fresh lime or lemon juice (or a mix of both)
- ¾ oz (22 ml) simple syrup
- 1 egg white
- Aromatic bitters

Shake all ingredients except the bitters with ice (some prefer to dry shake for a few seconds without the egg white for extra froth, then add it with the ice to finish) until frothy and well chilled, at least 20 seconds. Strain into a chilled coupe glass. Carefully place 3 dots of the bitters atop the egg white foam. Using a toothpick or cocktail pick, swirl them into the foam (optional, but encouraged).

# HANKY PANKY

- ⊕ 1918
- ⚑ LONDON, UK
- ⅄ ADA COLEMAN

- ⌂ AMERICAN BAR, SAVOY HOTEL
- ◊ GIN
- ⅄ NICK & NORA OR COUPE

In 1903, at a time when women bartenders were referred to as "barmaids" and rarely found behind the bar in the first place, Ada Coleman became the first female head bartender of the American Bar at the Savoy Hotel in London. It has been widely reported that the natural magnetism of the twenty-four-year-old, known by the nickname Coley, soon charmed the regular clientele, such as Charlie Chaplin, Mark Twain, the then Prince of Wales (later King Edward VII), and Marlene Dietrich, among many others.

Coley held the position well into the 1920s, famously overlapping with Harry Craddock, who had come over from New York. Around that time, the comedy actor Charles Hawtrey would often come to see her, and, according to a 1925 interview with her in *People* magazine, he would say, "'Coley, I am tired. Give me something with a bit of punch in it.' It was for him that I spent hours experimenting until I had invented a new cocktail." She eventually came up with the recipe for what became a cocktail menu staple around the world—the boozy, stirred combination of gin, sweet vermouth, and the bracing Italian amaro Fernet-Branca (the ingredient that delivers the "punch" bit).

The article reported that when Hawtrey took his first sip, he declared, "By Jove, this is the real hanky panky!" That phrase has a cheekier meaning now, but at the time it was slang referring to something wildly good. Indeed, it's a mixture of ingredients that don't sound as though they would work well together, but somehow, in the right proportions, it's quite the charmer.

- 1½ oz (45 ml) gin
- 1½ oz (45 ml) sweet vermouth
- 2 dashes Fernet-Branca

- Garnish: orange twist (this part really pulls the flavors together)

Add all ingredients to a mixing glass and stir with ice until well chilled. Strain into a chilled Nick & Nora or coupe glass, express the peel over the drink, and add to the glass.

# SIDECAR

⊕ 1918
⚑ PARIS, FRANCE
𐰬 "JOHN"

⌂ HENRY'S BAR
⌀ COGNAC
Y COUPE

The Sidecar is the world's most famous cognac cocktail. The recipe—cognac, triple sec, and lemon juice—was first published in the 1919 edition of Harry MacElhone's *Harry's ABC of Mixing Cocktails,* and soon after in Robert Vermiere's *Cocktails: How to Mix Them* in 1922. MacElhone claims it was invented by a bartender named "John" at Henry's in Paris (at the time, across the street from Harry's New York Bar) for an American soldier who was on leave from serving on the Western Front. The refreshing mixture immediately raced around the cafés of the city and was soon discovered by bartender Malachi "Pat" McGarry, a known travel enthusiast, who made it one of the signatures of Buck's Club in London.

Though the drink was reportedly christened with the name "Sidecar" because it was potent enough to "take you for a ride," it was considered the height of sophistication to order one.

According to *The Oxford Companion to Spirits & Cocktails,* Frank Meier of the Ritz Bar in Paris claimed in 1923 that it was their second most popular seller next to the Monkey Gland, invented by MacElhone. Meier was known to dazzle privileged clientele by mixing a super blingy $5 variation (about $85 in 2022) made with the Ritz's stash of precious vintage mid-1800s cognac from before the phylloxera epidemic forever changed the structure of grapes used for wine and brandy.

The original Sidecar was served without a sugar rim on the glass. The sugar-frosted rim was popularized in the US sometime in the 1930s, perhaps out of confusion with the Brandy Crusta, a close relative, but it stuck. These days, both variations are served in bars around the world, but as with Margaritas and salt rims, it can't hurt to state a preference for sugar or none when ordering one.

- 2 oz (60 ml) cognac
- ¾ oz (22 ml) triple sec
- ¾ oz (22 ml) fresh lemon juice

Shake all ingredients with ice. Strain into a chilled coupe glass.

# NEGRONI

- ⊕ 1919
- ⊳ FLORENCE, ITALY
- ⅄ COUNT CAMILLO NEGRONI/
  FOSCO SCARSELLI
- ⌂ CAFÉ CASONI
- ⍭ GIN
- ⅄ ROCKS

The Negroni, the most famous and riffed on equal-parts cocktail—gin, sweet vermouth, and Campari—hails from Florence, Italy, and was first mixed sometime around 1919. The earliest mention of it was discovered in a letter written by Count Camillo Negroni, a larger-than-life Florentine aristocrat (never verified as a count, by the way) whose resume includes a stint as a cowboy in the United States, where he was a professional high stakes gambler and fencing instructor. Gin historian Keli Rivers, in *Negroni: More Than 30 Classic Recipes For Italy's Iconic Cocktail*, says Camillo Negroni relocated there temporarily to avoid the Italian draft in World War I.

Once back at home in Florence after the war, he paid a visit to his local, Café Casoni, where he requested bartender Fosco Scarselli rev up his usual Americano (sweet vermouth, Campari, and soda water) with a splash of gin.

In 1947, American actor Orson Welles is famously quoted as saying, "The bitters are excellent for your liver, the gin is bad for you.

They balance each other." Though it's highly possible the ingredients combination made the rounds at the local cafés and beyond under many different names, including "Camparinette," it wasn't until well after World War II that the cocktail known as a Negroni was popularized as a counterpart to the chic Vespa-riding, café-sitting lifestyle movement known as *la dolce vita*, "the sweet life," and hit the jet set through the sleek graphics of 1950s and 60s Campari advertising posters.

While Negronis have been a staple at classic Italian restaurants since the mid-twentieth century, in the early 2000s it became one of the darlings of the modern cocktail movement, with thousands of bars the world over serving their own signature variation. It even inspired an annual Negroni Week, a worldwide charity initiative with Campari in partnership with bars serving Negronis and Negroni adjacent creations. Because devotees consider its red-hued presentation a thing of simple beauty, Negronis have inspired countless tattoos and other artworks.

- 1 oz (30 ml) dry gin
- 1 oz (30 ml) sweet vermouth
- 1 oz (30 ml) Campari
- Sparkling water
- Soda water, to top (optional)*

- Garnish: orange twist or orange wheel

Add all ingredients to a rocks glass. Add ice (best with 2 large, clear cubes) and stir. Top with a splash of soda water (optional) and garnish with orange.

*Since Negronis evolved from the Americano, early recipes call for a splash of soda, though most modern serves omit it.

# WHITE LADY

- 1919
- PARIS, FRANCE
- HARRY MACELHONE

- CIRO'S
- GIN
- COUPE OR COCKTAIL

Some say this gin and lemon cocktail is related to the Sidecar (page 80). Others maintain it's more of a sour. Either way, a White Lady is quite the treat if you've never tasted one, or haven't in a long while.

It was conceived by Scottish barman Harry MacElhone in 1919, when working at Ciro's Club in London, and was originally an almost entirely different recipe than the modern default one, using crème de menthe, triple sec, and orange juice.

That somewhat acrid combination of flavors would probably explain why MacElhone tweaked the recipe considerably by the time he was at Harry's New York Bar in Paris in the 1920s, using brandy in place of the crème de menthe.

However, the drink we know and love today is the recipe that, by 1929, was a signature of Harry Craddock at the American Bar in London's Savoy Hotel, swapping out the

brandy for gin. In most serves around the world, it is prepared with a frothy egg white, which adds a striking pearlescence to its presentation. However, at the Savoy, the preferred method is to shake the daylights out of it with ice, then possibly play with other flavorings or ingredients, even transforming it into a taller serve with fizz.

The White Lady was so popular in the mid-twentieth century that it was as common a drink order as a Martini or Manhattan. And it has certainly enjoyed its pop cultural closeup. Among many instances, it is called out in Ernest Hemingway's novel *Islands in the Stream* (originally penned in the early 1950s but posthumously published in 1970), and John LeCarré's *The Looking Glass War* in 1965. It is also the chosen libation of detective Hercule Poirot, played by Peter Ustinov, in a pivotal cocktail party scene in the 1982 movie *Evil Under the Sun*, based on the 1941 Agatha Christie mystery.

- 1½ oz (45 ml) London dry gin
- ¾ oz (22 ml) Cointreau or triple sec
- ¾ oz (22 ml) fresh lemon juice
- ½ oz (15 ml) simple syrup (optional—use only if more sweetness is desired)
- 1 egg white (optional)

- Garnish: lemon twist

Vigorously shake all ingredients with ice until cold and frothy. Strain into a chilled coupe or cocktail glass. Express lemon oils over the drink and rest the twist on the rim or discard.

# BEE'S KNEES

| | | | |
|---|---|---|---|
| ⊕ | 1920s | ⌂ | UNKNOWN |
| ⴲ | PARIS, FRANCE | ⸕ | GIN |
| ⅄ | MARGARET BROWN | ⴘ | COUPE |

....................................................................................................

This cocktail is one of the most famous from the Prohibition era, although its origins are commonly misunderstood.

It's true that the term "bee's knees" was popular 1920s slang indicating that something is truly superb or highly attractive. As in, "I think your new dress is just the bee's knees, *dahling*." What isn't true at all is that the drink was created to mask the taste of poor-quality gin.

Let it be a reminder that while Prohibition restricted access to liquor in the US and a handful of other countries, perfectly drinkable hooch could easily be enjoyed elsewhere. Scores of excellent drinks made with good-quality ingredients were born in that period.

The Bee's Knees is no exception. In the past few years, cocktail historian and Sipsmith Gin co-founder Jared Brown discovered an article about women-only bars in Paris, France entitled "Bars in Paris for 'Madame' Close Doors to Mere Male," published in Brooklyn's *Standard Union* on April 23, 1929. The piece describes a certain "Mrs. J.J. Brown of Boulder" who ordered a drink (though not at which specific bar) made of gin, lemon, and honey while living in that city.

Not only is the use of honey instead of sugar notable, so is further investigation into who exactly Mrs. J.J. Brown was. That would be none other than *Titanic* survivor Margaret Brown, aka "The Unsinkable Molly Brown," depicted by Kathy Bates in the 1997 movie.

In modern times, rather than focusing on the gin, the honey component in Molly Brown's signature takes on a more socio-ethical value. Vermont's Caledonia Spirits, producer of Barr Hall Gin, runs an annual Bee's Knees Week promotion to raise funds for causes associated with honeybee conservation. At the Parlour bar at the Intercontinental Hotel in New York City, Bee's Knees is prepared with smoked honey from the hotel's rooftop apiary.

....................................................................................................

- 2 oz (60 ml) dry gin
- ½ oz (15 ml) fresh lemon juice
- ½ oz (15 ml) honey syrup* (use more or less depending on desired level of sweetness)

Combine all ingredients in a shaker tin with ice. Shake until well chilled. Strain into a coupe glass.

*Honey syrup is prepared in the same manner as simple syrup, using equal parts honey and water. For a 2:1 or 3:1 honey syrup, use two parts or three parts honey to one part water.

# BLOODY MARY

🕐 1920s
⚑ PARIS, FRANCE
🧍 FERNAND PETIOT

⌂ HARRY'S NEW YORK BAR
🍶 VODKA
🍸 PINT, HIGHBALL, OR TUMBLER

The Bloody Mary is one of the most popular drinks on the planet. Its base recipe is built on vodka and spiced tomato juice, although there are hundreds of variations, ranging from the subdued to the blazingly spicy. There is some debate over its origins, but the story with the most traction bestows the honor on Fernand "Pete" Petiot, whose 1975 obituary in the *San Francisco Chronicle* mentions his experimentation with vodka drinks in Paris dating to 1920, saying he eventually mixed a drink of half vodka and half tomato juice then debuted it at Harry's New York Bar "… which was frequented by American newspaper correspondents and bankers. An American entertainer Roy Barton provided the name, saying it reminded him of a Chicago club, the Bucket of Blood." Incidentally, the "Mary" part is a reference to ruthless sixteenth-century British monarch Mary I.

Petiot's vodka and tomato combination, considered an ideal "reviver" (hangover cure), was popularized as a midday beverage,

(though it's suitable for any time of day), especially after he elaborated the tomato mix with spices and Tabasco and/or Worcestershire sauce. In 1934, Petiot took the recipe to the St. Regis Hotel bar in New York City as head bartender. This signature Bloody uses a gin base and goes by the less aggressive-sounding name Red Snapper.

Over the decades and all over the world, Bloody Mary became its own category of anything base spirit (vodka, gin, tequila, bourbon, etc.) + tomato (and all manner of spice components). While some establishments keep the garnish simple, fanciful ones abound, ranging from topiary-in-a-glass to mini sandwiches. Sobelman's Pub in Milwaukee, Wisconsin even serves a Bloody Mary with an entire fried chicken as garnish.

Everyone seems to know someone with a "secret" Bloody Mary mix recipe, but here's a basic one to build from, and it can be expanded to pitcher (jug) size for a crowd.

- 6 dashes Worcestershire sauce
- 3 dashes Tabasco sauce
- Pinch of salt
- Pinch of ground black pepper
- Juice of ½ lemon
- 5 oz (150 ml) tomato juice
- 2 oz (60 ml) vodka

- Garnish: lemon wheel or celery stalk (get as fancy as you like from there)

Option 1: add all ingredients to a pint or highball glass. Add ice, stir, and garnish.

Option 2: add all ingredients to a pint glass or tumbler with ice. Transfer ("roll") the mixture between glasses a couple of times to gently aerate and mix, then keep all ingredients and ice in one glass. Garnish.

# DAIQUIRI NO. 4 (AKA EL FLORIDITA)

- ⏱ 1920s
- ⚐ HAVANA, CUBA
- ⚘ CONSTANTINO RIBALAIGUA VERT
- ⌂ EL FLORIDITA
- 🍾 RUM
- 🍸 HURRICANE OR COUPE

Some may be unaware, but the iconic Daiquiri variation made in a blender is a younger cousin to the original prepared in a shaker (some even stir them). The icy take comes from Constantino Ribalaigua Vert, head bartender at El Floridita in Havana, Cuba, which, in the 1920s, was one of the first places in the world to serve drinks made with what was then known as an "electric mixer." After some tinkering, Constante, as he was known, discovered a measure of maraschino liqueur blended with the original rum sour recipe made it sing.

Hearing the tune most loudly was author Ernest Hemingway, who then lured his celebrity friends to his favorite bar. Blended Daiquiris repeatedly made cameos in his writings from this period (which almost certainly contributed to their eventual popularity stateside). They were also the template for Constante's 1930s variation the Hemingway Special (aka Papa Doble), made without sugar, more rum, and the addition of grapefruit juice, shaken. But it was El Floridita that set the "whirled" on fire, so to speak. One could even say Hemingway originated the "walktail" Daiquiri still popular in places like New Orleans—legend has it he would bring a thermos (flask) to have it filled with El Floridita's blended treats to go.

When the time-saving Waring Blender launched in 1938, El Floridita was one of its first customers. By the 1950s, frappéd Daiquiris were the default variation around the world, though they unfortunately led to a more synthetic flavoring trend for several decades. Today, however, sophisticated Daiquiris based on the El Floridita are the pride of certain high-end cocktail bars, with frosty flavors ranging from simple to fanciful, pale yellow to electric blue.

- 1½ oz (45 ml) white rum
- ¼ oz (7 ml) maraschino liqueur
- ¾ oz (22 ml) fresh lime juice
- 1½ tsp granulated sugar

- Garnish: paper straw

Add all ingredients to a blender with a scoop of crushed ice. Blend until smooth, about 15 to 20 seconds. Pour into a hurricane or deep coupe glass. Add a straw.

# BUCK'S FIZZ

🕐 1921  
⚑ LONDON, UK  
🧍 MALACHI MCGARRY  

⌂ BUCK'S CLUB  
🍶 CHAMPAGNE  
🍸 FLUTE  

......................................................................................................

Peruse the ready-to-drink aisle in a British supermarket and you will find bottled and canned versions of modern classics, such as Bramble, Espresso Martini, endless combinations of Gin &Tonic, and even a Porn Star Martini. And if you don't feel like purchasing separate bottles of bubbly and orange juice, you can also opt for ready-to-drink (RTD) Mimosas, or that distinctly British brunch classic, the Buck's Fizz.

Consider the Buck's Fizz the older, bubblier, British sibling to the Mimosa (page 100). It was invented in London in 1921 at the gentlemen-only Buck's Club by bartender Malachi "Pat" McGarry, who was known for popularizing French-born drinks, such as the Sidecar (page 80) and Monkey Gland in the UK.

According to drinks historians Anistatia Miller and Jared Brown in *Spirituous Journey: A History of Drink (Book Two)*, McGarry was the personal bartender of club founder Captain

Herbert John Buckmaster. An account from Buck's Club secretary Captain Peter Murison reports that while he was in the process of divorcing actress Gladys Cooper, Buckmaster often had McGarry with him while hosting parties with movie and theater glitterati as well as club members. One of the members, having heard tell of a certain peach and Champagne cocktail from "the continent," requested one from McGarry.

McGarry came up with his own concoction, replacing the peach with orange juice and adding a few ingredients the club keeps secret (Miller and Brown discovered a 1950s' recipe—"Champagne Buck"—which calls for the addition of gin and cherry brandy, which certainly can't hurt).

Champagne and orange juice—technically the same as a Mimosa, but with just a splash of juice instead of topping it off.

......................................................................................................

Traditional recipe

- 3½ oz (100 ml) Champagne or other dry bubbly
- ¼ oz (7 ml) orange juice (preferably fresh)

Fill a flute or wine glass with the bubbly. Top with the orange juice. Add an orange twist, if you're feeling fancy.

1950s Champagne Buck

- 2 oz (60 ml) fresh squeezed orange juice
- 3 oz (90 ml) Champagne or other dry bubbly
- Splash of London dry gin
- Dash of cherry brandy

- Garnish: orange twist

Build the drink in a flute or wine glass. Stir. Add the orange twist to garnish.

......................................................................................................

# BRANDY ALEXANDER

🕐  1922
⚑  LONDON, UK
👤  HARRY MACELHONE

⌂  CIRO'S
🝊  BRANDY
🍸  COUPE OR MARTINI

The Alexander is a type of cocktail using heavy (double) cream as a star ingredient. While creamy cocktails certainly existed in earlier drink recipes, the ingredient didn't have its own official genre until the early twentieth century. According to the *Oxford Companion to Spirits & Cocktails*, there was a real Alexander—Troy Alexander, bar manager of Rector's seafood restaurant in New York City—who is credited with creating the first recipe using gin when commissioned to fashion a cocktail for officials visiting from the Lackawanna Railroad. His muse was Phoebe Snow, a fictional character used in the railroad's advertising campaigns who wore a white gown to promote the railroad's use of "smokeless coal." Gin Alexanders became an "it" drink during the next decade, but Harry MacElhone, then at Ciro's in London (Harry's in Paris came later), thought cognac made for a better base. Since the publication of 1923's *Harry of Ciro's ABC of Mixing Cocktails*, brandy has been the default Alexander.

MacElhone also added crème de cacao to his recipe, which lends a boozy melted ice cream sensation to the sipping experience. Being so easily drinkable, by the mid-twentieth century, Brandy Alexanders became known as a "gateway drink" for those just getting used to drinking alcohol (famously demonstrated in the 1962 movie *Days of Wine and Roses* with Jack Lemmon and Lee Remick), and they were a constant presence in swinging singles bar scenes, such as the "fern" bars of San Francisco.

However, the postmodern cocktail culture has boosted the reputation of Brandy Alexanders once again. The late British barman and writer Gary "Gaz" Regan said in a Liquor.com article, "The Brandy Alexander was a darned popular drink when I was working Upper East Side bars in Manhattan during the 70s, and when carefully crafted, it can be a quality quaff."

---

• 1½ oz (45 ml) VSOP cognac (or another good-quality grape brandy)
• 1 oz (30 ml) white crème de cacao
• 1 oz (30 ml) heavy (double) cream

• Garnish: grated nutmeg

Shake all ingredients with ice until well chilled. Strain into a coupe or Martini glass. Grate nutmeg over the top, to garnish.

# MARY PICKFORD

🕐 1922
▻ HAVANA, CUBA
🧍 FRED KAUFMAN

⌂ SEVILLA-BILTMORE HOTEL
🍸 RUM
🍷 COUPE

Though not technically a cocktail writer, the British journalist and playwright Basil Woon was so infatuated by the confluence of personalities in 1920s Cuban cocktail culture, that it inspired him to write *When It's Cocktail Time in Cuba*. Rather than being a straightforward cocktail book, it chronicles his observations of the buzzy scene in its heyday.

One of the figures he centered on was Fred Kaufman, a charismatic, well-traveled bartender from Liverpool, England who worked with German-American bartender Eddie Woelke (known for his take on El Presidente [page 68], among other classics) at the Sevilla-Biltmore Hotel in Havana, Cuba.

Woon denotes that the majority of Kaufman's creations tended to center around rum and pineapple. The most famous of these was named for the Canadian-American silent screen starlet Mary Pickford, a lead in some of the highest grossing movies of the 1910s,

and in the 1920s one of the few women who directed and produced her own movies.

While Pickford did make movies in Cuba in the mid-1910s, Woon's account that Pickford vacationed there in the 1920s—beguiling the likes of Kaufman while flanked by friend Charlie Chaplin and her husband, Douglas Fairbanks, who would have been among scores of Prohibition-era, cocktail-seeking jet-setters—was debunked in the 2010s. According to filmmaker and Pickford-ologist Cari Beauchamp, Pickford was too vain about the effect of the island's high humidity levels on her famous curls to choose it as a vacation destination.

The Mary Pickford endures as one of the most popular classic Cuban cocktails of all time, found on menus around the world. While Kaufman's original is simply rum, pineapple juice, and grenadine, the modern variation adds some maraschino liqueur for texture.

• 2 oz (60 ml) white or gold rum
  (preferably real Havana Club from Cuba)
• 1½ oz (45 ml) pineapple juice
  (fresh, if possible)
• 5 to 6 dashes maraschino liqueur
• ½ oz (15 ml) grenadine

• Garnish: cocktail cherry, if desired

Shake all ingredients with ice until well-chilled and frothy. Strain into a coupe glass. Garnish with a cherry, if using.

# LINE COCKTAIL

<table>
<tr><td>🕓</td><td>1924</td><td>⌂</td><td>CAFÉ LINE</td></tr>
<tr><td>⚑</td><td>TOKYO, JAPAN</td><td>◊</td><td>GIN</td></tr>
<tr><td>🙎</td><td>YONEKICHI MAEDA</td><td>🍸</td><td>CORDIAL</td></tr>
</table>

The Line Cocktail is one of the earliest known signatures to come out of Japan. Created by twenty-seven-year-old bartender Yonekichi Maeda as the house cocktail of Café Line in Tokyo in 1924, it is a Manhattan-esque, gin-based, sweet-and-savory combination that's intended for small, cordial-size servings. In the same year, the original recipe was published in Maeda's book, *Kokuteeru*, the second ever cocktail book published in Japan (the book was not published in English until 2022).

The cocktail combines small equal parts gin, Bénédictine, and sweet vermouth with a couple of dashes of Angostura bitters. It is garnished not with citrus or cherry, but crushed pickled rakkyo, an allium similar to a shallot.

While most all-spirit cocktails are typically stirred with ice for dilution and strained into the drinking vessel to preserve their inherent flavor characteristics, Maeda instructs that the drink be shaken, à la the Stinger. This technique serves to aerate the ingredients (not "bruise" them), adding viscosity to the otherwise rich combination of flavors and making the sum of its parts refreshing rather than cloying. The rakkyo adds an intriguing layer of sweet-and-sour brininess, akin to the Spanish way of serving vermouth on the rocks with pickled olives and orange peel.

While there was no prohibition in Japan, this somewhat esoteric drink is nonetheless one that fell into obscurity for several decades but has since been recognized as a foundational recipe of modern Japanese bar culture. Its compact presentation makes it an ideal drink to serve on any menu offering mini cocktails and flights.

- 2 dashes Angostura bitters
- $^1/_3$ oz (10 ml) Bénédictine D.O.M.
- $^1/_3$ oz (10 ml) sweet vermouth
- $^1/_3$ oz (10 ml) dry gin

- Garnish: crushed rakkyo, if available (if not available, a small section of crushed pickled onion could stand in), with a thin twist of orange or lemon peel

Add all ingredients to a cocktail shaker with 2 to 3 pieces of ice and shake until very cold. Strain into a cordial glass and garnish with the crushed rakkyo, or its alternatives.

# MIMOSA

⊕  1925                          ⌂  RITZ HOTEL
⊳  PARIS, FRANCE                 ◊  CHAMPAGNE
ጸ  FRANK MEIER                   🍸  FLUTE OR WINE

There's a snag in the thread of history when it comes to iconic drinks such as the Manhattan, Martini, or even the Margarita. The recipe could have been attributed to this bartender or that, at this club or that venue, at this party for that guest, in this year or that one, etc. So, what may be surprising to some is that there is a definite trail leading to the invention of the world's most popular and simple signature Champagne-and-orange-juice cocktail, the Mimosa.

Drinks historians Anistatia Miller and Jared Brown say in *Spirituous Journey: A History of Drink Book Two* that prior to the version we are most familiar with, there was another orangy drink by the same name created in the early 1920s by Harry MacElhone at Harry's New York Bar in Paris, consisting of gin, curaçao, and dry vermouth.

In 1925, Frank Meier, head bartender at the Ritz Paris, began serving a concoction with Champagne, orange juice, and Grand Marnier that became an instant hit with Parisians. It's made with less fizz and more juice than its British cousin, the Buck's Fizz (page 92), invented in 1921. In 1936, Meier included the Mimosa recipe *sans* orange liqueur in his book *The Artistry of Mixing Drinks*.

By the 1940s, Mimosas had landed Stateside. Of course, the dark period of the mid-twentieth century meant that many of them were prepared with frozen concentrate OJ. However, by the 1990s, with the rise of TV cooking shows and gourmet magazines, the Mimosa saw several upgrades, made with specific citrus varieties, such as blood oranges, tangelos, satsumas, and tangerines (or a mixture thereof), and topped with higher-quality sparkling wines.

Meier's recipe

Put the juice of half an orange in a Champagne flute or small wine glass and fill with chilled Champagne.

Traditional recipe

Fill a flute or wine glass mid- to three-quarters of the way with fresh orange juice. Top with chilled bubbly.

For either version, add optional ingredients such as grenadine, cassis or other berry liqueur, or perhaps a splash of gin or vodka. Garnish with an orange twist, if you're feeling particularly festive.

# BOULEVARDIER

⊕ C.1927
⯈ PARIS, FRANCE
𝄢 ERSKINE GWYNNE

⌂ HARRY'S NEW YORK BAR
⌀ BOURBON
𝄼 COUPE

Often described as the "Bourbon Negroni," the Boulevardier is so much more than that. True, like its gin counterpart, it is equal parts base spirit (in this case bourbon), Campari, and sweet (red) vermouth. However, the similarities pretty much stop there.

It was invented at Harry's New York Bar, Paris in the mid-1920s. In 1924, a club known as the International Bar Flies (IBF) was formed there. Members had a secret handshake and wore an enamel pin, which was a rectangular shape with an ivory background to resemble a sugar cube; the initials IBF and an image of a fly were black, with all details outlined with gold. One of the members was Erskine Gwynne, an American-born writer who founded a monthly magazine in Paris called *Boulevardier*, a term loosely meaning "a man about town."

The Boulevardier is first mentioned in the 1927 book *Barflies and Cocktails* by Harry McElhone and IBF member, the British journalist D. B. Wyndham Lewis, aka "Wynn." A section contributed by Gwynne's magazine partner, Arthur Moss, called "Cocktails Round Town," describes the bar's regulars and their usual orders. Here, he says, "Now is the time for all good Barflies to come to the aid of the party, since Erskine Gwynne crashed in with his Boulevardier cocktail; ½ Campari, ⅓ Italian Vermouth, ⅓ Bourbon whisky."

The combination of ingredients, typically served up instead of on the rocks like a gin Negroni, is delightful, which is why the drink has endured and made the rounds.

Long Island Bar in Brooklyn, New York has few drinks on its menu, and some have been swapped out over the years to reflect changing tastes. However, whenever owner Toby Cecchini attempts to replace the house Boulevardier, a more high-octane version that uses two styles of rye whiskey instead of bourbon and two styles of sweet vermouth, there is so much pushback that it remains a constant signature.

These days the typical recipe calls for a splash more of the whiskey component.

- 1½ oz (45 ml) bourbon or rye whiskey
- 1 oz (30 ml) Campari or other bitter aperitivo
- 1 oz (30 ml) sweet (red) vermouth

- Garnish: orange or lemon twist

Add all ingredients to a mixing glass and stir with ice until well chilled. Strain into a chilled coupe glass. Express the citrus twist over the drink and add to the glass.

Cecchini's recipe

- 1 oz (30 ml) bonded rye
  (the bar uses Rittenhouse)
- 1 oz (30 ml) Old Overholt rye
- 1 oz (30 ml) Campari
- 1 oz (30 ml) red vermouth (⅓ Carpano
  Antica Formula and ⅔ Cinzano Rosso)

Prepare in the same way as the classic and serve up.

# MOJITO

🕐 1928
⚑ HAVANA, CUBA
👤 UNKNOWN

⌂ SLOPPY JOE'S
🍶 RUM
🍸 HIGHBALL

Those who have indulged in a thirst-quenching mix of muddled lime, mint, and sugar with rum and soda water likely haven't given much thought to how and when that preparation came about. Although after preparing dozens of them a night, the sore-armed bartender might have some thoughts. It's this preparation of the Mojito that's been the default since at least the late 1920s, rising to fame among locals and Prohibition-era American imbibers as the signature of Sloppy Joe's in Havana, Cuba, and subsequently landing on even small-town-America diner menus decades later.

The original Mojito from the 1910s, La Concha, also from Havana, was made without mint or muddling of any kind, and lemon or pomelo instead of lime, with Angostura bitters. However, by the 1930s, that version was far outshadowed by the Sloppy Joe's minty, and more theatrical, serve. Although the first recipe was published in 1929, two high-profile books that made the rounds—the 1936 *Sloppy Joe's Cocktails Manual* and the 1935 *Old Waldorf-Astoria Bar Book* by Albert Stevens Crockett—both define Mojitos as the rum and mint drink, and it stuck.

Mojitos were a popular club cocktail in the 1990s and, by the early 2000s, splashed right into the modern cocktail renaissance, and with far more rum options to choose from, resonated with authentic rum aficionados. As the drink is essentially a simple rum Rickey or rum cooler at heart, there are nearly infinite ways to improvise a Mojito—swap out or add to the fruit, use alternative herbs (such as basil), add additional flavors, spices, tinctures, sweeteners, make it stirred and boozy, blend it, can it, bottle it, form it into a jello (jelly) shot, chocolate truffle, hard candy, etc.

- 5 to 6 mint leaves
- 1 oz (30 ml) fresh lime juice
  (or add ½ lime, cut into pieces)
- 2 tsp sugar
- 1½ oz (45 ml) white rum
- Soda water, to top

- Garnish: mint sprig

In a tall glass, gently muddle the mint, lime juice, and sugar until well mixed but not too mushy. Add the rum and fill the glass with ice. Top with soda water and garnish with a mint sprig.

# SOUTHSIDE

| | |
|---|---|
| ◷ 1929 | ⌂ '21' CLUB |
| ⚑ NEW YORK CITY, USA | ◊ GIN |
| ⅄ JACK KRIENDLER AND CHARLIE BERNS | ⅄ COLLINS |

In 1929, cousins Jack Kriendler and Charlie Berns, aka "Jack and Charlie," ushered in the 30s by opening '21' Club on what has been documented as one of the most raucous New Year's Eves in New York City history. Yes, they opened a bar at the height of Prohibition. However, by this phase of the Noble Experiment, laws had become somewhat relaxed, and it wasn't that difficult to find a drink in the city if one knew where to look, and when and where to run. Their speakeasy famously featured a bar with automatically collapsing shelves that would discard bottles down a series of chutes into the sewer system below should the Feds come a-knocking. In the 1980s, when construction work began on the Paley Center next door, it was said the scent of alcohol emanated from the foundations.

The house drink at Jack and Charlie's previous bar, the Puncheon, was the Major Bailey. For '21' they decided on a Southside—essentially a gin Julep, or gin Mojito minus the muddling—originally invented at the South Side Sportman's Club on Long Island.

The Volstead Act was repealed in 1933, ending Prohibition, which allowed '21' to function as a normal bar and restaurant open to the public, and it famously became a regular haunt for well-known celebrities and politicians. The venue was renowned for its extensive wine list and other cocktails, but the '21' signature, and the most-ordered drink, remained the Southside.

As of this writing, although '21' survived the Great Depression and other economic disasters, including having to close for several months in 2018 to repair damage from a water main break, it did not survive the COVID-19 pandemic. However, the Southside lives on as one of the most beloved of gin refreshers, especially during the summer months, and has inspired countless variations through the decades.

- 2 oz (60 ml) dry gin
- 1 oz (30ml) mint simple syrup (add several sprigs of mint while preparing the standard 1:1 recipe, and strain)
- 4 to 5 fresh mint leaves
- Juice of 1 lemon
- Splash of soda water

- Garnish: sprig of mint

Vigorously shake all ingredients with ice until well chilled. Strain into a Collins glass over fresh ice and garnish with a mint sprig.

# BELLINI

🕐 1930s

📍 VENICE, ITALY

👤 GIUSEPPE CIPRIANI

🏠 HARRY'S BAR

🍷 PROSECCO

🍸 FLUTE

If asked to name alcoholic brunch cocktails, two immediately come to mind, and they both contain sparkling wine. One is the Mimosa (page 100); the other is without a doubt the Bellini, invented in Harry's Bar, Venice, Italy.

The name of the drink dates back to 1948, however its creator, Giuseppe Cipriani, had been serving the bubbly concoction as an elegant aperitivo to delight guests practically since the bar opened in May 1931. Before then, no one had thought to combine a purée of Italian white peaches (as opposed to the banal yellow ones), lemon juice, grenadine for color, and festive Prosecco.

For years it was simply the house aperitif. Then, in 1948, a grand exhibition of Renaissance artist Giovanni Bellini took place in Venice, and Cipriani was inspired to finally name the bar's most popular drink.

The white peaches used in the early decades of Harry's Bar were grown in the Venice area. Giuseppe's son, Arrigo (Italian for "Harry"), writes in the *Harry's Bar Cookbook* that it's "… never yellow peaches, better still if the white peaches are small with a pink skin." The reason for this distinction is that white peaches have subtle floral aromatics absent from the yellow ones.

This fruity, bubbly drink has become a staple on hundreds, if not thousands, of menus (including wedding receptions) the world over, particularly as an accompaniment to a weekend midday meal, but still also as an aperitif. While Harry's insists on using high-quality Conegliano Valdobbiadene Prosecco Superiore DOCG, or at the very least, a Prosecco DOC, these days most Bellinis are prepared with any number of sparkling wines from around the world—Champagne, of course, but also Cava, and other dry white styles.

At some point, the lemon and grenadine were omitted from the recipe, which is now simply white peach purée and Prosecco. (Use store-bought purée if white peaches aren't available.)

- 2 oz (60 ml) white peach purée
- 6 oz (180 ml) Prosecco

Pour the peach purée into a champagne flute, then add the Prosecco. Gently stir, and your peach Bellini is ready to be served.

# BIRD OF PARADISE FIZZ

🕐 1930s
▷ COLÓN, PANAMA
🗛 UNKNOWN

⌂ STRANGERS CLUB
🍶 GIN
🍸 HIGHBALL

Caribbean cocktails tend to be associated with tropical islands, however there are exceptions to the genre. One such is the Bird of Paradise Fizz, one of the few classic recipes hailing from Panama. It was first popularized by cocktail author Charles H. Baker, who came across "this colourful, eye-filling experience" of a drink in the 1930s while signing the guestbook at the Strangers Club in Colón, which many celebrities and dignitaries going the extra mile to imbibe during Prohibition had also done. He later published the recipe in his 1939 book, *The Gentleman's Companion Volume II: Being An Exotic Drinking Book.*

Considering its provenance, another of the cocktail's unique quirks is that it's based on gin, not rum. Like the Clover Club (page 20),

it's sweetened with raspberry syrup instead of sugar, but unlike that drink, it's made with lime instead of lemon. Like a Ramos Gin Fizz (page 48), it's made with fresh cream and shaken hard, served in a tall glass with a good head of foam. Similarly, it's prepared with orange blossom water, but the efflorescence is also visual in the form of a flower garnish.

Even though its origins are from the mainland, this is one of those cocktails that would almost certainly have been stranded on the Island of Forgotten Cocktails had it not been revived by the likes of Jeff "Beachbum" Berry, who included a version of the recipe in his 2013 book *Potions of the Caribbean: 500 Years of Tropical Drinks and the People Behind Them.*

- 3 oz (90 ml) dry gin
- 1 oz (30 ml) heavy (double) cream
- 1½ oz (45 ml) fresh lime juice
- 1 tbsp egg white (half a whole egg white)
- ½ oz (15 ml) raspberry syrup
- 3 dashes orange blossom water
- 1 oz (30 ml) club soda

- Garnish: edible flower (the original recipe suggests bougainvillea, however it's best to use something that would be safer to touch the drink, such as a pesticide-free orchid, available at specialty stores)

Add the gin, cream, lime juice, egg white, and raspberry syrup to a shaker filled three-quarters of the way with crushed ice. Shake "with extreme prejudice" (meaning vigorously, and for a long time until very frothy) and pour, unstrained, into a tall glass with some room at the top. Add the orange blossom water, then club soda, and stir. Garnish with an edible flower.

# FANCIULLI

- 1930s
- NEW YORK CITY, USA
- ALBERT STEVENS CROCKETT

- WALDORF-ASTORIA BAR
- BOURBON OR RYE
- COUPE

The Fanciulli cocktail is a variation on the Perfect Manhattan—bourbon or rye, and a split of sweet and dry vermouth—that replaces the dry vermouth with Fernet-Branca liqueur. The first published recipe appears in the book *Old Waldorf Bar Days* by Albert Stevens Crockett in 1931. In the book, Stevens notes that this signature, served at the prestigious New York City hotel bar, could have been named for the background singers who were in town performing the Giacomo Puccini opera "La Fanciulla del West" ("The Girl of the Golden West"). "Fanciulli" means "boys" in Italian, so it could have been a play on words, although given that the drink was first served prior to the premier of the opera in 1910, there is likely another, albeit still musically themed, origin story.

Former Waldorf bar manager Frank Caiafa, author of 2016's *The Waldorf Astoria Bar Book,* says its bartenders were known to name drinks after regulars. Francesco Fanciulli, an Italian maestro who lived in New York City after taking over the US Marine Band from John Philip Sousa in the 1890s, could very well have been one. The use of the bracingly bitter Italian ingredient Fernet would certainly make sense: Fanciulli famously had an ongoing fight with the US government to unionize and raise the pay of military band musicians. There was also an incident during an 1897 Memorial Day parade in Washington, D.C. when he took issue with being told what to play by Lt. T. L. Draper, told him off, and was subsequently court martialed (though Navy Secretary Theodore Roosevelt overturned the conviction). Fanciulli was known to harbor bitterness over this incident, hence the use of Italian Fernet to represent him.

Either way, the Fanciulli survives as a go-to Manhattan variation for those who lean toward the bitter flavor spectrum.

---

- 1½ oz (45 ml) bourbon or rye
- ¾ oz (22 ml) sweet vermouth
- ¾ (22 ml) Fernet-Branca

- Garnish: orange twist and cocktail cherry

Stir all ingredients with ice until well chilled. Strain into a chilled coupe glass. Express the oils from a piece of orange peel into the drink, skin side down, then twist the orange peel and thread a cocktail pick through it before adding the cherry and placing in the drink or balancing on the rim of the glass.

Larceny and Old Lace

This variation comes courtesy of Caiafa, who served it during his tenure.

- 1½ oz (45 ml) Larceny bourbon
- ¾ oz (22 ml) Carpano Antica Formula sweet vermouth
- ¾ oz (22 ml) Cynar liqueur
- 1 dash orange bitters

- Garnish: lemon twist and cocktail cherry

Follow the recipe on the left, replacing the orange twist with lemon.

# MEDIA COMBINACÍON

⊕ 1930s  
⌂ CHICOTE  
▷ MADRID, SPAIN  
◊ VERMOUTH; GIN  
𐎒 PEDRO CHICOTE  
𝒴 ROCKS

For many decades, vermouth was considered a supporting player in the cocktail realm, and a mistreated and misunderstood one at that. Vermouth is an aromatized and fortified wine after all, and should be treated as one would a good wine, refrigerated after opening to keep fresh, not growing dusty and oxidized on a back bar. Although vermouth has recently become cool again (literally), it was only in certain parts of Europe, particularly Italy and Spain, that it was always treated in bar culture with the respect it deserves. Still, one of Spain's most popular mid-twentieth-century aperitifs, Media Combinacíon, spent a few decades as out of fashion as flared trousers.

Writer and vermouth afficionado François Monti says this upscaled variation of Spain's classic vermut cocktail—*vermut rojo* (red), splash soda, olive—was perfected in Madrid in the 1930s by bartender Pedro "Perico" Chicote at his self-named bar. He claimed at the time that it was a variation of a cocktail he enjoyed while visiting Cuba in the 1920s. His version adds a pour of gin and a splash of curaçao, set off by Angostura bitters. By the 1950s, Perico's Media Combinacíon was considered the most sophisticated aperitif to order in Spain, and most bars offered their own take on it.

Although its popularity declined for a few decades, Media Combinacíon is now being celebrated via a new generation of bars and restaurants, particularly those with a strong vermouth program, such as the José Andrés Group. As with the mid-twentieth-century MC fad, most of the venues will serve their own spin on the basic recipe template.

- 2 oz (60 ml) red vermouth (Spanish for authenticity)
- 1 oz (30ml) London dry gin
- ¼ oz (7 ml) curaçao
- 2 dashes Angostura bitters

- Garnish: orange twist

Add all ingredients to an ice-filled rocks glass, then stir. Express the oils from a piece of orange peel into the drink, skin side down, then twist and place in the glass.

# OLOFFSON'S RUM PUNCH

⏱ 1930s        ⌂ GRAND HOTEL OLOFFSON
⮞ PORT-AU-PRINCE, HAITI      🍶 RHUM BARBANCOURT
🜨 JOSEPH CÉSAR        🍸 HIGHBALL

The Hotel Oloffson, situated at the top of a hill in Port-au-Prince, Haiti, has been described as resembling a giant gingerbread house. It's known for its rum punch, created by Joseph César, one of its original barmen from the 1930s. César died in 1981—and so did his secret recipe along with him. However, Oloffson's Rum Punch (mixed in an approximation to his original recipe) is still considered one of the most sacred drinks in cocktail history.

The hotel was built in the late nineteenth century as a private mansion for the Haitian president Guillaume Sam, who came from a wealthy, influential family and only served a few months before he was brutally assassinated. The ornate structure was converted to a hotel in the 1930s by Walter Gustav Oloffson. By the 1950s and 60s, it was attracting a star-studded clientele and was nicknamed the "Greenwich Village of the Tropics" for its roster of intellectually minded artists and writers. It was the setting for Graham Greene's 1966 novel *The Comedians* (the punch plays a cameo both in the book and movie adaptation), and various rooms are named for past guests, such as Jackie Onassis and Mick Jagger.

Tiki impresario Trader Vic positively *kvelled* over the rum punch and published an interpretation of the super-secret hush-hush recipe in the 1940s. Tiki historian Jeff "Beachbum" Berry's book *Potions of the Caribbean* features an adaptation of Vic's recipe, while the César's Rum Punch that originally appeared in a 1973 *Playboy* was the go-to variation for decades. He insists Rhum Barbancourt from Haiti would be the most authentic base regardless.

Oloffson's Rum Punch (1940s)

- 1 tsp white sugar
- ¾ oz (22 ml) fresh lime juice
- 2½ oz (75 ml) Rhum Barbancourt
- ¼ oz (7 ml) maraschino liqueur
- 1½ oz (45 ml) fresh orange juice
- Dark Jamaican rum, to float on top

Dissolve the sugar in the lime juice. Add all the other ingredients except the Jamaican rum and shake with ice. Strain into a highball glass filled with fresh ice. Using a barspoon, float the Jamaican rum over the top of the drink.

César's Rum Punch (1973)

- 1 tsp white sugar
- 2 oz (60 ml) fresh lime juice
- 2 oz (60 ml) Rhum Barbancourt
- 1 oz (30 ml) grenadine
- 3 drops Angostura bitters

- Garnish: pineapple wedge and cocktail cherry speared through cocktail pick

Dissolve the sugar in the lime juice. Add all the remaining ingredients and shake with ice. Strain into a highball glass filled with crushed ice. Garnish with a pineapple wedge and cherry.

# SEAPEA FIZZ

| | | | |
|---|---|---|---|
| ⊕ | 1930s | ⌂ | RITZ HOTEL |
| ⊳ | PARIS, FRANCE | ◊ | ABSINTHE |
| ⋏ | FRANK MEIER | ⟡ | COUPE |

..................................................................................................................

Frank Meier was the celebrated, "cracker jack" head barkeep at the Ritz in Paris, France. Born in Austria, he had worked in the hotel hospitality industry in both Paris and London from a young age, and was tapped to open the Ritz bar in 1920, serving there through World War II. The Seapea Fizz—which originally called for sweetened Anis "Pernod fils," lemon, and soda water—is one of the most famous cocktails featured in his stylish 1936 book *The Artistry of Mixing Drinks*, although the recipe has been tweaked over the years.

There is an entire section of *Artistry* devoted to the fizz genre of cocktails, including the "New Orleans Fizz" that closely resembles the Ramos Gin Fizz (page 48), and a raspberry liqueur and sloe gin "Ruby Fizz." The notation for this drink is "Seapea 'C.P.' — Special for Mr. Cole Porter, famous composer of lyrics and music." Does that mean Porter drank this tailor-made cocktail at the Ritz bar in Meier's presence? It's highly possible.

The original recipe, which lacks much sweetener and could use a binding agent of some sort, might not have people singing "You're the Top," but keep in mind that anis liqueur was *de rigueur* in 1920s and 30s France and Meier would have used a soda siphon for dramatic effect when serving. Modern variations of the Seapea Fizz use absinthe instead of Pernod, and additional simple syrup. Also, the drink was just begging for an egg white (perhaps it was even accidentally left out? Anything goes…). Therefore, contemporary recipes call for it, which not only makes the cocktail taste better, but truly lends it the aesthetic quality of sea foam.

..................................................................................................................

- ¾ oz (22 ml) absinthe
- ¾ oz (22 ml) simple syrup
- ¾ oz (22 ml) fresh lemon juice
- 1 egg white
- Soda water, chilled, to top

Add all ingredients except soda water to a cocktail shaker and shake without ice for at least 20 seconds. Add ice and shake for an additional 15 to 20 seconds. Strain into a coupe glass and top with soda water.

..................................................................................................................

# TEQUILA SUNRISE

⊕ 1930s                         ⌂ AGUA CALIENTE
⮞ TIJUANA, MEXICO               ⍭ TEQUILA
ᚨ UNKNOWN                       ⍭ HIGHBALL OR PINT

In his 2010 memoir *Life*, Rolling Stones guitarist Keith Richards writes that the epically debauched 1972 tour promoting the band's *Exile on Main St* album was nicknamed the "Cocaine and Sunrise Tour"—the "Sunrise" because of Mick Jagger's fondness for Tequila Sunrises (not mornings). They even stocked tequila in the limos. But in the 1930s, decades before the Stones would crash at the Playboy Mansion (or the county jail), the Tequila Sunrise was invented as an entirely different drink at Agua Caliente—a casino complex that even included a racetrack—in Tijuana, Mexico. It was a huge draw for alcohol-seeking tourists and celebrities as a south-of-the-border Prohibition retreat.

Agua Caliente's version is a tall refresher made with tequila, lime, grenadine, and crème de cassis, layered over ice in a highball glass. Once Prohibition ended, the Biltmore hotel in Phoenix, Arizona, which has also laid claim to its invention, was making a similar drink that enjoyed brief popularity and is still served there.

In 1970, bartender Bobby Lozoff at the Trident restaurant in Sausalito, California originated his variation, skipping the cassis, mixing the tequila with orange juice and a splash of gin, and finishing with a generous dollop of grenadine cascading through the glass for that sunrise effect. In 1972, he served one to Jagger, who preferred his without gin. By the mid-1970s, it seems, no turn of a barstool was left un-Stonesed. The Tequila Sunrise became as much a 70s icon as polyester and disco balls, forever associated with first tequila experiences and sugar-laden hangovers.

By the 2000s, cocktailians had refreshed the Tequila Sunrise for the modern era, although it still wears platforms. It's just made with less cloying ingredients, such as fresh juices, 100% blue Weber agave tequila, and homemade grenadine, among other variations that include "sunsets" and "twilights."

Tequila Sunrise (1930s)

- 2 oz (60 ml) 100% agave blanco or reposado tequila
- ½ oz (15 ml) grenadine
- 1 tsp crème de cassis
- ½ lime

Layer all ingredients except the lime in a highball glass over ice. Squeeze the lime over the drink and add to the glass. Sip through a straw.

Tequila Sunrise (1970)

- 1½ oz (45 ml) 100% agave blanco or reposado tequila
- 2½ oz (75 ml) orange juice
- ¾ oz (22 ml) dry gin (most are made without)
- ¼ oz (7 ml) grenadine (or more)

Shake the tequila and orange juice (and gin, if using) with ice until well chilled. Strain into a highball glass (though in most dive bars, it's a pint glass) over fresh ice. Add the grenadine and let it settle over the drink. Do not stir.

# VIEUX CARRÉ

- ⊕ 1930s
- ⚑ NEW ORLEANS, USA
- ⚇ WALTER BERGERON
- ⌂ CAROUSEL BAR, HOTEL MONTELEONE
- ⚗ WHISKEY
- ♈ COUPE

.................................................................................

The Vieux Carré is one of the quintessential signatures of New Orleans, a true representative of the Crescent City. The bright and spicy concoction was invented in the 1930s by Walter Bergeron, head bartender of the Hotel Monteleone Carousel Bar, during his second stint in that role, having left it during Prohibition. The name is a French translation of "old square" and refers to the French Quarter neighborhood where the hotel is located.

The recipe first appeared in print in Stanley Clisby Arthur's 1938 book *New Orleans Drinks and How To Mix 'Em*, and is a potent mix of North American rye whiskey, with French ingredients—cognac, sweet vermouth, Bénédictine D.O.M. liqueur—as well as both Angustura bitters from the West Indies and local Peychaud's bitters. The mixture is meant to represent the flavors of the Quarter, which Arthur describes as "… that part of New Orleans where the antique shops and iron lace balconies give sightseers a glimpse into the romance of another day."

Although it's always been a local Big Easy staple, the Vieux Carré (pronounced "Voo Ka-ray" in local parlance) is one of those cocktails that fell out of fashion elsewhere during the late 1960s and 70s. However, as if taking an extra slow rotation around the grand Carousel Bar, where it was born, it circled its way back into the hearts of a new generation of cocktail drinkers around the world, thanks to the rye whiskey boom of the early 2000s and the rise of Internet cocktail chatrooms and blogs. The drink is also treasured for its inclusion of cognac, which adds a unique extra layer to the typical single spirit + vermouth + liqueur formula of the Manhattan variation.

Give it a spin!

.................................................................................

- ¾ oz (22 ml) straight rye whiskey
- ¾ oz (22ml) cognac VS or VSOP
- ¾ oz (22 ml) sweet vermouth
- ¼ oz (7 ml) Bénédictine D.O.M. liqueur
- 2 dashes Angustura bitters
- 2 dashes Peychaud's bitters

- Garnish: lemon twist and/or cocktail cherry

Stir all ingredients with ice until well chilled. Strain into a chilled coupe glass. Express the oils from the lemon twist into the glass, and place in the glass with a cocktail cherry, if using.

.................................................................................

# CORPSE REVIVER NO. 2

- 1930
- LONDON, UK
- HARRY CRADDOCK

- AMERICAN BAR, SAVOY HOTEL
- GIN
- COUPE

To the unfamiliar, this cocktail sounds like it comes from a 1990s-era TGI Friday's' menu. However, "reviver" is a genre of cocktails that has been around since the 1850s, originating in the UK. The first known versions were served at a bar in Piccadilly, London, and intended to stimulate the palate during the early part of the day. Some referred to them as "anti-fogmatic," which is a stately way to refer to a hangover remedy.

The drink might have been lost to history entirely if it hadn't been for Harry Craddock, the New York bartender who relocated to the American Bar at the Savoy hotel in the 1920s, who included recipes for Corpse No. 1 and Corpse No. 2 in the 1930 *Savoy Cocktail Book.*

Having again gone out of rotation for decades, Corpse Reviver No. 2 was resurrected in the early 2000s by cocktail enthusiasts who found it in Craddock's book and favored this refreshing gin lemonade-like recipe over the stirred, often unctuous No. 1. Its rediscovery also happened to coincide with the Stateside legalization of real absinthe—an essential flavor component—and it became one of the "it" cocktails, particularly around 2008 into the early 2010s. These days, almost any decent bar with the necessary ingredients either has it on the menu already or will know how to make one, and there are ready-to-drink (RTD) versions as well. Of course, Corpse No. 2 is once again one of the stars of the Savoy, too.

- ¾ oz (22 ml) dry gin
- ¾ oz (22 ml) Lillet Blanc (or Cocchi Americano, closer to the original Kina Lillet recipe)
- ¾ oz (22 ml) orange liqueur
- ¾ oz (22 ml) fresh lemon juice
- 1 dash absinthe

- Garnish: lemon twist

Shake the gin, Lillet Blanc, orange liqueur, and lemon juice with ice, adding the absinthe via your chosen method,* and strain into a coupe glass before garnishing with a lemon twist.

*A word on incorporating the absinthe: bartenders use several methods. Some simply add a scant dash to the other ingredients before shaking them together. Some rinse the cocktail glass out with it. Others spray it over the finished drink with an aromatizer.

# CLARITO

🕐 1935
⚐ BUENOS AIRES, ARGENTINA
👤 SANTIAGO POLICASTRO

⌂ UNKNOWN
🍸 GIN
🍸 MARTINI

Just because something is popular doesn't necessarily mean it appeals to *everyone*. In the 1930s, the preferred serve for the dry Martini was up with an olive or twist. However, in Buenos Aires, Argentina, few locals ordered them, because they were turned off by the olives. So in 1935, bartender Santiago "Pichín" Policastro sought to modify the classic gin Martini for Argentine palates.

He ditched the olives altogether and instead would moisten the rim of the Martini glass with lemon rind and dip it into fine sugar, then add a long, continuous strand of lemon peel swirled against the glass before the final drink—from here essentially a dry Martini made with vermouth blanc and dry gin, stirred with more lemon—was chilled and poured in. His resulting innovation was somewhere between a lemony dry Martini and a sort of Gin Crusta, and it was a massive success. ¡*Claritos para todos*!

By the 1960s, the so-called "Argentine Martini" had fallen into near obscurity. By that time, most Claritos were served with the long peel minus the sugar rim. However, in the early 2000s, riding the wave of the classic cocktail revival, bartender Federico Cuco resuscitated the once-beloved national cocktail (opting to omit the sugar) at the Verne Cocktail Club in Buenos Aires. There was even a "Save the Clarito" campaign, started by Cuco in 2008. Since then, it has become one of the most ordered cocktails in Argentina.

The technique is a little tricky, but well worth the extra steps.

• ⅓ oz (10 ml) dry vermouth
• 3 oz (90 ml) dry gin
• 2 small pieces lemon rind

• Garnish: long lemon rind spiral

Add whole ice cubes to a mixing glass and let sit. Rub the rim of a Martini glass with a small piece of lemon rind and add the rind to a mixing glass. Set aside. Fill the Martini glass with crushed ice. Set aside. Strain off the excess water from the mixing glass, then add the vermouth and gin along with the second small piece of lemon rind, squeezing the oils into the mix. Stir until combined and well chilled. Discard the ice from the Martini glass, add the long spiral of lemon rind against the sides, and strain the contents of the mixing glass into the spiraled Martini glass.

# DEATH IN THE AFTERNOON

- ⏱ 1935
- ⚑ FRANCE
- ⍺ ERNEST HEMINGWAY

- ⌂ UNKNOWN
- ◊ CHAMPAGNE; ABSINTHE
- ⍶ FLUTE

Death in the Afternoon is a Champagne and absinthe cocktail that was conceived by the author Ernest Hemingway, who went through an absinthe phase in Paris in the 1920s. The recipe for his signature Champagne concoction was first published in 1935's *So Red the Nose, or, Breath in the Afternoon,* edited by Sterling North and Carl Kroch. All the cocktails featured in the book were contributed by famous writers of that period—Erskine Caldwell, Virginia Faulkner, Dorothy Aldis, and dozens of others—and can be counted as one of the first celebrity recipe compilations.

Although it is named for his 1930s treatise on bullfighting in Spain, the inspiration for Death in the Afternoon is a reflection on one of his naval adventures: "This was arrived at by the author and three officers of H.M.S. *Danae* after having spent seven hours overboard trying to get Capt. Bra Saunders' fishing boat off a bank

where she had gone with us in a N.W. gale." *Danae* was a British naval vessel that was later used in the South Atlantic and Indian oceans during World War II.

Hemingway instructs to drink "3 to 5 slowly." However, a note from the editors reads, "It takes a man with hair on his chest to drink five Absinthe and Champagne Cocktails and still handle the English language in the Hemingway fashion." Also, "After six of these cocktails, the *Sun Also Rises.*"

After 2007, when absinthe once again became legal in the US, a wormwood cocktail boom repopularized Death in the Afternoon on American cocktail menus, at least for a time. While in Europe, especially in the Czech Republic, where high-ABV absinthe is still popular, one sees a cloudy flute of bubbly and instantly recognizes the drink order.

- 1½ oz (45 ml) absinthe
- About 4 oz (120 ml) chilled Champagne (other dry sparkling wine will also do)

- Garnish: lemon peel (optional)

Pour the absinthe into a flute or white wine glass, then add chilled Champagne "until it attains the proper opalescence." Garnish with lemon peel, if using.

# TOM & JERRY

| | | |
|---|---|---|
| ⏱ | 1935 | ⌂ MILLER'S PUB |
| ⚑ | CHICAGO, USA | ◊ RUM OR BRANDY |
| ⋔ | UNKNOWN | ⨅ CERAMIC OR GLASS MUG |

The Tom & Jerry is a creamy, sweet, and spicy large-format winter concoction that resembles eggnog but is served warm. Recipes have existed since at least the 1820s and likely originated in the UK, though storied American barman Jerry Thomas, who included a recipe for the Tom & Jerry in his 1862 *Bar-tender's Guide*, laid claim to it. At the very least, he might be responsible for the tweaks that saw it evolve into the go-to standard. From the 1930s to the late 1960s or so, it was adopted as a traditional winter treat all over the US, served as soon as temperatures dropped. Its name, which pre-dates the cat and mouse cartoon characters by nearly a century, also refers to the sets of porcelain bowls from which it is ladled into matching mugs. By the end of the twentieth century, only a few establishments still served the labor-intensive hot punch, but it's still popular from the end of November to early spring in certain bars in the Midwest, particularly Miller's Pub in Chicago, which has ladled it out every winter since opening its doors in 1935.

According to drinks writer Robert Simonson, at the famous Loop neighborhood bar, "They even advertise it on their illuminated sign outside. The bowl sits right behind the bar near the cash register."

Recipes vary between using cognac (or other brandy) and rum, or both, as the base spirit, and like Bloody Marys the spice ratio diverges according to taste. No matter the preference, the ideal Tom & Jerry should be pillowy, like a freshly mixed egg batter, and warm, but not too hot.

Miller's exact recipe remains a secret, but it resembles this one, adapted from Audrey Saunders (who served them at NYC's Pegu Club every winter until it closed in 2020) via *The Oxford Companion to Spirits and Cocktails*. The Tom & Jerry mix makes enough for a crowd.

---

- 1 oz (30 ml) dark rum or brandy (or 1:1 split)
- 1 oz (30 ml) Tom & Jerry Mix
- Hot milk or hot water, to top

- Garnish: grated nutmeg

Preheat a coffee mug with hot water, then discard the water. Add the spirit of choice, Tom & Jerry mix, then top with hot milk or hot (not boiling) water. Grate nutmeg over the top.

For the Tom & Jerry Mix

- 12 eggs, separated
- 4½ cups (900 g) sugar
- 1 oz (30 ml) dark rum or brandy (or 1:1 split)
- 1½ tsp ground cinnamon
- ½ tsp each ground allspice and grated nutmeg
- ¼ tsp ground cloves

In a medium bowl, beat the egg whites until stiff peaks form. In a separate bowl, beat the yolks until pale yellow. Mix them together in a large bowl with the sugar, spirit of choice, and the spices. Stir until it resembles a cake batter. Refrigerate to cool and use within 4 to 6 hours.

# QUEEN MARY

🕐 1936
⚑ SOUTHAMPTON, UK
👤 "MUTCH"

⌂ RMS *QUEEN MARY*
🍶 GIN
🍸 DOUBLE ROCKS

RMS *Queen Mary* was an ocean liner run by the British Cunard-White Star Line and built by John Brown & Company in Clydebank, Scotland. While it occasionally visited other destinations during its main run between 1936 and 1967, the *Queen Mary*, named for Mary of Teck, the consort of King George V, traveled primarily on the Atlantic Ocean between New York City and Southhampton in the UK. The ship boasted two indoor swimming pools, dog kennels, paddle courts, a performance space/lecture hall, beauty salons, libraries, children's nurseries, and a "Jewish prayer" facility in what was then a rare show of religiously inclusive support. There was a grand main dining room for all classes, though the ship's star attractions were the smaller, more exclusive Art Deco lounge, the Observation Bar, and, on the upper deck, the Verandah Grill, which transformed into the Starlight Club at night. Naturally, all this floating finery deserved its own signature cocktail, which was stirred up on the maiden voyage in 1936 by a bartender known only as "Mutch."

The Queen Mary Cocktail consists of gin, a squeeze of lime, and ginger beer. Essentially a simple gin mule, what's significant about this recipe is that it precedes the vodka-based Moscow Mule by about five years, though both recipes can certainly be traced to the Mamie Taylor whiskey ginger highball from 1890s Rochester, New York.

Drink historians Jared Brown and Anistatia Miller discovered a 1942 notice in *Motor Boating* magazine that mentions Mutch went on to serve the Queen Mary cocktail aboard the *Laconia* in the 1930s before it was converted into a merchant cruiser in 1939. The gin mule cocktail as a species all but disappeared until its early 2000s revival, which includes the ever-popular Gin Gin Mule from Audrey Saunders' Pegu Club in New York City.

---

- 2 oz (60 ml) dry gin
- Juice of ½ key lime
  (or juice of 2 lime wedges)
- Ginger beer, to top

- Garnish: 2 lime wedges (if not using key lime juice)

Combine the gin and lime juice (if using the wedges, squeeze them into the drink, then add the wedges to the glass) in a double rocks glass. Stir. Add plenty of ice and top with ginger beer. Stir again.

# 20TH CENTURY

⊕ 1937
⚑ LONDON, UK
 A C. A. TUCK

⌂ CAFÉ ROYAL
⚗ GIN
Y COUPE

These days, even a first-class train ticket should come with a complimentary sanitary wipe. However, in the early 1900s, cross-country train travel was a posh affair. The 20th Century Limited Express, a passenger train that ran between New York City and Chicago from 1902 to 1967, was one of the snazziest ways to travel overnight in the US via "The Great Steel Fleet," with stunning, glitzy carriage interiors designed by Henry Dreyfuss.

The crown jewel of the Limited was its dining car. In the daytime hours, it was a luxurious setting in which to take morning and midday meals, and with a far less polluted view of the East-Midwest American landscape than we have now. However, in the evening, the car was transformed into Café Century, a nightclub on wheels rivaling any found in its destination cities. Of course, cocktails were in order, and they were consumed in vast quantities. Yet the drink named after this glamorous ride wasn't invented until the 1930s.

The recipe was first published in 1937 in the *Café Royal Cocktail Book* by William J. Tarling, who names British bartender C. A. Tuck as its creator. Essentially, the drink is a Corpse Reviver No. 2 made with crème de cacao instead of orange liqueur. Mixed with gin, Lillet Blanc (it was Kina Lillet back then), and fresh lemon juice, this might sound like an odd combination. However, the ingredients dance like a Lindy Hop—it turns out the crème de cacao adds an extra note of brightness rather than cloying sweetness.

- 1½ oz (45 ml) dry gin
- ¾ oz (22 ml) fresh lemon juice
- ½ oz (15 ml) Lillet Blanc
  or Cocchi Americano
- ½ oz (15 ml) white crème de cacao

- Garnish: lemon twist

Shake all ingredients with ice. Double strain into a chilled coupe glass. Garnish with a lemon twist.

# ALMOND BLOSSOM CRUSTA

- 🕐 1940s
- ▷ SANTIAGO, CHILE
- A UNKNOWN

- ⌂ HOTEL CRILLON
- 🍶 COGNAC; GIN
- Y COUPE

..................................................................................................

A crusta is a species of cocktail credited to Italian-born New Orleans bartender Joseph Santini in the 1850s during his tenures at the St. Louis Hotel and Jewel of the South. Early crusta recipes, first published in the 1862 edition of *Bar-tender's Guide* by Jerry Thomas, called for whisky and gin, though brandy later edged them out as the most popular base. The defining feature of any crusta is its presentation, with a lemon peel cut into a spiral and set inside a wine or coupe glass that has been crusted with a wide sugar rim. It can be argued that the Sidecar was born from the crusta, and with the most popular American serve of Sidecar using a sugar rim, the two are often confused with one another. However, one of the most interesting takes is the Almond Blossom Crusta, the signature cocktail of the Hotel Crillon in Santiago, Chile, first served in the 1940s.

The cocktail gained particular notoriety when it was published in *The South American Gentleman's Companion* in 1951 by roving cocktailian Charles H. Baker. The recipe, which he discovered at the Hotel Crillon during his travels, calls for both cognac and gin, with fresh lemon juice and the addition of orgeat (almond syrup), which adds a subtle marzipan-like layer to the drink.

The Almond Blossom Crusta is one of those cocktails that would have been lost to time had it not been discussed in online forums during the early days of the modern cocktail renaissance. Since then, the lavish cocktail has been adopted by bars and restaurants around the world and presented at drink conferences and other special events to showcase the gin and cognac brands used to prepare it.

..................................................................................................

- 1½ oz (45 ml) cognac
- ½ oz (15 ml) gin
- ¾ oz (22 ml) fresh lemon juice
- ¾ oz (22 ml) orgeat (homemade or store-bought)

- Garnish: orgeat and white granulated sugar to rim the glass,* orange or lemon peel, cut in a long spiral, to set in the glass

Rim a coupe glass by dipping it in a saucer of orgeat and another saucer of sugar. Set aside to dry. Cut off both ends of a whole lemon or orange and, using a peeler (not a wide one), peel off a single, long spiral. Place in the rimmed glass. Shake all ingredients with ice until well chilled and frothy, at least 15 to 20 seconds. Strain into the prepared glass.

*For best results, prepare the glass a few hours before making the drink to ensure a dried sugar rim.

..................................................................................................

# IRISH COFFEE

🕐 1940s            ⌂ FOYNES AIRPORT
⊳ IRELAND        ⌀ WHISKEY
🯅 JOE SHERIDAN     ⅄ HEATPROOF GLASS MUG

.......................................................................................

One of the highest volume cocktails on the planet is served every day in San Francisco, but the drink, and its countless variations around the world, was born in Ireland.

When Americans took transatlantic flights in the 1940s, one of the only available routes from the United States was via the Pan Am flying boat to Foynes airport in County Limerick, Ireland, which meant arriving in the dead of night, on the water. Joe Sheridan, head chef at the airport restaurant, would meet bleary-eyed, shivering passengers with coffee. At some point, he fortified it with Irish whiskey, sugar, and whipped cream.

Transatlantic flights were directed through nearby Shannon airport by 1945, where Irish Coffee, as it became known, had become a local staple. In the 1950s, *San Francisco Chronicle* travel writer, the aptly named Stanton Delaplane, experienced the boozy pick-me-up. He brought the basic recipe back to his hometown local, the Buena Vista Café, where it became the house drink, perfected by bar owners Jack Koeppler and George Freeberg.

It is said the Buena Vista now serves up to 2,000 Irish coffees a day, with dozens of glass mugs lined up on the bar, filled, and shuttled about, then the whole scene reset within what seems like mere seconds.

Irish Coffee was also the star of modern cocktail luminary Dale DeGroff's legendary St. Patrick's Day brunches at New York City's Charley O's in the 1970s, and it is now the quintessential house drink at The Dead Rabbit, prepared using his specs. Versions around the world swap out the whiskey for other base spirits, adding additional liqueurs, using spiced syrups, and/or even replacing the coffee with tea.

.......................................................................................

Original recipe

• Hot water
• 1 or 2 sugar cubes
• 6 oz (180 ml) freshly brewed, hot coffee
• 1½ oz (45 ml) Irish whiskey of choice
• Fresh whipped cream

Add hot water to a heatproof glass mug to warm it, then discard. Quickly add the sugar cube(s), then the coffee and stir to dissolve. Add the whiskey and stir again. Top with whipped cream. Engaging in debate over whether to garnish with grated nutmeg, grated cinnamon, or cocoa powder, optional.

# SCORPION BOWL

| | | | |
|---|---|---|---|
| ⏱ | 1940s | ⌂ | TRADER VIC'S |
| ⚑ | OAKLAND, USA | ◊ | GIN; RUM |
| ⚇ | VICTOR BERGERON | ⏑ | TIKI BOWL |

.........................................................................................................

The Scorpion Bowl, aka Scorpion, is a potent, communal tiki-era drink that is traditionally shared with long straws from one—typically ornate ceramic—vessel between four or more people. Tiki impresario Victor "Trader Vic" Bergeron popularized it in the 1940s on the menu at Trader Vic's in Oakland, California, after which it was imitated the world over.

A November 2019 essay in the *Daily Beast* by drinks historian David Wondrich traces the exact circumstances that inspired Trader Vic's Scorpion, the story as dizzying to read as the effects of sipping an entire bowl solo. The gist: Trader Vic was in the Manoa Valley of Honolulu, Hawaii in 1938 and attended a luau where, among the poi and the palm fronds, attendees used long straws to sip a communal drink made from the local Okolehao aguardiente-like distillate that had floating gardenias in it. *'O ke koena ka mo'oelo* ("the rest is history").

Trader Vic's version calls for rum and multiple spirits with fresh fruit juices and orgeat (almond syrup)—widely interpreted over the years and varying in sweetness from cloying to slightly sour. Some chuck it all in a blender with ice before serving, others prefer to just do it punch style. Some set it on fire, others do without the pyrotechnics. No one can really agree on an exact authentic recipe, but a successful Scorpion Bowl is all about fun and whatever tastes good.

This recipe is a mashup of several sources, based on the bones of Trader Vic's original. It's blended until the ice is chunky, not like a slushy. You will need plenty of small ice cubes on hand to prepare this drink.

.........................................................................................................

Serves 4

- 4 oz (120 ml) dry gin
- 4 oz (120 ml) gold rum
- 2 oz (60 ml) aged grape brandy or cognac
- 2 oz (60 ml) orgeat
  (homemade or store-bought)
- 1½ oz (45 ml) simple syrup
- 2 oz (60 ml) fresh lime juice
- 4 oz (120 ml) fresh orange juice

- Garnish: 3 mint sprigs threaded through the center of as many orange wheels, with edible orchids placed in the "bush" of the mint leaves; chunks of fruit such as pineapple, cocktail cherries, etc. (optional); flaming lime disk (optional)

Whack the mint sprig against the drinking bowl to release the aromas. Prepare the garnishes and set aside. Add all the ingredients to a blender without ice and blend until combined. Add 3 cups of ice and blend until chunky. Pour into the bowl. Add the prepared garnishes and any additional, as desired. Place 4 bamboo or metal straws into the bowl, fanning them out from the center.

If going for a flaming lime, scoop the pulp out of half a lime and float it shell-down in the middle of the bowl with a sugar cube and about ½ oz (15 ml) lemon extract or overproof 151 rum in it. Use a long match or lit wooden skewer to light. The flame will die down on its own, but if very thirsty, snuff it out before consuming. Sip away!

.........................................................................................................

# MOSCOW MULE

- 1941
- LOS ANGELES, USA
- UNKNOWN
- COCK 'N BULL CLUB
- VODKA
- MULE MUG

The Moscow Mule is one of the most popular vodka drinks of all time. That ubiquitous mix of vodka, lime, and ginger beer (the ingredient that gives the Mule a kick) served in a copper mug is the signature of the Cock 'n Bull Club in Los Angeles, where it was first served in 1941.

*The Oxford Companion to Spirits & Cocktails* documents two versions of its origin story. One is that the bar's owner, Jack Morgan, took a meeting with Smirnoff vodka rep John Martin and came up with the drink to boost sales of both the vodka and the bar's house-made spicy ginger beer. However, then head bartender Charles Wesley "Wes" Price reportedly claimed he came up with the concoction for actors Broderick Crawford and Rod Cameron. Regardless, Smirnoff put the cocktail on heavy promotional rotation for the next couple of decades.

As to how the mug became the drink's vessel of choice—whether it was to put the bar's stockpile of them to use or simply an act of creative genius on the part of Wes—since the 1940s, Moscow Mules have almost always been served this way at Cock 'n Bull and beyond.

A new wave of vodka brands emerged during the craft spirits boom of the 2010s and used Moscow Mules as one of the preferred serves. Bars all over the world were expected to stock the copper mugs to meet demand, though that resulted in widespread mug smuggling. Some venues were known to keep credit card details on file to ensure return of their vessels.

With such a simple combination, the Moscow Mule has inspired hundreds of spicy, gingery riffs, representing different cities as well as other, uh, burros. It is also one of the top flavors in the ready-to-drink (RTD) bottled and canned cocktail trend of the 2020s.

- 2 oz (60 ml) unflavored vodka
- ½ oz (15 ml) fresh lime juice
- 3 oz (90 ml) ginger beer (if made with ginger ale, that's a Buck!)

- Garnish: lime wheel (optional)

Combine all ingredients in a copper mug filled with ice. Stir. Garnish with the lime wheel, if using.

# SUFFERING BASTARD

- 1942
- CAIRO, EGYPT
- JOE SCIALOM

- SHEPHEARD'S HOTEL
- BOURBON OR BRANDY; GIN
- DOUBLE ROCKS

There is a science to great bartending. It's a study of flavors, experimenting with different combinations of ingredients to yield the desired results in the glass, understanding the properties of those ingredients and how they interact with one another, successfully mixing and presenting them, and all the while doing so with a command of the source material. Joe Scialom at the Shepheard's Hotel in Cairo, Egypt in the 1940s was a masterful bartender, but he also happened to be one with a degree in chemistry. As with many professionals outside the industry who learn to bartend, he discovered this skill was much more fun as a job than his intended field and stuck with it.

In 1942, at the height of World War II, this hotel bar was a popular hangout for British soldiers and the press. They were drawn to Scialom, an Egyptian-Jew who spoke many languages and had a gift for remembering names.

The Suffering Bastard (née Suffering Bar Steward) is Scialom's entry in the "reviver" genre of cocktails, those meant to wake one up after a long night of drinking. The drink—made from gin, brandy, lime juice, Angostura bitters, and ginger beer or ginger ale—was also apparently meant to be a "cure" for soldiers who complained of the poor quality of drinks in the area.

Scialom eventually changed bar locations to San Juan, Puerto Rico, and then Havana, Cuba, and took the recipe with him. Because of its slightly tropical and refreshing nature, cheeky name, and use of more than one spirit, his creation found its way into the tiki cocktail canon, though as an anomaly for being one of the few not automatically made with rum. At some point in its history, the brandy ingredient was changed to bourbon. Like the Sazerac or French 75, some establishments will ask customers which spirit they would prefer in the base.

- 1 oz (30 ml) bourbon or brandy
- 1 oz (30 ml) dry gin
- 1 oz (30ml) fresh lime juice
- 1 dash Angostura bitters
- Chilled ginger beer or ginger ale (depending on spice preference), to top

- Garnish: mint sprig and orange wedge

Shake all ingredients except the ginger beer with ice until well chilled. Pour unstrained into a double rocks glass. Top with ginger beer and stir. Garnish with a mint sprig and orange wedge.

# KIR

🕐 1945  
⚐ DIJON, FRANCE  
👤 FÉLIX KIR  

⌂ N/A  
🝮 CRÈME DE CASSIS  
🍸 FLUTE OR WINE  

To paraphrase Shakespeare, would a Kir known by any name taste as sweet? It is widely believed the original version of the Kir was created in Burgundy, France to promote two of its less fashionable products: Aligoté, the grape and white wine made from the much more acidic and rustic-tasting cousin to Chardonnay, and the unctuous berry liqueur, crème de cassis. In 1990's *Champagne Cocktails*, drink historians Jared Brown and Anistatia Miller explain that in the early 1900s, the concoction, consumed locally as a digestif, was referred to as *rince cochon*, which translates in English to "rinsed pig." In the 1920s, the purple-hued white wine cocktail became more elegantly known as Vin Blanc Cassis, but this was apparently to differentiate it from another drink, Vermouth Cassis.

It wasn't until 1945 that the drink was named after Félix Kir, the popular deputy-mayor of Dijon who rose to be the city's mayor until his death in 1968. By the 1960s, it became a chic thing to order in cafés across Europe and inspired numerous variations on the wine-plus-fruit-liqueur cocktail theme.

These days it's somewhat rare to see a Kir made with still white wine. Instead, the more popular variation is the Kir Royale, which swaps it out for brut Champagne (although the contemporary pour is with a less precious sparkler, such as Crémant de Bourgogne, Crémant d'Alsace, or cava). There are also variations changing up the fruit liqueur component to other fruit liqueurs or fruity syrups and shrubs.

### Kir (Classique)

- ¾ oz (22 ml) crème de cassis
- White wine, to top

Add the cassis to the bottom of a flute or wine glass. Top with the white wine.

### Kir Royale

- ½ oz (15 ml) crème de cassis
- Brut Champagne or other dry, white sparkling wine, to top

- Garnish: fresh raspberry or blackberry, or lemon twist

If using, pop the fresh berry of choice into the bottom of a flute or wine glass. Add the cassis. Top with bubbly. If using the twist instead, add it to finish.

# KENTUCKY CLUB MARGARITA

- ⏱ 1947
- ▷ JUÁREZ, MEXICO
- ⚲ LORENZO HERNANDEZ

- ⌂ KENTUCKY CLUB
- ⚗ TEQUILA
- ⍦ COUPE

As with the Manhattan and Martini, the precise origins of the drink we refer to as a "Margarita" are a bit foggy. However, as a house cocktail made in a particular iconic style that was subsequently popularized around the world, the Kentucky Club in Juárez, Mexico is considered a sort of Margarita Mecca.

"Margarita" means "daisy" in Spanish, and it is likely that a tequila-and-lime version of a Daisy-style cocktail—lemon, sugar, sometimes sweetened with additional liqueur—was served in Mexico long before it had an official name (the legend told at Kentucky Club is that a regular's girlfriend, enchanted with the drink, asked the name, and was told it was named after her, Margarita. Likely he was just being a good bartender—it's thought it was probably referred to as some combination of "tequila Margarita" long before). The American-style bar near the border, and the drink itself, gained attention from

American tourists and investors seeking to open business just outside of Prohibition territory. Riding this long wave of attention, in the 1940s, the Kentucky Club started serving its version of tequila Daisies in a signature salt-rimmed Champagne coupe—a recipe and flourish credited to bartender Lorenzo Hernandez, who would serve them there for fifty-seven years.

Following Prohibition, the elegant house Margarita drew attention from 1950s celebrities—including Marilyn Monroe and John Wayne, various Spanish celebrity bull fighters, and, in later years, boxing champ Oscar De La Hoya. It was also where GIs flocked to during World War II and the Korean and Vietnam wars.

In 2000, the Kentucky Club celebrated its 100th anniversary, and it is still serving Margaritas made with Cointreau served up in salted coupe glasses.

- 1½ oz (45 ml) silver or blanco tequila (use 100% agave versions)
- ¾ oz (22 ml) fresh lime juice
- ½ oz (15 ml) Cointreau orange liqueur

- Garnish: kosher or other coarse salt and lime wedge for the rim, lime wheel (optional)

If rimming the glass, spread a thin layer of salt in a small plate or saucer. Rub the rim of a coupe glass with a wedge of lime, then dip in the salt to make the salted rim. Set aside. Shake the tequila, lime juice, and Cointreau with ice until well chilled. Strain into the salted glass. Garnish with a lime wheel perched on the side, if using.

# BLACK RUSSIAN

🕐 1949
⚑ BRUSSELS, BELGIUM
👤 GUSTAV TOPS

⌂ METROPOLE HOTEL
◊ VODKA; KAHLÚA
🍸 ROCKS

Those of us who love the taste of coffee are naturally drawn to coffee cocktails. However, a freshly brewed, or even stale, batch of coffee isn't always available, hence the invention of coffee liqueur. Today, one of the most widely available brands is Kahlúa, made in Veracruz, Mexico, with a base of rum mixed with Arabica coffee and sugar. It first became commercially available via the Pedro Domecq liquor company in 1936.

By 1949, Kahlúa was available in Europe, and to show off this buzzy coffee liqueur, bartenders began creating signature cocktails with it. At the Hotel Metropole in Brussels, barman Gustav Tops served Perle Mesta, American Ambassador to Luxembourg, a simple little number he had whipped up with just Kahlúa and vodka, a spirit that was then closely associated with Russia. Thus, we have the Black Russian.

Made without the need for a separate brewed coffee component, the Black Russian is what lies between the Irish Coffee (page 138) and the modern-day Espresso Martini (page 190), *sans* foam or milk. After enduring the long war, a great-tasting beverage that could be prepared in a flash without much fuss was vastly appealing. For this cocktail, there's no need for extensive bartending skills, or even that much hand-eye coordination. Because it's built in the glass—no fancy tools required!—it's a drink almost anyone can make.

Of course, with anything this simple, the Black Russian has seen its fair share of more elaborate offshoots, with additional liqueurs as modifiers or using cold brew coffee or other local ingredients and bestowing it with a different regional name. Take the Colorado Bulldog, for≈example, which is a Black Russian with cola mixed in.

So what's the difference between a Black Russian and a White Russian? The White Russian is the one with the cream liqueur. And the Dude (think *The Big Lebowski*).

• 2 oz (60 ml) unflavored vodka
• 1 oz (30 ml) Kahlúa coffee liqueur

Add the ingredients to a rocks glass. Add ice, then stir until cold.

# DR. FUNK

🕐 1950s            ⌂ DON THE BEACHCOMBER'S
⚑ PALM SPRINGS, USA    ◊ RUM
👤 DONN BEACH         🍸 HURRICANE OR HIGHBALL

Dr. Funk, as we've come to know it, is a fizzy drink consisting of rum, lemon and lime juice, absinthe, and grenadine (or sometimes a mix of grenadine and passion fruit juice) with club soda or seltzer. It is said to be based on a rum-less absinthe limeade recipe by Dr. Bernard Funk, the German-born personal physician to nineteenth-century author Robert Louis Stevenson, an absinthe buff who originally concocted it to help Stevenson cope with the intense heat and humidity while he was living on the South Pacific Island of Samoa. The surviving rum-based version of Dr. Funk was popularized by Donn Beach (née Ernest Raymond Gantt), the adventurer and World War II veteran behind Don the Beachcomber's, the foundational Hollywood, California tiki palace. It's one of the few dozen or so cocktails that appeared on the original 1950s-era menu, deemed part of "Don's Drink Diaspora" by tiki expert Jeff "Beachbum" Berry in the 10th anniversary edition of *Sippin' Safari* (2017).

According to Berry, things get, well, funky, from here. Copycat versions of Don the Beachcomber's recipes, though kept well under wraps, still managed to show up at rival tropical drinks-themed habitats. In their late 1950s to 60s heyday, there were hundreds around the world. Dr. Funk begat Dr. Wong at the Luau in Beverly Hills, which begat Dr. Fong of Tahiti at the Kon-Tiki Ports restaurant in Chicago, etc, etc ...

Whatever the variation, the most important feature of Dr. Funk (or any of the other attending liquid physicians) is that it's one of the only cocktails made with absinthe (or anything absinthe adjacent, such as Pernod or Herbsaint) to survive the tiki era. To live up to its name, it's best prepared with a good, funky rum.

- 1½ oz (45 ml) Blackstrap rum (or split dark rum and white rhum agricole)
- 1 tsp absinthe
- ½ oz (15 ml) lemon juice
- ¼ oz (7 ml) lime juice
- ½ oz (15 ml) grenadine
- Club soda or seltzer, to top

- Garnish: mint sprig

Shake all ingredients except the club soda or seltzer with ice until well chilled. Strain over crushed ice into a hurricane or highball glass. Top with your fizz of choice, and garnish with a mint sprig.

# GOOMBAY SMASH

⊕ 1950s
⚑ GREEN TURTLE CAY, BAHAMAS
ጸ "MISS EMILY" COOPER

⌂ MISS EMILY'S BLUE BEE BAR
◊ RUM
Ⴓ ROCKS

Much like the original Bushwacker (page 186), the exact iteration of the first Goombay Smash—found at almost any spot in the Bahamas that serves alcoholic beverages, from beach stands to luxe resort bars—is a secret. The drink was conceived in the 1950s by "Miss Emily" Cooper, owner of Miss Emily's Blue Bee Bar on Green Turtle Cay, who is said to have wanted a house signature made with pineapple, a local staple, but didn't drink alcohol and was allergic to pineapples. On a rainy afternoon during a game of dominoes, she tried out the recipe she'd been tinkering with on a group of regulars who deemed it "very good." Relying solely on their judgment, she began serving the drink at her bar. In a short time, she had to revise the recipe to make it in larger batches, which is how it is served there to this day.

The consensus is that the original Goombay Smash recipe contained a mixture of dark rum, coconut rum, apricot brandy, pineapple, orange juice, lime juice, and Angostura bitters. However, there are so many establishments that make the tropical punch beyond the Bahamas, throughout the Caribbean, and the Florida Panhandle that recipes can vary widely, including a tendency not to include the apricot brandy or that flavor profile at all. Other venues opt instead to sub the apricot brandy or coconut rum with juices or other liqueurs.

Whatever the preference, the Goombay Smash has the power to conjure the sense of a sunny beach vacation in a glass. Perhaps that's why it's become one of the house cocktails, in, of all places, the Killington ski resort in Vermont.

• 1 oz (30 ml) dark rum
• 1 oz (30 ml) coconut rum
• ½ oz (15 ml) apricot brandy or liqueur
• 1½ oz (45 ml) fresh pineapple juice
• 1 oz (30 ml) orange juice
• ¼ oz (7 ml) fresh lime juice
• 2 dashes Angostura bitters
  (optional, but recommended)

• Garnish: pineapple wedge

Shake all ingredients with ice until well-chilled. Strain into a rocks glass over fresh ice. Garnish with a pineapple wedge.

# PINK SQUIRREL

🕑 1951
⚑ MILWAUKEE, USA
👤 UNKNOWN

🏠 BRYANT'S COCKTAIL LOUNGE
🍸 CRÈME DE NOYEAUX
🍸 MARTINI OR COUPE

The Pink Squirrel is a uniquely midwestern American cocktail that is in the same creamy dessert category as the Brandy Alexander (page 94) and Grasshopper, though it is truly an animal of a different color. Its hero ingredient is crème de noyeaux, a pink, almond-flavored crème liqueur, which can be tough to find. "Crème" means it has added sugar, not that it is made from cream. In Wisconsin, it's ice cream that makes it creamy, and this variation has been the signature of Bryant's Cocktail Lounge in Milwaukee since the 1950s.

Pink Squirrels made without ice cream have been around since at least 1951. In that year, an article from the June 11 Baton Rouge *State Times* entitled "Pink Squirrel Plugs Drink" details an event in New York City, where Bols liqueur company introduced their crème de noyeaux to the United States by, of course, having singer Betty Reed lead around a trained dyed pink squirrel at various Midtown bars to promote a drink of "two jiggers of Bols Crème de Noyeaux, one jigger of white crème de cacao, and one jigger of coffee cream." The squirrel was reported to have gone for the bar nuts instead.

The drink found its spiritual home in Milwaukee, the unofficial creamy drinks capital of the US, as well as other midwestern towns, where it's been a supper club staple since the 1950s. Bryant's claims its original owner, Bryant Sharp, invented the ice cream variation, and they sell more of them than any other venue. As with many retro mid-twentieth-century cocktails, the Pink Squirrel is finding new audiences, although the *State Times* article warns that anyone minding an actual squirrel shouldn't have more than three. "After that, you get the feeling to tell the squirrel to look after himself."

Serves 2

• 3 oz (90 ml) crème de noyeaux
• 3 oz (90 ml) white crème de cacao
• ⅔ cup (85 g) vanilla ice cream

• Garnish: cocktail cherry

Add all ingredients to a blender and process until smooth and creamy. Pour into Martini or coupe glasses. Serve with a cocktail cherry.

# VESPER

🕑 1951  
⚐ ORACABESSA, JAMAICA  
👤 IVAR BRYCE  

⌂ N/A  
🍶 GIN; VODKA  
🍸 COUPE

The word "vesper" refers to the evening hour when the star of Venus first makes an appearance. Vespers, the sixth of the seventh canonical hours of the divine office, harkens the sunset and twilight for evening prayer. In many settings, this is also the start of cocktail hour.

In his 1975 memoir *You Only Live Once*, author Ivar Bryce reveals that while traveling in Jamaica during World War II, his close friend, James Bond novelist Ian Fleming, met an elderly couple in Oracabessa, who beckoned him in for evening drinks. When the butler arrived with a tray of frozen rum beverages, he announced that "vespers are served." From here, a drink—and a fierce Bond girl—name was born. "To Ivar, who mixed the first Vesper, and said the good word" was the inscription from Fleming to Bryce in his personal copy of 1953's *Casino Royale*, where it makes its first literary appearance.

In the early 1950s, when vodka merely spiked tomato juice or ginger beer for Bloody Marys (page 88) and Moscow Mules (page 142), the Vesper (after all, Bond was not the Daiquiri type) was among the first cocktails to showcase the newly chic spirit in something as refined as a Martini variation. Bond's order as written in the book: "Three measures of Gordon's, one of vodka, half a measure of Kina Lillet. Shake it very well until ice-cold, then add a large slice of lemon-peel. Got it?"

Though also shaken, not stirred, the Vesper did not become Bond's signature order until later, however the popularity of Fleming's later works in the 1960s boosted sales of *Casino Royale* and it was briefly popularized in chic lounges. It was the 2006 movie adaptation starring Daniel Craig that gave the literary drink new life in a prominent scene, detonating it onto the modern cocktailsphere like a key fob bomb. Even though vodka was considered an unhip spirit by this time, the Vesper was the exception even the cocktail snobs could make peace with.

- ½ oz (15 ml) unflavored vodka
- ¼ oz (7 ml) Lillet Blanc  
  or Cocchi Americano
- 2 oz (60 ml) dry gin

- Garnish: lemon peel

Shake all ingredients with ice until well chilled. Strain into a chilled coupe glass (originally a "deep champagne goblet"). Garnish with lemon peel.

# GOLD CADILLAC

| | | | |
|---|---|---|---|
| 🕐 | 1952 | 🏠 | POOR RED'S |
| 🏴 | CALIFORNIA, USA | 🍾 | LIQUORE GALLIANO L'AUTENTICO |
| 👤 | FRANK KLEIN | 🍸 | 2 COUPES |

Pairing cocktails with food is nothing new. However, pairing a cocktail with a car? That happened in 1952, when a couple arrived at Poor Red's Bar-B-Q restaurant in El Dorado, California. They asked the bartender, Frank Klein, to mix up a drink that would match the chrome of their newly purchased gold-colored Cadillac. The bartender came up with a concoction made with Galliano liqueur, crème de cacao, and heavy (double) cream, served it in two Champagne coupes, and dubbed it the Gold Cadillac.

It was an instant hit among the visitors and locals in that tiny Sierra Nevada foothills town of only 1,400, and every order is still served in two coupes as an homage to its original customers.

According to Poor Red's website, noticing an unusually large spike in sales of Liquore Galliano L'Autentico to this single Northern California account, Galliano ran an advertising campaign from 1964 to 1967 with the recipe, which garnered worldwide fame. In 1999, Galliano claimed Poor Red's had the single highest-selling account, amounting to over 3 percent of its annual American market sales.

Although the original restaurant closed in 2013, then reopened in 2016 with new owners, it has been reported that the Gold Cadillac has never waned in popularity and Poor Red's continues to serve so many of them that they go through an entire bottle within an hour and a half.

Note: while the restaurant lists the drink as the "Gold Cadillac," it is known in the cocktail world and other menus as the "Golden Cadillac." Some versions are served with a garnish of orange bitters and/or chocolate shavings, but these are optional.

---

Serves 2 (halve the recipe for one serving, if you must)

• 2 oz (60 ml) Liquore Galliano L'Autentico
• 2 oz (60 ml) white crème de cacao
• 2 oz (60 ml) heavy (double) cream

• Garnish: chocolate shavings and/or 3 dashes orange bitters, swirled

Shake all ingredients with ice until well chilled and frothy. Strain into two coupe glasses. Grate chocolate over the drinks, if desired. If using orange bitters, artfully apply 3 drops in the foam and swirl using a toothpick or cocktail stick.

# CARIBE HILTON PIÑA COLADA

- ⏲ **1954**
- ⚐ **SAN JUAN, PUERTO RICO**
- ⚖ **RAMÓN MARRERO PÉREZ, PLUS BAR STAFF**

- ⌂ **CARIBE HILTON HOTEL BEACHCOMBER BAR**
- ◊ **RUM**
- ⏦ **HURRICANE OR PINT**

The 1970s musician Rupert Holmes might not have had a worldwide hit about getting caught in the rain and amorous midnight escapades with an ideal partner based on a shared love for Piña Coladas if it weren't for the commercialization of Coco López in 1954. In their 2017 book *Spirit of the Cane,* drinks historians Anistatia Miller and Jared Brown write that a version of the cocktail was served at the Caribe Hilton Beachcomber Bar in San Juan, Puerto Rico since its opening in 1949, where it attracted celebrity clientele. Movie starlet Joan Crawford once said it was "better than slapping Bette Davis in the face." However, its essential ingredient, coconut cream, is extremely tedious to render manually. So when Coco López canned cream of coconut was packaged by agricultural professor Ramón López Irizarry, this was the game changer. Caribe Hilton's Ramón "Monchito" Marrero Pérez is often credited as the sole creator of what became the perfected Piña Colada recipe using the product, though it's been said the final tweaks were a group effort by Hector Torres, Ricardo Gracia, Miguel Marquez, and other bar staff members.

Coco López was launched with Piña Colada recipe booklets that found their way around the world, setting the planet a-buzz with the mechanical whirr of blenders, which then spilled sweet, frosty nectar into glasses (and plastic cups, and hollowed out coconut shells, etc.).

If the Piña Colada is the national drink of Puerto Rico (official as of 1978), the Henny Colada—made with Hennessy in place of or in addition to the rum—is the borough drink of the Bronx in New York City. In the world's high-end establishments, fanciful variations abound, and so-called advancements have been sought in the coconut delivery system (water, clarified milk, etc.). But, as the song goes, "if you have half a brain," it's hard to top the original.

- 2 oz (60 ml) rum (light or dark)
- 1 oz (30 ml) coconut cream
- 1 oz (30 ml) heavy (double) cream
- 1 oz (30 ml) fresh pineapple juice
- ½ cup crushed ice

- Garnish: pineapple wedge and cherry

Blend the rum, coconut cream, heavy (double) cream, and pineapple juice in a blender. Add the ice and mix for an additional 15 seconds. Pour into a hurricane or other tall glass, or a pint glass. Garnish.

# VANCOUVER

🕐 1954  
⚑ VANCOUVER, CANADA  
🜨 UNKNOWN  

⌂ SYLVIA HOTEL  
🜩 GIN  
🍸 COUPE  

One would think that a signature cocktail named for its hometown would have stood the test of time. However, unlike the Manhattan, most city cocktails, such as the Los Angeles or the Toronto, had fallen into obscurity until recently. Another such cocktail is the Vancouver, which was the house cocktail of the Sylvia Hotel from 1954—reportedly when granted the city's first cocktail bar license—until the late 1960s or so.

The boozy, gin-based Vancouver has been compared to the Martinez, however, along with sweet vermouth, it also shares some of the flavor profile of a Vieux Carré, with its inclusion of subtly spicy Bénédictine liqueur. In a 2018 article for *Serious Eats*, drinks writer Paul Clarke says that legend has it that the swashbuckling actor Errol Flynn "knocked back a Vancouver just before expiring." However, he also notes that it's probably one of those "too good to be true" tales.

The Vancouver fell out of fashion for decades, but in 2006 things came full circle when bartender Steve Da Cruz was working at the Sylvia and a regular told him the cocktail's origin story—from that very bar! Da Cruz has since made it is his mission to share the recipe with the world. And it's working. If not already on the menu, it's one of those drinks bartenders keep in their back pocket for when they're asked to make something like a Martini or Manhattan, but different. It's also a great way to showcase the variety of craft gins to emerge from British Columbia in recent years.

By the way, that Errol Flynn story is just a myth. Although certainly potent, no ingredient in the Vancouver cocktail is lethal if consumed responsibly.

---

• 2 oz (60 ml) dry gin (preferably from the Vancouver area)
• ½ oz (15 ml) sweet vermouth
• 1 tsp Bénédictine D.O.M.
• 2 dashes orange bitters

• Garnish: lemon peel (optional)

Stir all ingredients with ice until well chilled. Strain into a chilled coupe glass. Express the oils from a piece of lemon peel over the drink, skin side down, and either discard or place in the glass, according to preference.

# BLUE HAWAII

🕐 1957
⚑ WAIKIKI (HAWAII), USA
👤 HARRY YEE

🏠 HAWAIIAN VILLAGE
🍸 BLUE CURAÇAO
🍸 HURRICANE

········································································

Blue Hawaii is a potent tropical cocktail consisting of white rum, vodka, fresh pineapple juice, sweet-and-sour mix, and blue curaçao liqueur, which lends a striking, deep blue-green hue to the presentation. It is understandably often confused with the Blue Hawaiian cocktail, which is a variation using coconut cream, but this drink is the original blueprint, as it were.

Harry K. Yee, head bartender of the Hawaiian Village hotel in Waikiki, came up with the recipe for the Blue Hawaii in 1957, when the Netherlands-based Bols liqueur company commissioned a signature drink showcasing the US debut of the product—a spirit infused with the peel of dried Caribbean oranges that has then been dyed blue—presumably as a marketing gimmick since it adds no additional flavor. What could have been a mere ripple in the cocktail ocean turned into a tidal wave, riding the success of the 1956 Elvis Presley

movie of the same name, and the exotic appeal of a blue drink at the height of the tiki era. In Yee's thirty years at the job, this is the cocktail he is best known for.

While Bols' original blue curaçao liqueur still exists, several spirits companies in the modern era have come up with their own recipes using natural ingredients, such as butterfly pea powder to cast the blue hue. Blue Hawaii, and its many variations, are still a fixture on the tropical drinks scene, particularly now that most venues are back to making fresh sweet-and-sour mix from squeezed citrus, instead of the powdered or concentrated variety that was more widespread in the late 1960s through to the 1990s.

Depending on who's making it, the recipe is either shaken or blended. The original was shaken, but a blended Blue Hawaii, to paraphrase the Elvis title track, is still heavenly.

········································································

- ¾ oz (22 ml) white rum
- ¾ oz (22 ml) unflavored vodka
- ½ oz (15 ml) blue curaçao liqueur
- 3 oz (90 ml) fresh pineapple juice
- 1 oz (30 ml) Sweet-and-Sour Mix (or use a prepared mix made with fresh citrus)

- Garnish: pineapple wedge and cocktail umbrella

Shake all ingredients with ice until well chilled. Strain into a tall glass over fresh ice. Garnish with a pineapple wedge and cocktail umbrella.

Alternatively, blend all ingredients with ice until smooth. Pour into a tall glass and garnish.

For the Sweet-and-Sour Mix

- 1 cup (200 g) granulated sugar
- 16 oz (480 ml) water
- 4 oz (120 ml) fresh lemon juice
- 4 oz (120 ml) fresh lime juice

Dissolve the sugar in the water in a saucepan over low heat, about 10 to 15 minutes, stirring occasionally. Pour into a jar and let cool. Add the citrus liquids and shake together. Keeps for about a week in the refrigerator and can also be frozen (freeze in cubes for individual cocktails).

········································································

# YUKIGUNI

🕐 1958
🏳 SAKATA CITY, JAPAN
🧑 KEIICHI IYAMA

⌂ KERN
🍶 VODKA
🍸 NICK & NORA OR CORDIAL

Yukiguni, composed of vodka, white curaçao, and lime, served with a minted cherry in a palm-sugar rimmed glass (the name translates to "snow country"), represents the rebirth of bar culture in 1950s postwar Japan. According to Emma Janzen and Julia Momosé in the 2021 book *The Way of the Cocktail*, in the early years following World War II, most bars in Japan, particularly cocktail bars, remained shuttered, because they were considered an unnecessary luxury. But by the mid-1950s, "Tory Bars" were popping up throughout big cities, such as Osaka and Tokyo, opened by Shinjiro Torii of Kotobukiya (now Suntory) as a way of promoting national whisky products in highballs and offering a casual, relaxed atmosphere to lure customers back into a bar setting. Outside of these cities, other bars began to open that incorporated Western spirits and ingredients in more classically elegant and slightly more upscale settings that served proper cocktails and snacks, such as katsu-sando (traditional fried pork sandwiches).

One such bar was Kern, opened in Sakata City by Keiichi Iyama in 1955. In 1959, he entered the Yukiguni into Kotobukiya's national cocktail competition, and it won. Not only did the drink become Kern's signature, but it is also considered a mid-century classic and a national staple.

The basic recipe has changed in the decades since its invention. At the time, fresh limes were scarce, and the original recipe calls for bottled lime cordial as well as a sweeter flavor profile. Janzen and Momosé say that Iyama himself (who passed away in 2021 at the age of ninety-five) tinkered with the recipe some sixty years after he created it to suit more modern palates, calling for a more spirit-forward serve with less sugar and fresher ingredients.

- 1 oz (30 ml) unflavored vodka
- ½ oz (15 ml) curaçao
  (a clear expression is preferred to capture the original presentation)
- ½ oz (15 ml) fresh lime juice

- Garnish: palm sugar and citrus wedge for the rim, green maraschino cherry (use red if green is unavailable)

Rim a Nick & Nora or cordial glass by rubbing a wedge of citrus around the rim, then dipping it in a small plate of palm sugar. Tap to shake off the excess. Shake all ingredients with ice until well chilled. Strain into the rimmed glass and garnish with a cherry.

# AIGUA DE VALÈNCIA

◷ 1959
⚐ VALENCIA, SPAIN
 man CONSTANTE GIL

⌂ CAFÉ MADRID
◊ VODKA; GIN
Y WINE OR GOBLET

Aigua de València (Spanish for "Valencian Water"), also referred to as "Agua de Valencia," is a cocktail consisting of cava or other sparkling wine mixed with orange juice and a measure of vodka and gin. Essentially, it's the Spanish version of a Mimosa (page 100) or Buck's Fizz (page 92), with an added boozy kick, and traditionally served by the pitcher and consumed from a wide glass goblet instead of a flute. Spanish culinary historian María Ángeles Arazo, in her 1978 book *Valenica Noche*, says the cocktail was first served by bartender Constante Gil in 1959 at Café Madrid de Valencia in the city of Valencia, Spain.

According to Arazo, the drink was concocted for a group of Basque travelers who were regulars at the bar. As with many cocktail origin stories, it was conceived following a request for a twist on the usual drink order, in this instance "Agua de Bilbao," referring to the house cava. On the spot, Gil suggested they try "Agua de Valencia" and mixed up a pitcher (jug) of cava with orange juice and the extra booze. The group of friends ordered it by the pitcherful on future visits, and eventually Gil began serving it to other guests at the café.

By the 1970s, Aigua de València was a popular order throughout the region. However, instead of becoming known as a brunch cocktail alongside its other orange juice and bubbly cousins elsewhere in the world, its most popular setting is within the Valencian nightlife scene. Until his death in 2009, Gil featured the drink's origin story as a part of his lecture series "Tertulias de Café," detailing his experiences at the bar. It has remained a popular local drink.

Single serving

• ¼ oz (7 ml) unflavored vodka
• ¼ oz (7 ml) dry gin
• ½ tsp simple syrup
• 1¼ oz (38 ml) fresh orange juice
• 4–5 oz (120–150 ml) brut-style cava or other dry, sparkling wine

• Garnish: half an orange wheel

Shake all ingredients except the cava with ice until well chilled. Strain into a wine glass and top with the bubbly. Garnish with half an orange wheel.

By the pitcher (serves 4 to 6)

• 1½ oz (45 ml) vodka
• 1½ oz (45 ml) gin
• ¾ oz (22 ml) simple syrup
• 8 oz (240 ml) fresh orange juice
• 26 oz (750 ml) bottle brut style cava or other, dry sparkling wine

• Garnish: orange wheels

Combine all ingredients in a pitcher (jug) without ice and chill in the refrigerator for at least 30 minutes or until ready to serve. Add ice and orange wheels just prior to service. Pour into wine or goblet glasses.

# BATANGA

🕑 1961
⚐ TEQUILA, MEXICO
👤 DON JAVIER DELGADO CORONA

⌂ LA CAPILLA
🍶 TEQUILA
🍸 HIGHBALL

There's a place in the cocktail canon for recipes with several ingredients, each—in careful measurements—imparting their own specific flavor profile in layered nuances.

Then there are the drinks that are like a great soup, made with small amounts of simple ingredients that are best when stirred together with love.

One such cocktail is the Batanga, which many refer to as the "Mexican Cuba Libre." It is simply cola, tequila, lime, and salt.

Batangas have been served at La Capilla (The Chapel) bar in Tequila, Mexico since 1961, where the drink was perfected by owner Don Javier Delgado Corona. He served them well into his eighties, ritualistically adding the ingredients to the glasses one by one. These days, adding salt to sweet ingredients like chocolate has become somewhat trendy, but this was unusual for the 1960s, when Don Javier demonstrated perfectly that bit of flavor magic, combining salty, sour, and sweet with the earthy, vegetal tones inherent in tequila.

At La Capilla, Batangas are theatrically stirred with the long wooden handle of a well-weathered knife that slices the limes, as well as other things that need cutting in a good Mexican bar, such as avocados, onions, jalapeños, and tomatoes. No doubt this technique contributes to the sipping experience particular to the place. However, the basic flavor combination also comes through with regular cocktail tools.

- Pinch of kosher or coarse salt, plus extra for a salt rim (optional)
- 1 freshly squeezed lime
- 2 oz (60 ml) tequila (preferably blanco or reposado)
- Cola of choice, to top (best when sweetened with sugarcane instead of corn syrup)

Build the drink in a tall glass. If a salt rim is desired, rub the rim with a wedge of lime and dip into a small saucer of coarse salt. Add the pinch of salt to the lime juice at the bottom of the glass and stir to combine until the salt is dissolved. Add the tequila, then fill the glass with ice and top with cola. Stir again before serving.

# JUMP UP AND KISS ME

- ⏱ 1968
- ⚑ ST. CROIX, VIRGIN ISLANDS
- ౭ WESTON HUGGINS
  AND TOM RUSSELL
- ⌂ BUCCANEER HOTEL
- ⚱ RUM
- ⅄ BRANDY SNIFTER

..............................................................................................................................

In the 2017 edition of *Potions of the Caribbean*, tiki drinks expert Jeff "Beachbum" Berry identified Jump Up and Kiss Me as the third cocktail to be defined as the "official cocktail of St. Croix." The first was the Miss Blyden—rum, sugar, and prickly pear cactus pulp fermented in a bottle buried underground for up to a year—in the eighteenth century, when the island was a Dutch colony; it was understandably knocked off the top spot by the second one, Sherry Cobbler, in the nineteenth century. However, Jump Up and Kiss Me, attributed to Buccaneer Hotel bartender Weston Huggins and bar manager Tom Russell in 1968, is considered the modern signature of the island.

The cocktail is one of a few from the era based on Galliano liqueur, such as the Harvey Wallbanger and Gold(en) Cadillac (page 160).

Berry found Jump Up and Kiss Me in a 1968 Galliano promotional recipe booklet. In it, Huggins says the drink is named for a flower resembling a miniature carnation that blooms on long vines throughout the island.

The cheery, juicy concoction, which is also one of the few showcasing apricot brandy, is typically prepared in a blender with ice and served in a brandy snifter. It was originally garnished with the flowers it's named for. It's still served at bars throughout the island, though these days the typical garnish is a wedge of pineapple and a cocktail cherry, protected under the shade of a mini umbrella. Some recipes are shaken rather than blended, and call for "frothee" in the ingredients list, which is just a descriptive term for egg white.

..............................................................................................................................

- 1 oz (30 ml) Galliano liqueur
- 1 oz (30 ml) gold Caribbean rum
- 1 oz (30 ml) unsweetened pineapple juice
- 1 egg white (optional)
- ¼ oz (7 ml) apricot brandy
- ¼ oz (7 ml) fresh lemon juice
- ½ cup crushed ice (if running through a blender)

- Garnish: cocktail cherry, pineapple wedge, mini umbrella

Option 1: add all ingredients to a blender and blend until smooth, about 45 to 60 seconds. Pour into a brandy snifter and garnish.

Option 2: omit the crushed ice and shake the ingredients with ice until well chilled. Strain over fresh ice into a brandy snifter, tiki mug, or double rocks glass. Garnish.

# THE CAESAR

🕐  1969
🏳  CALGARY, CANADA
👤  WALTER CHELL

🏠  CALGARY INN
🍸  VODKA
🍸  HIGHBALL

The combination of tomato juice, base spirit, Worcestershire sauce, and various spices (not to mention hot sauces and wild garnishes) was nothing new by the late 1960s. After all, the Bloody Mary (page 88) had been around since the 1920s, and its officially recognized gin cousin, the Snapper, since the 1940s. Nor was it uncommon to add savory modifiers such as broth or clam juice. However, in 1969, when Walter Chell was asked by the Calgary Inn to invent a signature cocktail for its new Italian restaurant, Marco's, it apparently took him three months to formulate his final recipe for what is now considered the national cocktail of Canada, The Caesar, aka The Bloody Caesar.

Chell's inspiration was spaghetti alle vongole, a dish that hails from the Campania region of Italy, in which pasta is flavored with the juices of freshly steamed clams and other herbs and spices. His technique was to mash the clams into what he referred to as a "clam nectar," and add his now not-so-secret ingredient oregano, one of the stars of the original dish. The final recipe consists of vodka, tomato juice, clam nectar, Worcestershire sauce, celery salt, and oregano. He was apparently not a fan of Tabasco but did use hot sauce on request.

Through the decades, The Bloody Caesar (that name stems from a British customer declaring the concoction "a damn good bloody Caesar," according to a 1994 interview with Chell in the *Toronto Star*) became a standard midday cocktail throughout Canada. In 2009, to celebrate its 40th anniversary, then Mayor of Calgary, David Bronconnier, declared each Thursday before Victoria Day Caesar Day, with Mott's Clamato Juice an official sponsor. Like the Bloody Mary or Snapper, venues pride themselves on their secret house recipes. The bar 1858 Caesar, with various locations throughout Ontario, Canada serves an astounding forty-five variations on the theme, including the Beet Drop, Pickled Peppered, Bacon Bomb, Maple BBQ, and C'est Chaud—yup, it's served warm.

- 1 oz (30 ml) unflavored vodka
- 2 dashes hot sauce (optional)
- 4 dashes Worcestershire sauce
- ¼ tsp salt
- ¼ tsp black pepper
- 4 oz (120 ml) clamato or other Caesar mix, such as Mott's (here's where the oregano comes in)

- Garnish: lemon and celery salt for the rim, celery stalk, lime wedges (or you can get creative)

Rim a tall glass with lemon and celery salt (or other rimmer of choice) by rubbing the rim with a wedge of lemon and dipping in a saucer of preferred salt mix. Fill the glass with ice, then add the other ingredients.

There are two options to mix: the easy one is simply to stir all the ingredients together in the glass, then garnish with the celery stalk and lime wedges. The preferred method is to "roll" the ingredients a couple of times between two glasses to aerate them slightly, then let them settle in the rimmed glass and proceed with the celery and lime wedge garnish.

A collection of 200 iconic drinks from around the globe, each of which has changed the culture of the cocktail – with recipes and stories from their original creators and mixologists

A signature cocktail is a bespoke drink that expresses the nature of the time, person, or place for which it was created. Covering the rich and full history of cocktail culture, the 200 easy-to-recreate recipes in this collection include well-known classics and instantly recognizable favorites such as the Bellini and Tequila Sunrise, alongside up-to-the-minute creations such as Twin Cities from New York's Dead Rabbit bar and the brand-new Phaidon 100 from The Connaught Bar in London. Each unique cocktail is accompanied by a fascinating insight or story and a stunning contemporary image to capture its very essence.

# JUNGLE BIRD

🕐 1970s
⚐ KUALA LUMPUR, MALAYSIA
👤 JEFFREY ONG SWEE TEIK

⌂ AVIARY BAR, HILTON HOTEL
🍶 RUM
🍹 ROCKS GLASS OR CERAMIC
    TIKI VESSEL

The Jungle Bird is a tropical cocktail that is one of the few that balances both fruity and bitter flavors. It was created by Jeffery Ong Swee Teik, head bartender of Malaysia's Kuala Lumpur Hilton Hotel Aviary Bar on Jalan Sultan Ismail. The bar looked on to a netted enclosure near the hotel's swimming pool where exotic birds were kept, and Jungle Birds were served as a welcome drink to greet guests from July 1973, which puts its time stamp just a few years past the golden tiki era.

The Jungle Bird gets its sunset orange hue from Campari, which is combined with pineapple and lime juices, dark rum, and sugar syrup. At the hotel, the cocktails were served in a striking, custom-made ceramic vessel shaped like a bird, and garnished with citrus, cocktail cherries, and an edible orchid.

Though it was a hit at the time, it wasn't until author Jeff "Beachbum" Berry first spotted the recipe in the 1980 edition of *The New American Bartender's Guide* that Jungle Birds flocked on to the modern cocktail scene. Intrigued by the unusual combination of flavors, he decided to include the recipe in his 2002 book *Intoxica* and the cocktail made an instant connection with tiki fans and amaro enthusiasts alike. Another aspect of its appeal is that it's quite simple to prepare and can be dressed up or down in presentation, as well as used as a template for other fruity and bitter drinks.

In the modern era, any bar serving tropical cocktails, such as Berry's Latitude 29 in New Orleans, serves the original Jungle Bird, or their own flights of fancy to play off the bitter and bright notes, including stirred (non-juice), coffee-based, and smoky variations.

- 1½ oz (45 ml) dark rum
- ¾ oz (22 ml) Campari
- 1½ oz (45 ml) fresh pineapple juice
- ½ oz (15 ml) fresh lime juice
- ½ oz (15 ml) Demerara syrup (omit if less sweetness is desired)

- Garnish: pineapple wedge, cocktail cherry, and/or citrus slices

Shake all ingredients with ice until well chilled. Strain over fresh ice into a rocks glass or ceramic tiki vessel of choice. Garnish as desired.

# LEMON DROP

⏱ 1970s             ⌂ HENRY AFRICA'S

⚑ SAN FRANCISCO, USA     🍸 VODKA

🧍 NORMAN JAY HOBDAY    🍸 COCKTAIL OR SHOT

The sweet, frothy Lemon Drop is often disparaged by cocktail purists as one of those "frilly" 1970s cocktails that's due for retirement. Technically, it's a Sidecar (page 80) with the cognac switched out for vodka. But considering how many of them are still consumed around the world on a nightly basis, its strategic creation could be argued as an act of genius.

Before there was the Cosmopolitan, or even the Fuzzy Navel, the Lemon Drop was the original good-time singles' drink. The recipe is credited to former New York state native Norman Jay Hobday, owner of Henry Africa's in San Francisco. In 1969, short on a renovation budget for the bar, he filled it with cheap plants and salvaged, ornate lamps interspersed with various knick-knacks to make it appear more attractive to anyone looking for a safe spot for a solo night out. This style of shabby chic bar caught on and became known as a "fern bar"—meccas of the 1970s and 80s swinging singles scene.

Hobday created the candy-based beverage for adults sometime in the 1970s, when brown spirits such as whiskey, brandy, and rum were considered "old man drinks," and fruity vodka- (hardly ever gin)-based drinks reigned supreme. Though it can certainly be ordered as a full cocktail, the most common Lemon Drop serve is one split up in shot glasses among multiple bar patrons.

The popularity of the Lemon Drop helped make Henry Africa's such a success story that it was national news when Hobday sold the business in 1983, and at some point, Hobday even legally changed his name to Henry Africa.

---

- 1½ oz (45 ml) unflavored vodka
- ¾ oz (22 ml) Cointreau
- ¾ oz (22 ml) fresh lemon juice (unlikely to have been fresh in the original, but for best results, it should be)
- 1 barspoon rich syrup

- Garnish: lemon wedge and granulated white sugar for the rim

Rub the rim of a cocktail glass with a wedge of lemon. Add a thin layer of granulated white sugar to a saucer, then dip the rim of the glass in the sugar. Shake all ingredients with ice until well chilled. Strain into the sugar-rimmed cocktail glass. Or split between 3 to 4 smaller glasses as shots.

# FLAME OF LOVE

- 1970
- LOS ANGELES, USA
- PEPE RUIZ

- CHASEN'S
- VODKA
- COUPE OR MARTINI

Before there was Spago, or Craigs, or the Polo Lounge, there was Chasen's. Mid-twentieth century Hollywood celebrities weren't interested in deconstructed pizza or dishes bubbling with foam; they wanted a good bowl of chili and a cold Martini, and that's what they got there. It was originally opened on Beverly Boulevard by comedian Dave Chasen in 1936, at the urging of his close friend, Academy Award-winning director Frank Capra.

In the 1960s (when they weren't in Vegas), Chasen's was a favorite haunt of the Martini-guzzling Rat Pack. The story goes that in 1970, tired of the ordinary Martini preparation, Dean Martin requested bartender Pepe Ruiz serve him an upgrade. Chasen's was no stranger to pyrotechnics, what with a barbecue pit in its backyard and a famous altercation between

Orson Welles and John Houseman involving a thrown, lit Sterno can—so Ruiz plopped some Fino sherry in Martin's glass, flamed an orange peel into it, then poured chilled vodka into it.

Far out, man!

Impressed with both the presentation and the flavor, Flame of Love soon became the Rat Pack's favorite order. Frank Sinatra loved it so much he famously demanded a round for all the guests attending his birthday party (a number that has been reported as being anywhere between 52 and 200). With the repopularization of flaming orange garnishes in the early 2000s, the drink is once again a local favorite, even though the venue has closed for good.

You can prepare this cocktail in one of two ways. If you prefer a stirred Martini with a flaming orange over the finished drink, make it this way:

- 1½ oz (45 ml) unflavored vodka
- ¾ oz (22 ml) dry sherry, such as Fino or Manzanilla
- Piece of orange peel, 1 inch (2.5 cm) or longer

Stir the vodka and sherry in a mixing glass with ice until well chilled. Strain into a chilled cocktail glass. Flame the orange oils from the peel over the top of the drink and discard.

Or try Chasen's way:

- ¼ oz (7 ml) dry sherry
- Large twist of orange peel
- 1½ oz (45 ml) unflavored vodka

- Garnish: orange twist, couple dashes orange bitters (optional)

Pour the sherry into a chilled glass, swirl to coat, then discard. Flame the orange peel into the glass and discard. Shake the vodka with ice until well chilled and strain into the glass. Garnish with a fresh orange peel twist and a couple of dashes of orange bitters, if desired.

# NEGRONI SBAGLIATO

- 1973
- MILAN, ITALY
- MIRKO STOCCHETTO

- BAR BASSO
- VERMOUTH; CAMPARI
- ROCKS OR FLUTE

"Negroni. Sbagliato . . . With Prosecco in it." Thus sayeth Emma D'Arcy to *House of the Dragon* co-star Olivia Cooke in the TikTok interview that broke the Internet and launched hundreds, if not thousands, of memes in 2022—from existing fans of the HBO series, who just thought it sounded cool coming from one of their favorite actors, to cocktail cognoscenti poking fun at the sheer redundancy of the statement. After all, a Negroni Sbagliato, credited to Mirko Stocchetto at Bar Basso in Milan in 1973, already *has* Prosecco in it. It's like ordering fried chicken with chicken in it.

The word "*sbagliato*" in Italian translates to "mistake." Negroni Sbagliato is a Negroni—a 1919 cocktail also hailing from Italy with equal parts gin, sweet vermouth, and Campari—made with Prosecco instead of gin. Given the Italian predilection for spritzes, it is highly possible the cocktail already existed in some form for decades. But it wasn't until the

mid-1970s that the name became official, when Stocchetto, whose workstation at the bar was not in the order he was used to, accidentally reached for the Prosecco bottle instead of the gin, shrugged it off, and continued to build the drink as if he meant to make it that way.

In an October 2022 interview with *Slate*, Stocchetto's son Maurizio, who took over from his dad at Bar Basso, says that, in reality, his Negroni-loving father thought it was sacrilege to alter the drink, but he carried on making them. Besides, there is really nothing technically wrong with it. And "Sbagliato" sounds catchy.

In the present day, like the drink it evolved from, the Negroni Sbagliato is sipped in many sparkly (even clear!) variations around the world, and is a popular style for the ready-to-drink (RTD) market.

- 1½ oz (45 ml) sweet vermouth
- 1½ oz (45 ml) Campari or other aperitivo
- Prosecco or other dry sparkling wine, chilled, to top

- Garnish (up): orange or lemon twist
- Garnish (on the rocks): orange or lemon wheel

Served up: stir the vermouth and Campari in a mixing glass with ice until well chilled. Strain into a flute glass, top with bubbly, and garnish with an orange or lemon twist.

On the rocks: in a rocks glass, add the vermouth and Campari and briefly stir with ice. Top with bubbly and garnish with an orange or lemon wheel.

# BUSHWACKER

🕐 1975
⚐ ST. THOMAS, VIRGIN ISLANDS
𝗔 ANGIE CONIGLIARO

⌂ SHIP'S STORE
◊ VODKA
𝖸 HURRICANE OR PINT

The original Bushwacker was invented in 1975 by bartender Angie Conigliaro at the Ship's Store on St. Thomas in response to a request for a tropical variation on a White Russian. What she came up with—vodka, Kahlúa, crème de cacao, Coco López, a dash of triple sec, and whole (full-fat) milk blended with ice and topped with grated nutmeg—was what Conigliaro herself deemed a "kick butt" version of a Piña Colada. It went by a variety of names, but sometime around 1977, the drink was named after a customer's Afghan hound, Bushwack, and it stuck.

About the same time, American bartender Linda Taylor (now Murphy) discovered the concoction on a trip to the island and attempted to re-create it at her hometown gig at the Sandshaker Lounge in Pensacola, Florida. She swapped the vodka for Mount Gay rum and topped it with whipped cream, a drizzle of chocolate syrup, and a cherry. The locals swooned and the Bushwacker transformed the once-sleepy Sandshaker into a destination spot, inspiring hundreds of local copycats.

What happened next, according to drinks writer Aaron Goldfarb, "is like a Coen Brothers movie set in the beach bars of the Florida Panhandle." Bushwackers became a local staple on both the Alabama and Florida coasts, but Murphy's exact recipe is still a secret—the others are inventions on the theme. From here a twisted tale involving recipe spies (recipionage?), trademark disputes over an annual Bushwacker beach festival, and even a cocaine ring ensued.

Despite the drama, and even in the wake of major hurricanes and other natural disasters, the Bushwacker continues to rule the Gulf Coast. In 2010, President Barack Obama, in the area to survey the damage from the Deepwater Horizon oil spill, was photographed sipping one at Tacky Jacks in Orange Beach with the caption "Cherry On Top."

• 2 oz (60 ml) vodka (or substitute with dark rum)
• 1 oz (30 ml) coffee liqueur
• 1 oz (30 ml) crème de cacao (white or dark)
• 2 oz (60 ml) whole (full-fat) milk
• 1 oz (30 ml) coconut cream
• 1 dash triple sec or other orange liqueur

• Garnish: grated nutmeg (or to "Murphyfy" it, add whipped cream, a drizzle of chocolate syrup, and a cherry)

Add all ingredients to a blender with a scoop of ice and blend for at least 30 seconds until smooth and frothy. Pour into a hurricane or pint glass and garnish as desired.

# DAWA

🕐  1980s
⚑  NAIROBI, KENYA
ዶ  UNKNOWN

⌂  CARNIVORE
◊  VODKA
Y  ROCKS

One of the most popular drinks in Kenya is the Caipirinha, a Brazilian cocktail made from the cane spirit cachaça with muddled fresh limes and sugar. In the 1980s, with some drinkers preferring the crisper taste of vodka over cachaça (and the myth that it lessens the severity of hangovers), the Caipivodka gained equal popularity throughout the country. The Nairobi restaurant Carnivore is famous for inventing its own take on the Caipivodka, Dawa, which has since become not only the house signature, but is now considered the national cocktail.

The story goes that sometime in the 1980s, one of the bartenders at Carnivore was experimenting with the recipe—which, along with vodka, limes, and sugar, incorporates honey as a nod to local beekeeping traditions—and served it to the restaurant's landlord, who was sitting at the bar. He was so taken with the drink, he asked for another, referring to it as his *dawa*, which is Swahili for "medicine." The name stuck and the sweet, refreshing mixture soon made the rounds.

The cocktail is now so popular throughout Kenya that, like the iconic copper mugs for Moscow Mules, most venues serve Dawa with its own signature accessory, the Dawa stick, a short, chunky piece of wood or plastic that is dipped in a small amount of honey for the drinker to stir into the cocktail as it is consumed. If a Dawa stick is not available, chopsticks, short straws (metal or bamboo), espresso spoons, popsicle (lollipop) sticks, or even half a dried bucatini pasta strand will work in its place.

It is also important to note that aside from the Dawa stick, in Kenya the drink is traditionally served with plenty of ice in the glass.

- 1 whole lime, cut into quarters
- 1 to 2 tsp granulated sugar (according to preference)
- 2 oz (60 ml) vodka

- Garnish: Dawa stick (or equivalent) dipped in 1 tsp honey

Add the lime quarters to a rocks glass and muddle with the sugar until the quarters are somewhat flattened and the sugar is mixed in. Add the vodka and enough ice cubes to fill the glass. Stir. Dip the Dawa stick (or equivalent) into the honey and place, honey-side down, into the glass to serve.

# ESPRESSO MARTINI

⏱ **1983**
📍 **LONDON, UK**
👤 **DICK BRADSELL**

🏠 **SOHO BRASSERIE**
🍸 **VODKA**
🍸 **COUPE OR MARTINI**

........................................................................................................

"Being conclusive can, at sometimes, be somewhat difficult," says a handwritten notation from legendary British bartender Dick Bradsell, included in the 2022 book *Dicktales or Thank Yous and Sluggings,* as he introduces the story of the genesis of the Espresso Martini at London's Soho Brasserie in 1983. The story goes, surrounded by coffee grounds leaking into his well after a coffee training, a young woman later identified as an American model by one of his friends (no one knows for sure which one, though rumors abound) approached Bradsell and famously said, "Give me a drink that will wake me up, then f**k me up."

What he presented was first referred to as the "Vodka Espresso" and contained the backbone ingredients of what came later—vodka, Kahlúa, dash of sugar, "extra, extra strong" espresso—shaken and served on the rocks.

It was sometime afterward, at London's Match EC1, that the now ubiquitous variation known as the Espresso Martini (sometimes called

"Pharmaceutical Stimulant") was developed to be served up. Bradsell, who died in 2015, notes in the posthumously published *Dicktales* that this version was formulated during a period when almost any mixed cocktail was called a "Martini." He says he used the original Brandy Alexander (page 94) ratio to develop the final recipe, this time with the signature three-coffee-bean garnish. The modern standard tweak came about at his final bar, the Pink Chihuahua, when a customer requested it "her way," with more liqueur, *sans* sugar syrup, and it stuck.

Espresso Martinis are one of the most shaken up and wildly interpreted recipes on the planet, taking all forms, including clarified variations, ready-to-drink (RTD) versions, and even chocolate truffles and jellybeans. Speaking of the buzzy rush from sipping them, Bradsell writes, "Moderation ... These espresso + alcohol things are dangerous ... Oh yeah. That's why I invented it."

........................................................................................................

Pink Chihuahua recipe

- 2 oz (60 ml) vodka
- 1 oz (30 ml) Kahlúa
  (other coffee liqueur will also work)
- 1 oz (30 ml) "double strength" espresso, cooled
- 1 tsp sugarcane syrup
  (if more sweetness is desired)

- Garnish: 3 espresso coffee beans

Shake all ingredients (including the sugar, if desired) with ice until well chilled and very frothy. Strain into a chilled coupe or Martini glass. Garnish with coffee beans set in the foam.

........................................................................................................

# JAPANESE SLIPPER

🕐 1984
⚑ MELBOURNE, AUSTRALIA
🄰 JEAN-PAUL BOURGUIGNON

⌂ MIETTA'S
◊ MIDORI
🍸 COUPE OR MARTINI

The Japanese Slipper cocktail is to Midori what sour apple liqueur is to the Appletini. The neon green drink was created in 1984 by French bartender Jean-Paul Bourguignon at Mietta's in Melbourne, Australia. The venue is named for co-owner Mietta O'Donnell, a food writer and consummate host who was considered a catalyst for the culinary arts scene in that city until her death from a car accident in 2001. Along with her partner, Tony Knox, they transformed the two-floor space—upstairs was a modern French restaurant, with a bar downstairs—into a destination salon/gallery, which hosted a variety of musical performances (opera, pop, jazz, cabaret), poetry readings, visual arts shows, and comedy acts.

Bourguignon was trained at the Parisian outpost of theater, gastropub Joe Allen, where he was not only trained to make classic cocktails but became accustomed to serving crowds with a similar mindset to that of Mietta's. The place needed a signature—one that was both showstopping and easy to drink. It had to look cool to sip, too; nothing brown or clear.

With its glowing, hubba-hubba lime green hue, Midori, the Japanese melon liqueur that was relatively new on the scene, was the answer. He mixed it in equal parts with Cointreau, a nod to his French heritage, and fresh lemon juice to cut through all that sweetness. Learning to speak English at the time, Bourguignon got "slipper" from a book he was reading, oddly enough about a Japanese woman and her slippers. It was a fit to rival that of Cinderella.

The Japanese Slipper soon became one of the "it" cocktails of 1980s Australia and, thanks to Bourguignon's subsequent consulting gigs, some shores beyond. Although it fell out of favor during the more purist cocktail age of the early 2000s, like its sour apple cousin, and many bands of the era, the Japanese Slipper is making the rounds again in the 2020s.

- 1 oz (30 ml) Midori melon liqueur
- 1 oz (30 ml) Cointreau or other orange liqueur
- 1 oz (30 ml) fresh lemon juice

- Garnish: melon ball or cocktail cherry

Shake all ingredients with ice until well chilled. Fine strain into a chilled cocktail glass. Place the garnish at the bottom of the glass.

# DUKES MARTINI

🕐 1985
⚑ LONDON, UK
👤 SALVATORE CALABRESE

⌂ DUKES HOTEL
🍶 VODKA OR GIN
🍸 MARTINI

Martini service is a ritual unto itself, but the specific method by which a Martini is presented at Dukes Hotel bar in London is a legitimate ceremony. Served tableside from a cart, the base spirit of vodka or gin can be requested according to preference; however, the remainder is prepared in only one way. The dry vermouth, a house blend that is custom-made for the bar by an English producer, is swirled around the glass, then ritualistically dumped right onto the carpet (it's cleaned often). Next, a full 3½ oz (100 ml) of vodka or gin is poured directly into the glass from a frozen bottle, chilled to the core and slightly viscous. The final touch is the peel of a lemon imported from the Amalfi coast, the oils expressed into the drink before placing it in the glass. The effect is at once exquisite, exhilarative, distinctly silky, but brutal, if more than one is consumed.

The method came about in 1985 when journalist Stanton Delaplane, a regular who wrote for the *Los Angeles Times* and *San Francisco Chronicle*, complained his Martini wasn't cold or dry enough. Frustrated, head barman Salvatore Calabrese then prepared what he referred to as a "direct martini." The rest is history. Very potent and delicious history.

Though nothing can possibly compare to the experience of being served by current head barman (as of this writing), the effortlessly witty Alessandro Palazzi, at the source, the Dukes Martini is now considered its own style in the genre. Most recently, it was adopted by the Lobby Bar in the Chelsea Hotel in New York City, but with only one type of frozen gin or vodka. And no Amalfi lemons, although guests can choose their own garnish adventure of lemon peel, olive, or both.

- The driest possible dry vermouth
- Bottle of gin or vodka of choice, frozen overnight (the alcohol content ensures it will not become solid)

- Garnish: lemon peel (from Amalfi, if possible)

Add vermouth to a Martini glass and swirl to coat, then dump out. Add 3½ oz (100 ml) frozen vodka or gin to the glass. Garnish by squeezing oils from the lemon peel, skin side down, over the drink, then place in the glass.

# COSMOPOLITAN

🕐 **1988**
▷ **NEW YORK CITY, USA**
🛆 **TOBY CECCHINI**

⌂ **ODEON**
🛆 **VODKA**
Ⴘ **COUPE OR MARTINI**

"Boyfriend, give us those pink drinks!" Back in the late 1980s and early 90s, that's how Madonna and gal pal Sandra Bernhard would order Cosmopolitans from bartender Toby Cecchini at downtown hot spot the Odeon in New York City. Cecchini had perfected the cocktail in 1988 after hearing about a concoction called the Cosmopolitan that was wildly popular in San Francisco nightclubs, made with vodka, Rose's lime cordial, and cheap grenadine. A brand-new vodka product, Absolut Citron, had just landed at the bar, so he went about transforming the rail Cosmo into a modern sour, incorporating the citrus-flavored vodka with fresh lime, cranberry juice cocktail, and for a touch of sweetness and extra depth, Cointreau.

Others have laid claim to the same recipe, saying they invented it years earlier—except Absolut Citron was not marketed until 1988. The fetching pink drink became the "it"

cocktail of the 1990s—chic because it was served in a Martini glass, cool because it wasn't too sweet, and ubiquitous because it was relatively simple to make quickly with easy-to-get ingredients. By 1998, Cosmos were as much of a regular fashion accessory for the characters Carrie, Samantha, Miranda, and Charlotte on the TV series *Sex and the City* as Jimmy Choos or Louboutins.

As with any classic, there are hundreds of variations that swap out juices and other ingredients, but Cecchini (who says he's never seen a single episode of *Sex and the City* ) always keeps a bottle of cranberry juice cocktail handy at Long Island Bar in Brooklyn, where he is now owner, because it simply works best. Just ask the Barefoot Contessa, Ina Garten, herself. Though we tried to hide from Coronavirus in the spring of 2020, there was no escaping the hilarious video of her with the Cosmo in the gigantic Martini glass.

• 1½ oz (45 ml) Absolut Citron vodka
• ¾ oz (22 ml) fresh lime juice
• ¾ oz (22 ml) Cointreau
  (or other orange liqueur)
• ¾ oz (22 ml) cranberry juice cocktail
  (100% cranberry juice will be too tart.
  If using instead, add at least 1 tsp/5 ml
  simple syrup to taste)

• Garnish: lemon twist

Shake all ingredients with ice until well chilled. Strain into a chilled coupe or Martini glass (it's iconically served in the "V" glass). Garnish with a lemon twist.

# BRAMBLE

🕐 1989
⚑ LONDON, UK
ᴀ DICK BRADSELL

⌂ FRED'S CLUB
◊ GIN
🍸 DOUBLE ROCKS

"I wanted to invent an English drink, a British cocktail," wrote Dick Bradsell. While perhaps the *vivantest* of all *bon vivants* was working at Fred's Club in London's Soho in 1989, a rep for Briottet liqueurs presented him with their crème de mure (a blackberry liqueur). In the book *Dicktales or Thank Yous and Sluggings*, Bradsell says in handwritten passages about his creation, "First sip and I had a 'Madeleine moment'. It reminded me of childhood foraging for blackberries in East Cowes Isle of Wight… blackberries in autumn or summer covered in purple."

He modeled his recipe using the "spirit, soured, sweetened and flavoured template" from the Singapore Sling recipe served at the members-only Zanzibar Club. Their interpretation used gin, lemon, and sugar syrup served over crushed ice in a Pilsner glass with a float of Cherry Heering (in a typical serve the Heering is mixed in with the rest).

Almost every bar imaginable now serves a version of Bradsell's Bramble as a template. Some are staunchly religious about following Bradsell's formula using real crème de mure. Others have made it their own, the—insert name of bar/occasion/other reference here—Bramble, subbing out one or more of the ingredients.

Bradsell's book features two Bramble recipes. One uses more gin than the other, but another important distinction is that the first version is served in a large pint glass while the one with less gin is served in a double rocks glass, which is what is more commonly seen today.

Most people would agree that the version with slightly more gin is the way to go, no matter the glass or amount of ice.

---

- 1¾ oz (50 ml) good, dry gin
- ⅞ oz (25 ml) fresh lemon juice
- ⅓ oz (10 ml) simple syrup
- ⅜ oz (12.5 ml) crème de mure (Bradsell mentions raspberry liqueur will also work)

- Garnish: lemon slice and fresh blackberry or raspberry

Add crushed ice to a double rocks glass. Shake the gin, lemon juice, and syrup in a shaker with ice. Strain over the ice-filled glass. Top with the crème de mure and garnish with a lemon slice and fresh berry.

Note: Bradsell also mentions that if working a busy bar service, "you can just pour it all in on top of crushed ice mass production style… it really helps."

# TOMMY'S MARGARITA

🕐 1990s
⚑ SAN FRANCISCO, USA
👤 JULIO BERMEJO

🏠 TOMMY'S MEXICAN RESTAURANT
🍶 TEQUILA
🍸 ROCKS

The classic 1930s recipe for a Margarita consists of tequila, lime juice, and orange liqueur (typically Cointreau or another curaçao). Yet, as the cocktail was popularized in the US throughout the twentieth century, great liberties were taken with the recipe, and most venues opted for mixto-style tequilas—the type many people associate with bad hangovers, made with sugary additives—over products using 100% Blue Weber agave, the plant which tequila is distilled from.

In a 2021 online article for *Punch*, drinks writer Robert Simonson explains that, by the late 1980s, when Julio Bermejo took over Tommy's Mexican Restaurant in San Francisco from his parents, the house Margarita had already nixed the curaçao in favor of simple syrup but was still using mixto. By the 1990s, not only had Bermejo replaced the mixto with his favorite 100% agave tequila, Herradura, which he valued for its purity, he also began using agave syrup in lieu of those made with processed sugar, discovering both the healthier alternative and the way it boosted the natural flavors of the spirit to make a more balanced Margarita.

By the early 2000s, Bermejo, who also invented the Spicy Margarita, was consulting for bars in other parts of the country, and Tommy's Mexican Restaurant had a reputation as an essential Bay Area stop for beverage industry insiders, such as Tony Abou-Ganim, who went off to preach the gospel of 100% agave to their own customers in other cities, which, in turn, opened the door for new tequila and mezcal brands to launch Stateside. The Tommy's Margarita is now considered a particular method, and is served on hundreds of menus not only in the States, but also in Europe and other international destinations.

- 2 oz (60 ml) 100% agave tequila
  (blanco or silver is standard, but reposado also works well)
- 1 oz (30 ml) lime juice
- ½ oz (15 ml) agave nectar

- Garnish: lime wedge and coarse salt for the rim (optional), an additional lime wedge (optional)

If rimming the glass with salt, spread an even layer of salt on a small plate or saucer, rub the rim of a rocks glass with the lime wedge, and coat with salt; another option is to coat only one half of the glass. Set aside. Shake the remaining ingredients with ice until well chilled. Strain over fresh ice in the prepared rocks glass and garnish with an additional lime wedge, if desired.

# FITZGERALD

🕐 1994
⚑ NEW YORK CITY, USA
👤 DALE DEGROFF

⌂ RAINBOW ROOM
🍶 GIN
🍸 ROCKS

Modern cocktail luminary Dale DeGroff famously kicked off his mixology career in New York City as the head bartender at the Rainbow Room in the 1990s. The space has closed and reopened at least a couple of times since, but in those days, the opulent venue, high above the city in 30 Rockefeller Plaza, was reserved by tourists and New Yorkers alike for special occasions; it also had a real functioning bar area, not just a service area. It was in the Promenade Bar on a particularly busy and balmy summer evening that DeGroff was asked by a customer who was bored with his usual G&T to come up with a new refreshing gin drink.

DeGroff mixed what was essentially a gin sour, but with a few healthy dashes of Angostura bitters to add more nuance.

As it seemed like the sort of libation literary characters in 1920s American novels might sip at a fictional lawn party, DeGroff named his creation Fitzgerald. Not only did it quench the thirsts of Rainbow Room patrons from that point on, but it also accompanied him to other gigs, and eventually found its way onto menus across the planet. DeGroff, in his 2021 book *The New Craft of the Cocktail* (an update of the 2002 original), credits that phenomenon to the Internet.

Drinks writer Robert Simonson notes that while many bars in the US serve Fitzgeralds, it is especially at home as the signature cocktail of the Commodore in St. Paul, Minnesota. This Art Deco beauty is a place where F. Scott Fitzgerald actually drank, and, therefore, a perfect spot to enjoy one.

- 1½ oz (45 ml) dry gin (DeGroff says he likes NY Distilling's Dorothy Parker, especially for the literary connection)
- ¾ oz (22 ml) simple syrup
- ¾ oz (22ml) fresh lemon juice
- 4 dashes Angostura bitters

- Garnish: thin lemon wheel

Shake all ingredients with ice until well chilled. Strain into a rocks glass over fresh ice. Garnish with the lemon wheel perched on the side of the glass or over the drink.

# GINGER ROGERS

⊕ 1995
⚐ PORTLAND (OREGON), USA
𝄞 MARCOVALDO DIONYSOS

⌂ ZEFIRO
🍸 GIN
🍸 DOUBLE ROCKS OR HIGHBALL

...................................................................

The Portland, Oregon restaurant Zefiro "landed on the corner of NW 21st and Glisan in 1990 like an undiscovered planet," said food writer Karen Brooks in a 2016 article in *Portland Monthly*. Lasting only a decade, it was one of the original venues in the city's burgeoning avant-garde food scene and became one of its first culinary destinations, specializing in cuisine from far off lands, such as Morocco, Tuscany, France, and parts of Asia. It became the closest thing to a Hollywood hang in Portland, with sexy lighting, spare but shiny décor, and cool, loungey music. With its unapologetic informality dusted with glitzy details, it was also the perfect setting in which to create a spicy signature cocktail named after the most famous dancing starlet of the 1930s and 40s, Ginger Rogers.

In 1995, bartender Marcovaldo Dionysos did just that, by transforming the conventional Mojito into something far more vivacious. He replaced the traditional rum with light and aromatic gin and tamed the acid component by swapping the more astringent lime for lemon, then added snappy ginger syrup along with ginger ale. To paraphrase the famous quote from the lady herself, a man did a thing, but he did it better, and put it in heels.

When Dionysos moved to San Francisco a couple of years later, the drink became the most ordered at Absinthe Brasserie & Bar, and then tapped its way around town with him to venues such as Bourbon & Branch, Tres Agaves, Harry Denton's Starlight Room, Rye, and Smuggler's Cove. With its effervescence and relative ease of preparation, the Ginger Rogers is now considered one of the essential modern classics.

...................................................................

- 10 to 12 fresh mint leaves
- 2 oz (60 ml) London dry gin
- ¾ oz (22 ml) fresh lemon juice
- ¾ oz (22 ml) ginger syrup (homemade or store-bought—steep peeled, chopped fresh ginger in simple syrup for 20–30 minutes, then strain)
- 2 oz (60 ml) ginger ale

- Garnish: mint sprig, thin slice of lemon

Gently muddle the mint leaves in the bottom of a double rocks or highball glass (be careful not to break the glass). Pour in the remaining ingredients. Fill with crushed ice and stir. Garnish with the mint sprig and lemon slice.

# ORANGE CRUSH

- ⏱ 1995
- ⚑ OCEAN CITY (MARYLAND), USA
- ⌂ HARBORSIDE BAR & GRILL
- 🍸 VODKA
- ♙ CHRIS WALL, LLOYD WHITEHEAD, KELLY FLYNN, AND JERRY WOOD
- 🍸 PINT

In the autumn of 1995, when coupe glasses were still considered relics from *Thin Man* movies, no one blinked at hot-pink maraschino cherries, and bars only kept bitters on hand to help cure the occasional case of the hiccups, the Orange Crush was born at the Harborside Bar & Grill in Ocean City, Maryland. According to writer Drew Lazor in a July 2016 article in *Punch*, on a slow Sunday afternoon, bar owners Chris Wall and Lloyd Whitehead, bartender Kelly Flynn, and regular Jerry Wood decided to play around with a newly available bottle of Stoli O. They mixed the orange vodka with triple sec, and if that wasn't orangy enough, added the juice of a crushed orange and a splash of Sierra Mist soda (for those unfamiliar, it's lemon-lime flavored). Since they're easy to make and even easier to drink, Orange Crushes and dozens of variations on the theme soon became a dive and sports bar staple up and down the Eastern Seaboard. As of this writing,

the Harborside reportedly still sells thousands a year.

The name stems not only from the association with the American soda-pop brand—the Harborside uses an industrial press to flatten and juice the oranges (it's been said the bartenders who work there have more defined muscles on their crushing arm).

Orange Crush made several lists of the top drinks prepared at home during pandemic lockdowns in 2020, and, as if they aren't easy enough to mix manually, it's been a popular ready-to-drink (RTD) flavor, even in "skinny" form. The drink also briefly inspired an infamous "Crush Tour" from an anonymous Twitter account, attempting to review every bar's variation, with at least fifty documented as of this writing. Among the qualifications: "juice *must* be squeezed in your presence."

- 2 oz (60 ml) orange-flavored vodka
- 2 oz (60 ml) triple sec or other orange liqueur
- juice of 1 orange
- lemon-lime soda, to top

- Garnish: orange wheel (optional)

Combine the vodka and triple sec in a pint glass filled with ice. Squeeze the orange juice directly into the glass, then top with the lemon-lime soda. Stirring optional. Garnish if desired.

# PERIODISTA

◴ 1995
⚐ BOSTON, USA
𐤀 JOE MCGUIRK

⌂ CHEZ HENRI
◊ RUM
🍸 COUPE

Periodista is one of those "Ernest Hemingway drank these" cocktails that originated in Cuba sometime in the early twentieth century. The name is Spanish for "journalist," and it's even possible that Harry Craddock's cocktail recipe for The Journalist in the 1930 *Savoy Cocktail Book* is a gin offshoot of it. Speaking of journalists, the drink, essentially a dark rum and apricot Daiquiri (page 54), has been reported as being a favorite with American reporters stationed in Havana in the 1960s to cover the missile crisis.

However, Periodista never enjoyed the worldwide fame of the Daiquiris and Mojitos (page 104), or even the Mary Pickford (page 96). If you live outside the Boston, Massachusetts area, you might wonder why Periodista should even be counted among the signatures of the world. But if you do come from Boston, you would berate the exclusion of this downright delicious cocktail that was revived in the mid-1990s and has been a darling of the local scene ever since.

According to drinks writer Robert Simonson, the Periodista renaissance began when Joe McGuirk, head bartender at the French-Cuban bistro Chez Henri, was tasked with coming up with a Latin drinks-themed menu and had gotten wind of a recipe that was found in a vintage spirits company promotional pamphlet. He included it with his own tweaks on the menu, and somehow it took off all around the Boston area. Just about every bartender there is familiar with it, even if they don't already include one on a menu.

McGuirk originally prepared the drink with Rose's lime juice and added sugar. He has since overhauled the recipe to reflect contemporary mixology standards with fresh lime and no additional sweetener.

- 1½ oz (45 ml) dark rum
- ½ oz (15 ml) triple sec
- ½ oz (15 ml) apricot liqueur
- ½ oz (15 ml) fresh lime juice

Shake all ingredients with ice until well chilled. Strain into a chilled coupe glass.

# CABLE CAR

🕐 1996

⚑ SAN FRANCISCO, USA

A TONY ABOU-GANIM

⌂ STARLIGHT ROOM

◊ RUM

Y COUPE

In 1996, around the same time Dale DeGroff was revamping the bar program at New York City's Rainbow Room, across the country Tony Abou-Ganim was working with Harry Denton to open the Starlight Room in what was then the Sir Francis Drake Hotel in San Francisco. A year or two shy of what would become a robust online cocktail culture, Abou-Ganim says, "Every recipe had to be found in books, and even then, there weren't too many sources. All the 1990s drinks were Sex on the Beach, Woo Woos, Purple Hooter, etc."

Abou-Ganim says he no longer remembers the exact source, but the recipe for the Brandy Crusta, on which the Sidecar (page 80) is based, inspired the Cable Car. With Captain Morgan Spiced Rum then a trendy ingredient, Abou-Ganim decided to use it in place of the brandy, and instead of the traditional sugar-coated rim, continue the sweet spice theme with a rim of cinnamon and superfine (caster) sugar. Denton had come up with the Starlight's slogan "between the stars and the cable cars," and from there a modern classic was born.

The success of the Cable Car and other Starlight Room signatures earned Abou-Ganim further consulting gigs in the early 2000s. Even though it seemed so inherently San Franciscan, the Cable Car was introduced to the Wynn Group in Las Vegas, first at the Bellagio, where he says it became a popular order, although it wasn't officially on the menu. To this day, having celebrated its 25th anniversary in 2021, the Cable Car continues its showstopping run in Las Vegas cocktail bars, as well as in Detroit, where it debuted at Highlands. At time of writing, Abou-Ganim is consulting on the reopening of the Starlight Room, which closed in 2019, ushering in a new era for the Cable Car's original home.

---

• 1½ oz (45 ml) spiced rum
• ¾ oz (22 ml) orange curaçao
• 1 oz (30 ml) fresh lemon juice
• ½ oz (15 ml) simple syrup
• 1 tbsp egg white (half a whole egg white)

• Garnish: cinnamon sugar for the rim, orange twist

Rim a coupe glass with an orange wedge and dip the rim into a saucer spread with an even layer of cinnamon and superfine (caster) sugar mix. Set aside. Shake all ingredients with ice until well blended and chilled. Strain into the cinnamon and sugar-rimmed cocktail coupe. Garnish with a twist of orange peel.

# TENDER GIMLET

🕘 1997
⚲ GINZA, JAPAN
👤 KAZUO UYEDA

⌂ TENDER
🝊 GIN
🍸 COUPE

It's a bit of a cliché at this point, but observing a bartender who is well trained in the art of the hard shake is like watching a ballet that's been choreographed and painstakingly rehearsed at the highest level. The shaker is held in the fingers of one hand while the thumb of the other secures the top. In this position, the tin is undulated away from the body, then snatched back toward the chest in a repetitive motion, completely linear, not up and down, for a good 15 seconds or so. With this technique the ice hits both the top and bottom of the shaker, while the liquid simultaneously aerates and emulsifies, chilling it without overdilution. The hard shake was perfected by bartender Kazuo Uyeda and is best exemplified by the simple art of the house gimlet served at Tender, in the Ginza district of Tokyo, Japan, which he opened in 1997.

The quiet, elegant cocktail den is located on the fifth floor of the Kanze (Ginza) Noh Theater building, overlooking Sotobori-dori, and is one of the few bars in town that still requires men to at least wear a button-down shirt, if not also a tie. While drinks have been known to run a little on the wild side, the most-ordered cocktail is the gimlet. This is one of those cocktails that is not merely a signature; it's a ritual.

Mr. Uyeda's recipe—made with gin, simple syrup, and lime juice—is one of the first sours in the modern era to be served in a coupe with a wide circumference over a single large ice cube or sphere. This detail enables the gimlet to maintain the proper temperature and wield all the benefits of that beautiful hard shake.

• 1½ oz (45 ml) London dry gin
• Scant 1 tsp simple syrup
• ½ oz (15 ml) fresh lime juice

Place a large ice cube or sphere in a wide-rimmed coupe glass (not one of those dainty, delicate ones or it could break). Place all the remaining ingredients in a cocktail shaker with ice and hard shake for at least 15 seconds. Strain into the coupe over the ice.

# AWAMORI LEMON TEA

- 2000s
- HONG KONG, CHINA
- JAY KHAN

- COA
- VODKA
- HIGHBALL

In 2017, bartender and Mexican spirits enthusiast Jay Khan opened COA in Hong Kong, China with the intention of putting Mexican-focused drinks on the Asian cocktail map. The name refers to the sharp, heavy machete-like tool used to harvest agave plants in the field. The venue's candlelit wood, brick, and concrete design elements with red and green accents are meant to transport guests to an Oaxacan drinking den in the heart of Asia. A mural of Mayahuel, the goddess of agave and fertility, watches over the space. As dedicated as most of the menu is to spirits such as tequila, mezcal, raicilla, and bacanora, as well as agave-adjacent ones such as sotol and bacanora, it also features Asian cocktails that fit the flavor profile and theme. One such cocktail is the signature Awamori Lemon Tea, which combines agave-like flavors with local tea traditions.

Awamori is the native spirit of Okinawa, Japan, made from indica rice, though not brewed as a sake, but distilled in the style of shochu. Although it's miles away from Mexico, awamori's distinct, slightly smoky and funky flavor profile—due to the use of black koji mold in its production process—has been described as tasting similar to pechuga-style mezcal, which is steam-infused with meat or fruit and spices during distillation. For Awamori Lemon Tea, the spirit is mixed with black tea egg-washed vodka and lemon cordial—to represent the local summer tradition of iced black tea with lemon—served highball style with club soda.

The process for making the black tea egg-washed vodka involves using egg whites, which will curdle. Don't be alarmed! Once strained, it is safe to consume, and is akin to a clarified milk for punch.

- 1 oz (30 ml) Black Tea Egg-Washed Vodka
- ¾ oz (22 ml) awamori (can substitute with shochu)
- 1 oz (30 ml) lemon cordial (homemade or store-bought)
- Club soda, to top

- Garnish: lemon wheel

Add the first three ingredients to a highball glass filled with ice and stir to combine. Top with club soda and stir briefly. Garnish with a lemon wheel.

For the Black Tea Egg-Washed Vodka

- 17 oz (500 ml) unflavored vodka
- 1/3 cup (25 g) loose leaf black tea
- 1 egg white, gently beaten

In a glass or plastic container, infuse the vodka with the tea for at least an hour. Strain and add the egg white, which will curdle instantly. Strain through a coffee filter or cheesecloth (muslin) until clear (you may need to do this more than once).

# WHITE LINEN

🕐 2000s
⚐ SACRAMENTO, USA
🧍 RENE DOMINGUEZ

🏠 SHADY LADY SALOON
🍸 GIN
🍸 HIGHBALL

The trendiest flavor combination of the early 2000s cocktail scene is largely defined by the success of two new brands that launched within several years of one another: Hendrick's Gin (1999) and St-Germain elderflower liqueur (2007). Hendrick's distinguishes itself by using cucumber and rose petals in its botanical makeup, while St-Germain is a liqueur made with elderflower blossoms harvested in the French countryside. Both brands used viral marketing tactics—a robust mix of traditional advertising, social media, and in-person tastings—to launch their somewhat esoteric niche products into the cocktailsphere.

And it worked. By 2009—the year the speakeasy-style Shady Lady Saloon in Sacramento, California opened—it was nearly impossible not to fall into a puddle of cucumber-and-elderflower-tasting drinks of some sort at any bar or restaurant. St-Germain even became known as "bartender's ketchup."

One of the defining cocktails from this era is the White Linen, first created by Shady Lady bartender Rene Dominguez. This long, highball-style drink incorporates all the *au courant* flavors of the time, with the addition of fresh cucumber to make it even more fashionable and to provide some verdant eye candy.

The Shady Lady is still Sacramento's top high-volume cocktail bar, and although collective tastes have changed since then, the White Linen continues to be a bestseller. It's served all over Sacramento, and the recipe is well known farther afield. In 2017, Can-Can cocktails even launched a ready-to-drink (RTD) version.

- 1½ oz (45 ml) dry gin (try to use Hendrick's for authenticity's sake)
- ½ oz (15 ml) elderflower liqueur (such as St-Germain)
- ¾ oz (22 ml) fresh lemon juice
- ¼ to ½ oz (7 to 15 ml) simple syrup, depending on desired level of sweetness (St-Germain is already quite sweet)
- 3 fresh cucumber slices
- Soda water, to top

- Garnish: 1 to 3 cucumber slices

Combine all ingredients except the soda water in a shaker filled with ice. Shake until well chilled. Strain into a Collins glass over fresh ice and top with soda water. Garnish with additional cucumber slices lining the inside of the glass.

# GOLD RUSH

🕓 **2000**
⚐ **NEW YORK CITY, USA**
👤 **SASHA PETRASKE
AND T. J. SIEGAL**

⌂ **MILK & HONEY**
◊ **BOURBON**
🍸 **ROCKS**

---

A post-shift drink is a standard ritual for those who work in the service industry. While many partake of it at their place of employment, the wind-down nightcap is often enjoyed away from work, at a bar on the way home. Rarely does a shift drink with a hastily improvised recipe become a world-renowned modern classic, but that's exactly what happened one night in New York in 2000.

After working a Midtown restaurant shift, T. J. Siegal stopped in at his local speak-easy-style joint in Manhattan's Lower East Side called Milk & Honey, owned by Siegal's childhood buddy, Sasha Petraske. Petraske was set to prepare Siegal's typical bourbon sour drink order, but mentioned he'd been playing around with a syrup using honey instead of sugar. Siegal then had Petraske prepare the sour with his proprietary specs using the honey syrup and bourbon.

Zing!

For a bar that famously never had a drinks menu, the yummy honey bourbon sour, henceforth dubbed by Siegal as the Gold Rush, became a standard order by the early 2000s.

As Petraske's little bar empire expanded to other menu-less venues, such as Greenwich Village's Little Branch, the Varnish in Los Angeles, and the London location of Milk & Honey, the Gold Rush was a staple drink order. When Petraske opened Double Seven with Jared Brown and Anistatia Miller in NYC's Meatpacking District, the paper menu changed every night, but it always featured a Gold Rush. Eventually the drink was served at other venues around the world—if not on the printed menu, it was easily recognized, if requested.

---

• 2 oz (60 ml) good-quality bourbon
  (best at 45% ABV or higher)
• 1 oz (30 ml) fresh lemon juice
• ¾ oz (22 ml) 3:1 honey syrup (page 86)

• Garnish: lemon twist

Shake all ingredients with ice until well chilled and frothy. Strain into a rocks glass over fresh ice (preferably one large cube). Garnish with the lemon twist.

# OLD CUBAN

○ 2001
▷ NEW YORK CITY, USA
ᴀ AUDREY SAUNDERS

◰ BEMELMANS BAR, CARLYLE HOTEL
◊ RUM
🍸 COUPE OR COCKTAIL

Some refer to the Old Cuban as a "rum French 75," but Audrey Saunders has often said of her creation that it's "a Mojito in a little black dress."

In 2001, when Dale DeGroff was ending his consultancy at Bemelmans Bar in the Carlyle Hotel, New York City, he brought in Saunders to revamp his menu. A swank location begged for an equally snazzy cocktail, and using Champagne seemed a natural counterpart to the various Martinis.

The Old Cuban (named for its use of dark rum instead of the white typically used in Mojitos) was an instant hit. Soon after, Saunders brought the drink to The Carlyle's British sister property, London's Ritz, which was hosting a Bemelmans pop-up. British drink journalism was way ahead of those in North America at the time, and reports of Saunders' creation appeared in various publications, such as the *Financial Times*. The Old Cuban impressed the international cocktail scene and soon landed on menus all over Europe. Back in the States, it became a staple at places like the Zig Zag Café in Seattle. And by the early 2000s, the burgeoning online cocktail community was also smitten with the refreshing, rummy sparkler.

But it's much more fun to drink it than it is to read about it. By the time Saunders opened Pegu Club in 2005 back in New York (named for the early-twentieth-century officer's club in what was then Burma, now Myanmar), it became one of the signatures. Even with that bar now gone, the Old Cuban is still on the menu at Bemelmans and dozens of other bars around the world.

---

• ¾ oz (22 ml) fresh lime juice
• 1 oz (30 ml) simple syrup
• 6 whole mint leaves
• 1½ oz (45 ml) dark rum
• 2 dashes Angostura bitters
• 2 oz (60 ml) Champagne

• Garnish: small sprig of mint

In a mixing glass, muddle the lime juice, syrup, and mint. Add the rum and bitters, then shake with ice until well chilled and frothy. Double strain into a coupe or cocktail glass, then top with Champagne. Garnish with a small sprig of mint.

# WHITE NEGRONI

⏲ 2001  
⚐ BORDEAUX, FRANCE  
ⵣ NICK BLACKNELL  
   AND WAYNE COLLINS

⌂ N/A  
🝮 GIN  
🍸 ROCKS

..................................................................................................................

Along with the Negroni Sbagliato (page 184), the White Negroni is one of the most popular Negroni adaptations to hit the modern cocktail mainstream. It was created on a whim in 2001 by then Plymouth Gin brand manager Nick Blacknell and Wayne Collins, a prominent London bar consultant, while the pair were in Bordeaux, France for the Vinexpo trade conference. Cocktail author Robert Simonson writes in an October 2020 *Punch* article that the event took place during a hot spell, and the pair were craving Negronis to cool off. However, the small village they were staying in didn't serve cocktails. With plenty of Plymouth on hand back at the hotel, they only needed to shop for the necessary mixers, which in the traditional recipe would have been Campari and sweet vermouth.

But Blacknell had a "when in Bordeaux" moment and decided to switch things up by using French mixers, in this case the bitter, earthy gentian aperitif Suze instead of Campari,

and Lillet Blanc instead of red vermouth. They garnished this new, paler, and rather delicious variation with wedges of pink grapefruit instead of orange. Blacknell's promotionally minded instincts were thus sparked, and he suggested they market the drink as the White Negroni when back in the UK.

The White Negroni wasn't an instant hit. It was one of those early 2000s "bartender's handshake" recipes, the delayed reaction largely because many international markets had trouble sourcing the necessary Suze ingredient. But, by the early 2010s, Suze's (and Plymouth's) importing company, Pernod Ricard, righted that wrong, and made it more accessible after the recipe was published in 2011 by PDT bar manager Jim Meehan in the vastly successful *The PDT Cocktail Book*.

Now the variation is as much a standard as the classic. And yes, even in Sbagliato form "with Prosecco in it."

..................................................................................................................

- 1½ oz (45 ml) dry gin (originally Plymouth)
- 1 oz (30 ml) Lillet Blanc
- ½ oz (15 ml) Suze gentian liqueur

- Garnish: lemon or grapefruit twist

Stir all ingredients with ice until well chilled. Strain into a rocks glass over fresh ice (preferably one large cube). Garnish with a citrus twist.

..................................................................................................................

# EL CAPITÁN

⊕ 2002
⊳ LIMA, PERU
ⴷ ROBERTO MELÉNDEZ

⌂ CAPITÁN MELÉNDEZ
◊ PISCO
Ⴌ COUPE

In nineteenth-century Peru, establishments known as *pulperias* could be found throughout the country, serving as both general stores and saloons. Pisco expert Nico Vera recounts how, during World War I, military cavalry captains in the Peruvian sierras would order an aperitif of sweet vermouth and pisco—first popularized by the Italian immigrants who flocked to the country in the 1850s and used the Cinzano Rosso they had brought with them—served in a shot glass at room temperature to ward off the cold during night rounds. The drink was called "20 centavos," the country's smallest coin, because over the years the Cinzano had been replaced with low-end vermouth. The barkeeps would serve the drink by saying, "For you, my Captain," and the name morphed to El Capitán over time. Though by the mid- to late-twentieth century, it had fallen out of favor.

In 2002, Roberto Meléndez, owner of Capitán Meléndez, brought the cocktail back in to the mainstream, but as a more sophisticated variation served in the style of a Manhattan, stirred with ice. As a nod to the original Italian ingredient, he uses Cinzano Rosso and Quebranta pisco, a style blended with two distinct grapes (Acholado), to add complexity while retaining a fruit-forward flavor profile.

Meléndez notes that just as with a Manhattan, El Capitán can be served in the classic way, or as a "perfect" variation, using a split of dry and sweet vermouth. Unlike a Manhattan, the cocktail is garnished with an olive instead of a cherry or citrus twist. Says Vera in a 2018 article in *Imbibe*, "Green olives are a must because, according to Meléndez, a bite of an olive invites you to take another sip."

• 1 oz (30 ml) pisco
  (Acholado-style preferred)
• ½ oz (15 ml) sweet vermouth
• ½ oz (15 ml) dry vermouth
• 1 dash Angostura bitters

• Garnish: green olives

Stir all the ingredients with ice until well chilled. Strain into a chilled coupe glass. Garnish by threading the desired number of olives on a pick and placing in the glass or over the rim.

# LONDON CALLING

⏱ **2002**
⚐ **LONDON, UK**
👤 **CHRIS JEPSON**

⌂ **MILK & HONEY**
🍸 **GIN; SHERRY**
🍸 **COUPE**

In 2002, when Sasha Petraske opened the London outpost of New York City's premier modern speakeasy Milk & Honey, certain ingredients, such as sherry, still exuded a somewhat enigmatic aura. Outside of its native Spain at that time, the fortified wine and all its various styles, from bone dry to sweet, were only understood by people who worked in the Spanish wine trade, or wine geeks in general. The cocktailians were just getting hip to sherry and how to incorporate the various styles into recipes. It was in that same year that M&H bartender Chris Jepson used it as a secret weapon in London Calling (gin, Fino sherry, lemon juice, simple syrup, and grapefruit bitters), a winning entry for a competition held by the publication *Drinks International*. From that point on, the public couldn't get enough of this gin sour with the nutty yet dry aromatic flavor profile, and it remained on the menu until the bar's closing in 2020.

Although the bar is gone, London Calling has continued its run as a mascot of sorts for both the dry sherry and gin categories. The modern classic—its name is a reference to both the catchphrase of the BBC World War II news announcements and the 1979 classic anthem by the punk band The Clash—has made it to "faraway towns" and inspired numerous variations. It's on the Hawksmoor international steakhouse chain's "Sacred Six" menu as a house highball. And at London's Dandelyan in 2018, it was mixed with banana liqueur for Banana Calling.

But no matter how one dials up the ingredients, gin and Fino are the main connection.

Here's the classic recipe.

- 1½ oz (45 ml) dry gin
- ½ oz (15 ml) Fino sherry
- ½ oz (15 ml) lemon juice
- ½ oz (15 ml) simple syrup
- 2 dashes grapefruit bitters (orange bitters will also work beautifully)

- Garnish: grapefruit twist

Shake all ingredients with ice until well chilled. Strain into a chilled coupe glass. Express the oils from a piece of grapefruit peel into the drink, skin side down, then twist and place in the glass.

# PORN STAR MARTINI

🕓 2002
⚑ LONDON, UK
👤 DOUGLAS ANKRAH

⌂ TOWNHOUSE
🍶 VODKA
🍸 PASSION-FRUIT HALF
AND WINE GLASS

---

The Porn Star Martini is so bright and delicious that we would likely still be talking about it even if British bar man Douglas Ankrah had gone with its original name, the Maverick Martini. In 2002, the co-owner of London's popular LAB (London Academy of Bartenders) bar, which opened in 1999, was working on his book *Shaken and Stirred* and preparing to open another venue—Townhouse—in Knightsbridge, when he took a trip to Cape Town, South Africa. After a visit to Maverick's Gentlemen's Club, it dawned on him that although a new era of serious cocktails had taken shape, there was no reason a new bar concept couldn't be playful and cheeky, but still considered chic. Townhouse needed a signature cocktail to match those qualities, and the name was changed from Maverick to Porn Star upon his return to London.

The Porn Star Martini is made with a combination of vanilla-flavored vodka, Passoã (Brazilian passion fruit liqueur), passion fruit purée, lime juice, and vanilla simple syrup, served in half a hollowed-out passion fruit with a side of sparkling wine. The drink was wildly successful at both bars, so much so that then bartender (now drinks consultant) Colin Asare-Appiah has said they couldn't shake them fast enough.

By the time of Ankrah's untimely passing in 2021, the Porn Star Martini was such a popular modern classic, with worldwide recognition and numerous riffs on the original recipe, that it had inspired a passion fruit and vanilla-flavored gin (BLOOM) and become a trendy ready-to-drink (RTD) flavor in its native UK. However, for British retail giant Marks & Spencer's, the RTD's name was changed to "Passion Star Martini" for political correctness—close enough to be recognized for what it is, but much easier for the public to identify than if they had they changed it back to "Maverick."

---

- 1½ oz (45 ml) vanilla-flavored vodka
- ½ oz (15 ml) passion fruit liqueur
- 2 oz (60 ml) passion fruit purée
- 2 tsp vanilla sugar or ½ oz (15 ml) vanilla simple syrup (1:1 sugar and water with split vanilla bean/pod, strained)
- 2 oz (60 ml) dry sparkling wine, served on the side

- Garnish: half passion fruit, pulp and seeds scooped out

Shake all ingredients except the sparkling wine with ice until well chilled. Strain into the prepared passion fruit half. Serve with a small wine or cordial glass of sparkling wine.

---

# DRIED FRUIT SANGRIA

🕐 2004
🏳 BARCELONA, SPAIN
👤 DIEGO CABRERA

⌂ RITZ CARLTON HOTEL
🍷 RED WINE
🍸 WINE

Sangria is a cocktail consisting of red or white wine mixed with liqueur or brandy, a variety of sliced fruits, juice, and either sparkling water or lemon-lime soda. Though it has its roots in ancient Rome, in modern times it is one of Spain and Portugal's most iconic drinks, and runs the gamut from sweet to dry, cheap to pricey, and from delicious to, well, not so much. The best sangrias are those made from a base wine that one would happily consume on its own, the freshest fruits, and a good brandy in the right proportions. At the Ritz Carlton Hotel in Barcelona, sangria gets a modern, elegant update using dried fruit, aged brandy, and good red wine.

The Dried Fruit Sangria was created in 2004 by bartender Diego Cabrera, who says he was challenged "to make a more interesting and,

above all, more foodie Sangria. So, we made it with a more elaborate base, with macerations, dried fruits, dried apricots and figs. It's inspired by the Sangria that is drunk at village festivals, where each one is different, and as in those villages, the recipe is homemade. Ours is more unctuous, tastier, and with more gastronomic nuances."

Another challenge was to create a recipe that didn't depend on only local fresh ingredients. "When everyone was thinking of combinations with fresh fruit, I thought of something with more intensity," says Cabrera. "I wanted the ingredients to be more accessible and easier to find, as well as timeless, because they are available all year round, regardless of the season of each fruit."

Note: make one day ahead.

Serves 4 to 6

- 4 (25 g) dried apricots
- 4 (30 g) dried figs
- 1 orange
- 1 lemon
- 2 tbsp red raisins
- 1 cinnamon stick
- ½ cup (100 g) granulated sugar
- 2 oz (60 ml) aged brandy
  (Spanish preferred)
- 2 oz (60 ml) orange liqueur
- 25 oz (750 ml) bottle good-quality
  dry red wine
- 4–6 oz (120–180 ml) lemon-lime soda

- Garnish: diced fresh apple and mint sprig

Cut the dried apricots and figs in half. Quarter the orange and lemon. Combine all ingredients except the soda in a nonreactive container, cover, and refrigerate for 24 hours. When ready to serve, strain into a punch bowl or large pitcher (jug). Pour into large wine glasses over fresh ice and top with the soda. Garnish with apple and mint.

# BLACK MANHATTAN

⊕ **2005**
⊳ **SAN FRANCISCO, USA**
A **TODD SMITH**

⌂ **CORTEZ**
🍶 **WHISKEY**
Y **COUPE**

The Manhattan is a perfect template for boozy and stirred drinks. It's traditionally prepared with American whiskey, rye preferred, but bourbon is almost as common these days. Then there are the variations that swap out the whiskey entirely for another base spirit. These are mixed with a smaller measure of sweet vermouth and bitters. To make it "perfect," split the vermouth dry and sweet and omit the bitters (though many people prefer to leave them in), and garnish with a cherry or lemon. Both are technically correct.

People have been drinking Manhattans since the last quarter of the nineteenth century, and bartenders have been riffing on them since then. However, it wasn't until 2005 that the possibilities of a darker side entered the mainstream. Sipping digestifs, such as the various forms of amaro, has been commonplace in parts of Europe for centuries, but the early 2000s is when bitter liqueurs became a thing in the US.

Bourbon & Branch, in San Francisco's Tenderloin district, is where Todd Smith had the idea to replace the vermouth quotient from a Manhattan with Averna—a dark, viscous, bitter orangey liqueur from Sicily that was making the rounds. The richness of that amaro lends a roasty, more intense flavor to the drink, without the need for additional sweetness, as well as a subtle chocolatey-ness without any actual chocolate. It was gospel at all the cool cocktail joints around the country and beyond by the time Smith opened ABV in the Mission district in 2014 with Ryan Fitzgerald and Erik Reichborn-Kjennerud, with the Black Manhattan as one of its signatures.

With its name firmly in lights, the Black Manhattan inspired hundreds of signature Manhattan variations using bitter components. Here is the foundational recipe for the modern age.

- 2 oz (60 ml) rye whiskey
- 1 oz (30 ml) Averna liqueur
- 1 dash Angostura bitters
- 1 dash orange bitters

- Garnish: cocktail cherry

Stir all ingredients in a mixing glass with ice until well chilled. Strain into a chilled coupe glass. Garnish with a cherry either in the glass or pierced through a pick balancing over the rim.

# PENICILLIN

🕐 **2005**
🏳 **NEW YORK CITY, USA**
👤 **SAM ROSS**

⌂ **MILK & HONEY**
◊ **SCOTCH**
🍸 **DOUBLE ROCKS**

........................................................................................

The Gold Rush cocktail (page 218), created in 2000 by Sasha Petraske and T. J. Siegal at Milk & Honey on New York City's Lower East Side, had already been declared a modern classic by the time young Australian bartender Sam Ross began his stint there in 2005. He started playing around with the recipe—bourbon, honey syrup, lemon—as though rearranging the architecture of a Lego set. New brands of blended Scotch, such as Compass Box, were just hitting the scene to shake up long-held prejudices of the category and win over diehard single malt aficionados. Thus, in some sequence of thought that incorporates elements of the Gold Rush with modern Scotch culture and the New York Sour, which features a float of wine at the top, Ross came up with the Penicillin—an ice-cold, shaken sour with flavors of hot honey ginger tea and a float of smoky Scotch over the top.

In those nascent days of the cocktail renaissance, any drink with flavors deemed "challenging" was passed around like a secret handshake. Bartenders in other venues had heard tell of this wild concoction, and the potently spicy homemade ginger syrup needed for Penicillin prep became a back bar staple worldwide within a couple of years. By the next decade, Penicillins were their own category of cocktail—hot, cold, tall, short, even dessert-like iterations—that riffed on the sour, spicy, smoky float formula.

In 2017, Ross and Michael McIlroy, who had taken over Milk & Honey as Attaboy, opened Diamond Reef in Brooklyn. Its featured cocktail was the frozen Penichillin. Sadly, that bar closed in 2021, but like its predecessor in the modern sour movement, the cocktail transcends the neo-blender era.

........................................................................................

- 2 oz (60 ml) blended Scotch, such as Compass Box Asyla
- ¾ oz (22 ml) fresh lemon juice
- ¾ oz (22 ml) Honey Ginger Syrup (page 382)*
- Drop of peated Scotch, to float on top (such as Laphroaig, Lagavulin, or Compass Box Peat Monster)

- Garnish: candied ginger

Add all ingredients except the peated Scotch to a shaker and shake with ice for 15 to 20 seconds until well chilled and frothy. Strain into a double rocks glass over fresh ice. Add the peated Scotch to a barspoon and carefully drizzle over the drink. Thread a cocktail pick through a piece of candied ginger and place over the glass.

*Note: if making the syrup is too much trouble, muddle a few pieces of peeled, fresh ginger in the shaker tin before preparing the drink and use plain honey syrup instead (page 86). Double-strain to serve.

........................................................................................

234

# GIN EST BELLE

🕐 2006
⚲ VALENCIA, SPAIN
🄰 ESTHER MEDINA-CUESTA

⌂ CAFÉ MADRID
◊ GIN
🍸 COUPE

Gin est Belle is a house cocktail featured at Café Madrid in Valencia, Spain. The drink, designed by Spanish-born bartender and founder of EMC drinks consultancy, Esther Medina-Cuesta, is essentially a deconstructed hybrid of a Negroni and a Gibson, with a main component of dry gin and Spanish ambré vermouth served with a side of cocktail onions soaked in amaro.

The concept was developed in 2006, when Medina-Cuesta was bartending at both The Player and Milk & Honey in London. During a post-shift drink at the latter, having started with a Negroni, but craving a Gibson next, it occurred to her to assemble the two together in some way. "The bartender thought I was mad when I asked him to make me what Embury's [David Embury's *The Fine Art of Mixing Drinks*, 1948] called a 'Sweet Martini' but with ambré vermouth, lemon twist discarded, and silver-skin onions soaked in classic Italian amaro on the side. But he made it," she recalls. "I was pleasantly surprised with the outcome: the interaction of pickles with amaro resulted in a bittersweet symphony that raised the Martini to a completely new level."

Gin est Belle, christened by drinks historians Jared Brown and Anistatia Miller, was soon featured at both The Player and M&H and has since become Medina-Cuesta's signature for her consulting business, including pop-ups at the 2014 Moscow Bar Show, and spirits and cocktail conventions across Europe.

"Drink it as you wish!" Medina-Cuesta says of the best way to approach the drink. "Soak an onion in the Martini, sip the amaro then the Martini, do it the other way around, mix it all together. I change the way I drink mine depending on my mood, the weather... Every combination will add a new flavour layer."

- 2 oz (60 ml) dry gin
- 1 oz (30 ml) ambré vermouth (if none can be found, Medina-Cuesta suggests mixing 1:1 French and Italian sweet vermouth styles)

- Garnish: lemon twist, Amaro-Soaked Onions

Prepare the amaro-soaked onions. Stir the gin and vermouth with ice until well chilled, then strain into a chilled coupe glass. Express the oils from the twist into the drink, skin side down, then discard. Enjoy with onions as desired.

For the Amaro-Soaked Onions

In a small separate glass, such as a cordial glass or saucer, add 3–5 small, silverskin pickled cocktail onions to 1 oz (30 ml) amaro or aperitivo of choice (Campari, Ramazzotti, Lucano, Montenegro, Meletti, Sibilia, etc.). Let sit for a few minutes before enjoying alongside the drink.

# JULIET & ROMEO

- ⊕ 2007
- ⚑ CHICAGO, USA
- ⚲ TOBY MALONEY

- ⌂ VIOLET HOUR
- ⚭ GIN
- ⚱ COUPE

When it opened in 2007, the Violet Hour was credited with being the first "serious" cocktail bar in Chicago. It was a period in cocktail history when bartenders thought it was their sworn duty to shift public tastes away from vodka sodas and introduce more complex spirits and ingredients. One of the biggest campaigns at the time was to highlight gin as a base spirit beyond the Martini or G&T, demonstrating that with a good-quality gin, the juniper aromatics and other botanicals serve to enliven whatever is mixed with it, rather than overpower. Gin could *do* things in a drink that unflavored vodka simply couldn't.

When New York City bartender Toby Maloney co-founded the Violet Hour, he sought to bring a taste of the NYC speakeasy scene to Wicker Park, with its heavy periwinkle curtains separating the rooms and a much more formal vibe in which to imbibe than Chicago had previously been known for.

His creation—a menu staple since its invention and served and imitated the world over—is essentially what you get when you cross a Mojito with a gin Martini (served up) and add cucumber and a hint of sweet rose. Maloney has said he wanted it to taste like "walking through an English garden."

Juliet & Romeo has accomplished exactly what it set out to do—making gin haters fall in love with gin, although not in such a star-crossed way as the name would suggest. After all, the real tragedy would be to make one with vodka.

- Pinch of salt
- 3 slices fresh cucumber
- 1 mint sprig
- 2 oz (60 ml) London dry gin
- ¾ oz (22 ml) fresh lime juice
- ¾ oz (22 ml) simple syrup

- Garnish: mint leaf, dash of rosewater, 3 dashes Angostura bitters

Muddle the salt with the cucumber and mint in a mixing tin. Add the remaining ingredients and shake with ice until well chilled. Strain (double strain if you want to lose more of the leafy bits) into a chilled coupe glass. Dash in the rosewater and bitter garnishes over the top (try to make neat little dots with the Angostura) and add the mint leaf.

# BLUSHING LADY

⏱ 2008
⚑ BELFAST, NORTHERN IRELAND
ᴀ LISA MCCARRON

⌂ THE MERCHANT HOTEL
◊ VODKA
Ⴘ COUPE

In 2008, the bar at The Merchant Hotel in Belfast, Northern Ireland broke the Guinness World Record for serving what was up to that point the most expensive cocktail in history: a $1,475 Mai Tai made with an ultra-rare seventeen-year-old Wray & Nephew rum. While that drink had the intended result of garnering all sorts of attention for a city that was then a fledgling blip on the cocktail map, head bartender Jack McGarry—who would years later move to New York City to open the Dead Rabbit with Merchant general manager Sean Muldoon—and the talented bar team were finding other ways to earn accolades for the bar and help boost Belfast destination tourism. In that same year, they encouraged junior bartender Lisa McCarron to travel to New Zealand to enter a 42Below Vodka cocktail competition. Her entry, the Blushing Lady, not only won first place but became one of the Merchant's (far more affordable) signatures for years to come.

McGarry reminisces that the drink was christened with that name because McCarron was so overcome with the pressure of having journeyed so far for an in-person competition, that she was flushed with terror the moment she was put in the spotlight. Cool heads prevailed, however.

The Blushing Lady is a balanced mix of unflavored vodka, fresh pomegranate juice, fresh lemon juice, a dash of rosewater, and the twist: a house mix of white grapefruit sherbet and orgeat biz (a term regularly used in early 2000s cocktail bars indicating a house-made sweetener) garnished with a rose petal. It's no wonder it became a bestseller: with its beguiling presentation, the Blushing Lady's flavors form a transportive tropical vibe for sophisticated palates, yet the Cosmo-like cocktail also holds appeal for vodka drinkers.

• 2 oz (60 ml) unflavored vodka
• ½ oz (15 ml) fresh pomegranate juice
• 1 oz (30 ml) fresh lemon juice
• ¾ oz (22 ml) 1:1 mix of white grapefruit sherbet/orgeat biz (homemade—there are many recipes online—or store-bought)
• 1 dash rosewater

• Garnish: pesticide-free rose petal

Shake all ingredients with ice until well chilled. Strain into a chilled coupe glass. Top with a rose petal.

# CAB CALLOWAY

◷ 2008
⚑ ATLANTA, USA
🜨 TIFFANIE BARRIERE

⌂ ONE FLEW SOUTH
◊ SHERRY
🍸 ROCKS

By the time the One Flew South restaurant opened in Atlanta's Hartsfield-Jackson airport in December 2008, the golden age of commercial plane travel—described as "cocktail parties on wings"—was a thing of the past, and travelers, especially in American airports, had come to expect mediocre food and drink offerings. However, this restaurant, in Concourse E of one of the world's busiest hubs, sought to revive the high-end airport dining experience with top-notch regional Southern cuisine and terrific cocktails to match. When Tiffanie Barriere took over the bar program a couple of years after the venue opened, signature cocktails such as her Cab Calloway were deemed destination-worthy. Suddenly travelers *wanted* to be stranded in Atlanta, if only to have more time at One Flew South than just a flyover.

The Cab Calloway cocktail is named for the legendary showman and Cotton Club band leader of the 1920s through to the late 1940s, who famously toured the Jim Crow South on charter train. He was one of the most recognizable and well-educated jazz performers of his day (he attended law school in Chicago), with hits such as "Minnie the Moocher" and "The Ghost of Smoky Joe" sprinkled with his trademark "hi-de-ho" scat singing.

Barriere's tribute cocktail is a stirred, boozy number combining dark sherry, rye whiskey, apricot liqueur, dry vermouth, and bitters. It's the sort of drink one could imagine sipping in a smoky jazz club. However, even if sipping one while waiting for that connecting flight to finally be announced instead, the Cab Calloway cocktail's comforting flavor profile feels like a first-class upgrade. Sure beats a sad Martini with mushy olives.

- 1½ oz (45 ml) Pedro Ximenez (PX) or sweet Oloroso sherry
- ½ oz (15 ml) rye whiskey
- ¼ oz (7 ml) dry vermouth
- ¼ oz (7 ml) apricot liqueur
- 2 dashes Angostura bitters
- 2 dashes orange bitters

- Garnish: lemon or orange peel (or both!)

Combine all ingredients in a mixing glass and stir with ice until well chilled. Strain into a rocks glass over fresh ice. Express the oils from the citrus peel over the drink, skin side down, then twist and add to the glass.

# CONNAUGHT MARTINI

○ 2008
⚑ LONDON, UK
A AGOSTINO PERRONE

⌂ CONNAUGHT
◊ GIN OR VODKA
Υ MARTINI

The Connaught Martini was invented for the opening of the Connaught Bar in 2008 by Agostino "Ago" Perrone and Erik Lorincz, and soon became the signature. Says Perrone, "After fifteen years, we (along with Maura Milia, Giorgio Barfiani, and the team) are still serving this wonderful drink that encapsulates the essence of hospitality with creativity and personalization."

One of the hallmarks of world-class cocktails in London's hotel bars is the bar cart. What started in the nineteenth-century Victorian tea-trolley era was adopted by certain bars to deliver tableside cocktails in style. Aside from nods to fine dining with white-glove service and exquisite bar ware, what sets the Connaught Martini trolley experience apart from others is the opportunity for guests to choose their own Martini adventure by selecting from five proprietary aromatic bitters: tonka bean (vanilla-almond for those in the States), relaxing lavender, zesty ginger, aromatic cardamom, or the trademark Dr. Ago, a combination of Italian bergamot and ginseng.

As with the Dukes Martini, it's a ceremonial experience. Gin or vodka is stirred with the bar's clear, "slow-frozen" ice, and then poured with one hand in an impressively long cascade while the other hand simultaneously and poetically spritzes the falling liquid with citrus before it lands in a frozen etched glass that has been anointed with the bitters.

The resulting Martini is crisp, cold, yet uniquely flavorful. "The biggest achievement of the Connaught Bar is not changing," said Perrone in a 2018 interview with 50 Best (the bar is consistently in the top 10). "We go back to the beginning, always focused on our guests and on the style we wanted to have since the beginning, with no arrogance, a humble approach and an open mind."

• 2½ oz (70 ml) gin or vodka
• ½ oz (15 ml) dry vermouth
• 3 dashes bitters of choice

• Garnish: olive or lemon peel (or both)

Freeze a Martini glass for at least 15 minutes. Stir the vodka or gin and vermouth in a mixing glass with ice chunks until well chilled. Add the 3 dashes of bitters to the frozen glass. Hold the mixing glass at least a foot above the frozen glass and, using a strainer, let it fall gently into the glass (if possible, express the oils from a lemon peel at the stream of liquid with the other hand, but you could always do this after it's safely in the vessel). Garnish as desired.

# GIN BASIL SMASH

⊕ 2008
⚑ HAMBURG, GERMANY
👤 JÖRG MEYER

⌂ LE LION
🍶 GIN
🍸 DOUBLE ROCKS

Gin Basil Smash is a modern, more aromatic interpretation of a Southside (page 106) by way of a Whiskey Smash, using basil instead of mint. It was created in the summer of 2008 by Jörg Meyer at Le Lion in Hamburg, Germany, where it was first referred to as "Gin Pesto." Since then, the muddled refresher has become one of the most popular drinks in all of Germany. According to a June 2021 article by Robert Simonson in *Punch*, sore-armed bartenders throughout the country call it "Meyer's Curse."

Meyer first wrote about his recipe in the online forum "Bitters Blog," which he ran with Stephan Berg of Bitter Truth. Meyer says he was inspired to use basil after spotting another recipe using a basil garnish instead of the traditional mint. He originally built the specs around bourbon, based on cocktail luminary Dale DeGroff's Whiskey Smash, but was unhappy with the taste profile. However, Meyer was much more successful pairing its specific savory-herbaceous flavor with gin, specifically Rutte Celery Gin.

Gin Basil Smash remains one of the top sellers at Le Lion (reportedly they sell 22,000 a year and go through over 3,000 bottles of gin) not only because it hits the spot on a warm day, but it also sparked culinary intrigue with its bright green hue and use of basil. The cocktail also became a recipe staple for gin brands, not just Rutte, at promotional events and cocktail festivals in Germany and throughout Europe and the UK. In 2012, the Instagram-famous words "Cradle of the Gin Basil Smash" were painted outside the restaurant, a nod to La Floridita's "La Cuna del Daiquirí" in Havana, Cuba.

Meyer has said that when preparing the recipe, it is better to use too much basil than not enough.

---

• 12 fresh basil leaves
• 2 oz (60 ml) dry gin (Rutte Celery for authenticity)
• 1 oz (30 ml) fresh lemon juice
• ¾ oz (22 ml) simple syrup

• Garnish: basil sprig

Muddle the basil leaves in the bottom of a shaker tin until well smooshed. Add the remaining ingredients and shake with ice until well chilled. Fine strain into a double rocks glass filled with fresh ice. Garnish with a basil sprig.

# OAXACA OLD FASHIONED

🕐 2008
🏴 NEW YORK CITY, USA
👤 PHIL WARD

⌂ DEATH & CO/MAYAHUEL
🍸 TEQUILA
🍸 ROCKS OR COUPE

The Oaxaca Old Fashioned—composed of both tequila and mezcal with agave nectar and aromatic bitters—is one of a select few famous signature cocktails that didn't spend months in research and development, and didn't require tweaking before it was a hit. Its creator, Phil Ward, is quoted in a November 2020 *Punch* article as saying it was a "right off-the-cuff humdinger." It debuted on the menu at Death & Co in New York City in 2008, at a time when mezcal was just beginning its approach into the cocktailsphere. Largely thanks to the Internet and social media, in just a couple of years, almost any bar in the world that served mezcal (by then it was quite a number) had a version of the Oaxaca Old Fashioned on its menu.

Ward was later deemed one of American bartending's first agave spirits experts and opened his own Mexican-spirits-focused venue, Mayahuel, in 2009. But two years earlier, when the Oaxaca Old Fashioned was first served to a Death & Co regular, who was keen to try something off menu, Ward reportedly had used only mezcal in a couple of drinks he was experimenting with. The cocktail was officially christened by David Kaplan, one of the bar's owners, who said he just liked the name "Oaxaca" (referring to the Mexican state where the spirit is produced), though the rest is the very definition of the drink itself.

The versatile Oaxaca Old Fashioned, or variations of it, is now considered a teaching tool of sorts for bartenders around the world, as a way of introducing the earthy, smoky flavors of mezcal to unconditioned palates. With so many expressions of mezcal and tequila and the other ingredients available now, it's easy to experiment with flavors using the base recipe as a template.

- 1½ oz (45 ml) tequila reposado
- ½ oz (15 ml) mezcal joven
- 1 tsp agave nectar
- 2 dashes aromatic bitters

- Garnish: orange twist

Stir all ingredients with ice until well chilled. To serve on the rocks: strain into a rocks glass over ice. To serve up: strain into a chilled coupe glass. For both, express the oils from a piece of orange peel into the drink, skin side down (you can also flame the orange while doing this for extra smoky flavor), then twist and place in the drink.

# SAFFRON SANDALWOOD SOUR

🕐 2008
⚐ SEATTLE, USA
ㅅ ANU APTE

⌂ ROB ROY
◊ GIN
� COUPE

The Saffron Sandalwood Sour is a twist on the classic gin sour, with flavors traditionally found in Eastern Indian cuisine. It was invented in 2008 by Navy Strength Talent consulting company co-founder Anu Apte, a year before she opened Rob Roy in Seattle, Washington, one of the city's first modern cocktail bars, where it has remained on the menu as a signature and fan favorite.

"I was inspired to create a drink that used some of my favorite Indian ingredients," says Apte. "Saffron sharbat was a staple in the fridge where I grew up. In the summer we could mix it with soda water and a squeeze of lemon and when we had the ingredients on hand or when my parents were throwing a potluck party."

Apte says she wanted to invent something slightly upscale that was on par with her favorite cocktail, the Martini, and a silky egg white sour based on gin and luxurious, aromatic spices seemed the way to go. She was very conscientious about the details, including the use of bitters to add pop to the other spices. As for the sandalwood, "I cross-referenced Ayurvedic and homeopathic medicinal books and made sure that the type of sandalwood I was using was OK to use, but just in small quantities." She says the bonus of having it rested on top of the egg white is that it's the last thing sipped as the glass empties, allowing for that aromatic experience. "By the time the liquids are gone below the egg white, the sandalwood is still nestled on top and not ingested," she notes.

- 1½ oz (45 ml) dry gin
- ½ oz (15 ml) lemon juice
- ½ oz (15 ml) lime juice
- ½ oz (15 ml) Saffron Sharbat
- 1 barspoon Angostura bitters
- 1 egg white (Apte suggests using aquafaba for a vegan option)

- Garnish: sandalwood powder (optional)

Dry shake all the ingredients in a cocktail shaker for about 15 seconds. Add ice and shake again until well chilled and frothy, another 15 to 20 seconds. Strain into a chilled coupe glass. To garnish, sprinkle powdered sandalwood over the top of the drink, if desired.

For the Saffron Sharbat

- ¼ tsp saffron threads
- 1 tbsp boiled water
- 2 cups (400 g) sugar
- 2 oz (60 ml) rosewater

Crush the saffron threads between your thumb and index finger, then add to the boiled water. Let the saffron steep for at least 15 minutes. Mix the sugar and 10 oz (300 ml) water in a small, heavy saucepan. Cook, stirring, over medium heat until the sugar has dissolved. Add the rosewater and the saffron mixture to the sugar syrup. Simmer over medium heat for 5 minutes. Remove from the heat and let cool. Transfer to a jar or plastic container and store, covered, in the refrigerator, for up to 3 months.

# THE SHARK

🕐 C.2008
⚐ NEW YORK CITY, USA
👤 JOHN DEBARY

⌂ PDT
🍶 RUM
🍸 ROCKS

The Shark cocktail was conjured up by John deBary in 2008 during the early years of New York City's PDT (Please Don't Tell), a bar (now not-so) secretly stashed behind a hot dog joint on St. Mark's Place in the East Village that's accessed through a phone booth. He began working there while contemplating law school at a time when the fuse was just being lit on the cocktail boom. As one of his first creations, The Shark had a lot of firsts going for it: it was one of the first modern tiki style cocktails served in a nontiki bar setting; one of the harbingers of the fat-washed spirit era; and one of the first cocktails from a "serious" contemporary cocktail bar to unapologetically, defiantly showcase blue curaçao, not to mention Frangelico.

In his 2020 book *Drink What You Want*, deBary says he set out to invent a tiki-style drink that had a wintry rather than tropical flavor profile. As he was consulting with bar manager Jim Meehan on final tweaks, he says his first instinct to use apricot liqueur as a modifier was shot down because "apricot isn't tiki." "How about blue curaçao?" deBary countered, fully joking, he says. Meehan called his bluff.

Another staff member tried the drink and suggested adding a touch of cream to give it body, which also tames the electric blue curaçao hue. The final recipe, which has since been deemed a PDT classic and as deBary says "might be the most notorious cocktail I ever created" finally came together with butter-infused rum, overproof rum, blue curaçao, Frangelico, lemon, pineapple, and bitters.

In the end, deBary decided to skip law school. Bartending was now his nighttime "day job."

Serves 4

- 6 oz (180 ml) Butter-Infused Rum
- 3 oz (90 ml) overproof Jamaican rum
- 2 oz (60 ml) blue curaçao liqueur
- 2 oz (60 ml) Frangelico hazelnut liqueur
- 1½ oz (45 ml) cane syrup
- 3 oz (90 ml) fresh lemon juice
- 1½ oz (45 ml) pineapple juice
- 1 oz (30 ml) heavy (double) cream
- ¾ oz (22 ml) pimento-style bitters

- Garnish: lemon wheels, cocktail umbrellas

Combine all ingredients in a blender with 2 scoops of ice. Blend on medium speed until fully combined and smooth. Pour into 4 prechilled rocks glasses and garnish each with a lemon wheel and umbrella.

For the Butter-Infused Rum

- 6 oz (180 ml) aged white rum
- 2 tablespoons (30g) unsalted butter, melted

Combine the rum and butter in an airtight container. Let sit, covered, at room temperature for a minimum of 8 hours or overnight. Transfer to the freezer and chill for at least 1 hour to let the butter solidify.

Strain the infused rum through a cheesecloth (muslin) or coffee filter into another airtight container, discarding the solids. It can be stored in the refrigerator for up to 1 month, and in the freezer for up to 6 months.

# SIAM SUNRAY

- 🕐 2008
- ⚐ BANGKOK, THAILAND
- ⚇ SURASAKDI PANTAISONG

- ⌂ N/A
- 🍸 VODKA
- 🍸 HIGHBALL

Siam Sunray was invented in 2008 by bartender Surasakdi Pantaisong, and in 2009 was named the official national drink of Thailand by the Tourism Authority of Thailand (TAT) and the Thai Hotels Association (THA). They said in a joint statement, "It is hoped that the drink will become recognized as the signature cocktail of Thailand, with visitors sipping on a Siam Sunray as they gaze out on the Chao Phraya River or watch the sun glisten off the Andaman." It is now served at hotels and resorts in key tourist destinations throughout the country.

This highball-style cocktail, which has been called "Thailand in a glass," contains vodka, coconut liqueur, lemongrass, ginger, Thai peppers, lime, and soda water. Aside from the vodka, these are many of the same ingredients and flavors found in one of the most popular Thai dishes, tom kha gai soup, and lend complex layers of spice, tang, and sweetness to many other classic preparations.

Coconut liqueur is an ingredient that may be hard to come by in some locales. In a 2009 *Washington Post* article, spirits columnist Jason Wilson recommends using a good-quality coconut rum if one can't be sourced. Also, don't be surprised by the Siam Sunray's peppery heat! Although only a sliver of Thai pepper is used in the drink itself, it goes a long way. Additionally, be warned that the soda water paradoxically works as a spice delivery system rather than an extinguisher — use only a splash and let the beauty of the other ingredients cast their delicious flavor rays.

- 1 thin strip red Thai chili pepper, seeded
- 3 thin slices peeled fresh ginger
- 1 lime leaf
- 3 slivers lemongrass (white parts only)
- 1 oz (30 ml) vodka
- 1 oz (30ml) coconut liqueur
- ½ oz (15 ml) simple syrup
- 3 drops lime juice (squeezed from a wedge)
- Soda water, to top

- Garnish: 1 whole red Thai chili pepper, small strip of lemongrass, slice of lime

Muddle the chili pepper strip, ginger, lime leaf, and lemongrass together in a shaker. Add the remaining ingredients except the soda water, and shake with ice until well chilled. Strain into a highball glass over fresh ice. Top with soda water and arrange the garnishes in the glass.

# BARBACOA

⏲ **2009**
⚑ **LOS ANGELES, USA**
👤 **JULIAN COX**

⌂ **RIVERA**
🍶 **MEZCAL**
🍸 **ROCKS**

In the early 2000s, a significant change to the cocktail scene came, oddly enough, in the form of restaurants, which not only focused on elevating diverse global cuisines but offered drink programs to match. One of the most prominent examples is Rivera, which opened in Los Angeles in 2009. Named for its head chef John Rivera Sedlar, who was previously behind the kitchens at St. Estephe, Bikini, and Abiquiu, the venue was known for its well-focused Latin-themed dishes with authentic origins, its ceviche bar, and colorful presentations.

Bar manager Julian Cox was tasked with developing a cocktail menu that reflected the restaurants's modern take on crowd-pleasing favorites. With such a bountiful kitchen pantry at his disposal, he decided to use it as inspiration, and focused on lesser-known Latin spirits. Certain cocktails, such as Blood Sugar Sex Magic, inspired by the smash album by local band Red Hot Chili Peppers and made with rye, red bell pepper, and fresh basil, were an instant hit. But the house drink that resonated the most was Barbacoa, made with mezcal, chipotle pepper, bell pepper, and ginger, and garnished with beef jerky, a nod to its name, which refers to spiced meat.

In a June 2010 article for *Imbibe*, "A Star is Re-born: Los Angeles Bars and Cocktails," Cox tells writer Paul Clarke: "There's such a following at Rivera that people come and say, 'Oh, they have food here?' Which makes me laugh, because it's a restaurant that's got a cocktail following."

Soon, other LA restaurants, Latin-focused or not, were serving Barbacoas, and bars had to start carrying bell peppers, chilis, and beef jerky to appease the masses. Certain venues even came up with their own riffs using different types of produce, including Avocado Barbacoas.

Sadly, the restaurant was gone by 2015, but the Barbacoa has lived on as one of LA's most-ordered modern classics.

- 3 slices red bell pepper
- 3 lime wedges
- ½ teaspoon chipotle purée
- ½ oz (15 ml) lemon juice
- ½ oz (15 ml) ginger syrup (page 204)
- ¾ oz (22 ml) agave nectar
- 2 oz (60 ml) mezcal

- Garnish: piece of beef jerky

Muddle the bell pepper slices, lime wedges, chipotle purée, and lemon juice in the bottom of a cocktail shaker. Add ice and the remaining ingredients and shake until well chilled. Add everything to a rocks glass and garnish with a piece of beef jerky.

# BUCK BUCK MULE

🕒 2009

⚐ VANCOUVER, CANADA

🁢 JOSH PAPE

⌂ THE DIAMOND

🍸 GIN

🍸 HIGHBALL

Let's begin by settling a debate. Buck vs. Mule? Some maintain that the buck is the one with the base spirit plus ginger ale instead of its spicier cousin, ginger beer. Incorrect. OK, so either a buck or a mule can be made with ginger beer *or* ginger ale? Some say it depends on the vessel; the mule is meant to be served in a copper mug, à la the Moscow Mule (an offshoot of the popular late nineteenth-century Mamie Taylor ginger and Scotch highball), while the buck (think Dark 'n Stormy or Horse's Neck) is always served long, in a highball glass. Buck? Mule? Rather than call the whole thing off, or at least picking a side, in 2009, Josh Pape created the Buck Buck Mule for the opening menu at The Diamond in Vancouver. It's remained on the list ever since.

The name of the cocktail did indeed derive from the great mule vs. buck debate and wordplay. "Originally we couldn't decide if we wanted to use ginger ale or ginger beer," Pape told *Spirited* author Adrienne Stillman in 2019. "In saying it repeatedly 'buck or mule, buck or mule' it's just kind of happened" (by the way, they went with ginger beer in a highball glass). What distinguishes this drink is the addition of Fino sherry to dry out the other flavors, and cucumber juice for an additional layer of aromatics.

Pape suggests that if cucumber juice is not readily available, it's OK to muddle a few cucumber slices in the shaker before adding the other ingredients. Just be sure to double strain to avoid pieces of floating cucumber in the final presentation.

- 1 oz (30 ml) dry gin
- 1 oz (30 ml) Fino sherry
- ¾ oz (20 ml) cucumber juice (or 4 to 5 slices, muddled)
- ⅓ oz (10 ml) lime juice
- ⅓ oz (10 ml) simple syrup
- 4 oz (120 ml) ginger beer, to top

- Garnish: cucumber peel

Combine all the ingredients except the ginger beer in a shaker with ice and shake vigorously for 10–15 seconds. Strain (if using muddled cucumber, double strain) into a highball glass over fresh ice. Top with ginger beer and garnish with a twist of cucumber peel.

# CHINATOWN SOUR

⊕ 2009
⊳ VANCOUVER, CANADA
A KEENAN HOOD

⌂ KEEFER BAR
◊ BOURBON
Y COUPE

The Keefer Bar, which opened in Vancouver, Canada's Chinatown in 2009, specializes in modern cocktails with a Chinese herbal apothecary twist (the menu features a helpful glossary of ingredients, such as yun zhi, hydrosol, and nin jiom). The wide range of drinks, which explore the full flavor spectrum from dry to sweet, are meant to be enjoyed alongside a mini tour of Asian-influenced dishes, such as Sichuan chicken bao, various dumplings, and Japanese cream puffs. An array of syrups, bitters, and various infusions are made in-house using herbs, roots, teas, and fruits traditionally found in Chinese medicine. One of the bar's signature cocktails since the Keefer first rose among the neighborhood's night market scene is the Chinatown Sour, created by Keenan Hood.

This cocktail's DNA is rooted in the traditional whiskey sour, yet takes a cue from the Mai Tai, sweetened with orgeat (almond syrup)—although in this instance it's enhanced with astragalus root. At the time the cocktail was created, the bracingly bitter herbal liqueur Fernet-Branca was a few years into its emergence from Argentina's ever-popular Fernet and Coke culture, and a generous measure of it is used in the Chinatown Sour.

The bar is now recognized on various "top" lists, with cocktails such as this one boosting its reputation. Though the ingredients may sound as if they would steer the flavor profile too far into the bitter herbal/medicinal spectrum, the proportions pull the drink together beautifully.

It's worth making the astragalus orgeat syrup from scratch. The root, typically sold in dried strips, can be purchased at Asian groceries and online.

---

- 1 oz (30 ml) overproof bourbon (the bar uses Wild Turkey 101)
- 1 oz (30 ml) fresh lemon juice
- ¾ oz (22 ml) Fernet-Branca
- ¾ oz (22 ml) Astragalus Orgeat Syrup

Shake all ingredients with ice until well chilled. Strain into a chilled coupe glass.

For the Astragalus Orgeat Syrup

- 4 oz (120 ml) water
- 2 x 5-inch (10 cm) astragalus strips
- ½ cup (100 g) granulated sugar
- 6 oz (180 ml) prepared orgeat

In a small saucepan, boil the water, then remove from the heat. Add the astragalus strips and steep for about 10 minutes. Fine strain into a resealable container, add the sugar, and stir to dissolve. Add the orgeat and let cool before using.

# KODAK MOMENT

🕐 C.2009
⚐ NEW ORLEANS, USA
👤 LIZ KELLEY

⌂ CURE
🍶 WHISKEY
🍸 DOUBLE ROCKS

From such a simple template of whiskey, lemon juice, and sugar, whiskey sours—consumed in the United States since the nineteenth century—can take on many forms. As the name would suggest, sour is one of them. But sometimes they veer toward the sweet side (especially those prepared with commercial sour mix). Some sport a head of creamy froth when prepared with egg white, while those made without can go down more like a boozy lemonade made with whiskey. At Cure cocktail bar in New Orleans, the Kodak Moment, the house whiskey sour from bartender Liz Kelley, stretches the texture and flavor profile of the classic to unexpected levels.

Kodak Moment has been a consistent bestseller at the bar, which in 2009 was one of the first high-profile venues in the city to open in the modern cocktail era. In the 2022 book *Cure: New Orleans Drinks and How to Mix 'Em*, the bar's co-owner, Neal Bodenheimer, says most whiskey sours can "be a little bit hardy, but here [it] is refreshing and summery." Perfect for the Crescent City, where it's warm and humid most months of the year.

Along with the traditional ingredients for the typical American whiskey sour—rye whiskey, lemon juice, sugar syrup, and egg white— Kelley adds an earthy, savory layer of flavor with aquavit, and further brightens the palate with Pasubio anaro, a wine-based liqueur made with blueberries. Of course, the Kodak Moment lives up to its name: the drink is a stunning sunset orange with a pillowy egg white froth on top. It happens to be highly Instagrammable.

- ½ oz (15 ml) fresh lemon juice
- 1½ tsp egg white
  (quarter of whole egg white)
- 1 oz (30 ml) rye whiskey
- ¾ oz (22 ml) Cappelletti Pasubio amaro
- ½ oz (15 ml) aquavit (the bar uses Svol)
- ¼ oz (7 ml) rich Demerara syrup

- Garnish: lemon peel (expressed and discarded)

Dry shake (without ice) the lemon juice and egg white in a shaker tin for 30 seconds. Add the remaining ingredients and shake with ice until well chilled and frothy. Double-strain into a double rocks glass over a large cube. Squeeze the lemon peel over the drink, skin-side down to express the oils, then discard.

# TIGER MOM GIMLET

🕐  2010s
⚑  LOS ANGELES, USA
⚕  CARI HAH

⌂  BIG BAR
◊  GIN
Y  COUPE

.............................................................................................................................

The Tiger Mom Gimlet is one of the standout cocktails of the contemporary Los Angeles bar scene. "Tiger mom" is slang used in Asian culture to describe a pushy parent, one who demands stratospherically high levels of achievement from their child or children. The drink's creator is Cari Hah, the self-described "Tiger Mom of LA," a former investment banker who is known for her strict hospitality ethics. Tough as she is, she is also known for being a nurturing champion of the local bar community.

Hah's signature cocktail was created in the late 2010s at Big Bar, an expansive outdoor garden bar and restaurant which grew out of the widely popular Alcove café in the Loz Feliz district. Hah—who previously worked behind the bar at the iconic venues Cole's, Clifton's, the Varnish, and Three Clubs—took over the bar in 2015. Her mission was to create a menu

of complex yet playful drinks that feel at home in a snazzy So-Cal patio setting.

The Tiger Mom Gimlet is built from the classic gimlet recipe consisting of gin and lime cordial, a drink which for many decades was relegated to bartenders reaching for the bottled, synthetic variety in lieu of homemade cordial. For her fresh herb garden-inspired take, Hah shakes up fresh lime juice, lemongrass syrup, quinaquina, and bergamot bitters to boost the aromatics of its gin base.

The drink is deeply emblematic of Hah's cocktail-making ideology. "The cocktail philosophy for me is centered around the ethos to respect the spirits that are in the drinks," said Hah in a 2018 interview for *VoyageLA*. "I do not create cocktails to 'cover up the taste' of alcohol. Our drinks [for Big Bar] showcase and respect the beauty of the spirit."

.............................................................................................................................

• 2 oz (60 ml) Bombay Sapphire gin
• ¾ oz (22 ml) fresh lime juice
• ¾ oz (22 ml) Lemongrass Syrup
  (store-bought or homemade)
• ¼ oz (7 ml) quinaquina (aromatized wine,
  such as Cocchi Americano)
• 2 dashes bergamot bitters

• Garnish: lime leaf

Shake all ingredients with ice until well chilled. Strain into a chilled coupe glass. Garnish.

For the Lemongrass Syrup

• 1 cup (200 g) white sugar
• 8 oz (240 ml) water
• Grated zest and juice of 1 lime
• 1 lemongrass stalk, white part only, halved
• 2 coin-sized slices peeled fresh ginger
• 1 lime leaf, roughly torn

Add all ingredients to a saucepan and heat over low-medium heat. Stir until all the sugar has dissolved, about 5 minutes. Remove from the heat and let stand for a few hours at room temperature to infuse the flavors. Strain into a sealable container or bottle. Store in the refrigerator for up to 10 days.

.............................................................................................................................

# YIPPEE KI YAY MOTHER F****R!

---

⊕ 2010s
⊳ NEW YORK CITY, USA
⅄ NICO DE SOTO

⌂ MIRACLE ON 9TH
◊ RUM
Ⴘ SANTA PANTS MUG

---

'Twas the month before Christmas, and all through the world, cocktails were shaken (though some only swirled). In 2014, Greg Boehm and his team at Cocktail Kingdom transformed Mace bar on East 9th Street in New York City into Miracle, a winter holiday-themed cocktail bar. Every night a line formed for holiday cheersing with Christmapolitans, Snowball Old Fashioneds, On Dashers, and Dreidel! Dreidel! Dreidel!s, served among the kitschy décor that included a mechanical hip-shaking St. Nick. It was such a hit that it returned the following year, along with Sippin' Santa, a tiki surf-themed pop-up at nearby Boilermaker. Over the next few years, Miracle and Sippin' Santa bars popped up in other spots in the city, then across the US, eventually going global in Canada, the UK, Mexico, Netherlands, and Panama.

One of the bestselling cocktails from the series is Yippee Ki Yay Mother F****r!, an impressively campy, yet seriously constructed tropical rum and cachaça punch made with purple yam/coconut orgeat and pineapple acid served with a festive sprinkle of powdered (icing) sugar over pebble ice in a Santa Pants mug (now sold commercially through Cocktail Kingdom). It was originally created by Mace bar co-owner Nico de Soto.

The name is inspired by the famous Bruce Willis battle cry from the 1988 movie *Die Hard* (edited for network TV as "Yippee Ki Yay, Melon Farmer!"). Of course, the cocktail is on the menu based on the very true premise shared by millions that although *Die Hard* is an action movie, it is also very much a Christmas movie.

---

- ¾ oz (22 ml) rum (the bar uses Plantation Rum Barbados)
- ¾ oz (22 ml) suro cachaça (the bar uses Yaguara)
- ½ oz (15 ml) overproof rum (the bar uses Plantation Overproof)
- 1 oz (30 ml) Purple Yam/Coconut Orgeat
- 1 oz (30 ml) Pineapple Acid

- Garnish: mint sprig and powdered (icing) sugar

Dry shake (without ice) all ingredients in a cocktail shaker. Strain into a Santa Pants mug (or other vessel) and fill with crushed/pebble ice. Garnish with a mint sprig and sprinkle with powdered (icing) sugar for a snow effect.

### For the Purple Yam/Coconut Orgeat

Note: scale down as needed

- 35 oz (1 liter) unsweetened coconut milk

- 1 tsp kosher salt
- 5 cups (1 kg) caster sugar
- ⅓ oz (10 g) almond extract
- ½ oz (15 g) purple yam (ube) extract
- ⅓ oz (10 g) coconut extract
- 20 drops orange flower water

In a saucepan, combine the coconut milk, salt, and sugar. Cook over medium heat, stirring, until the sugar has dissolved. Remove from the heat and stir in the extracts and orange flower water. Let cool, bottle, and store in the refrigerator for up to 10 days.

### For the Pineapple Acid

- 8¼ oz (250 ml) fresh pineapple juice
- ⅓ oz (10 g) citric acid

Measure out the fresh pineapple juice and add the citric acid. Bottle and store as above.

---

# DEATH FLIP

🕐 2010
⚑ MELBOURNE, AUSTRALIA
👤 CHRIS HYSTED-ADAMS

⌂ BLACK PEARL
🍾 TEQUILA
🍸 COUPE

Certain young mixologists from the modern era tend to gravitate toward specific spirits that outsiders might deem just a tad too weird and esoteric for their tastes. In 2010, while working at Black Pearl in Melbourne, Australia, bartender Chris Hysted-Adams was very into blanco tequila, Jägermeister, and Chartreuse, and obsessed with finding ways to combine them in drinks. One problem: when his customers requested the bartender's choice, after prompting them for taste preferences, if he told them any of those ingredients were in the drink he planned to prepare, he was often told to make something else.

According to Hysted-Adams, his frustration inspired him to think, "Bugger it, I'm gonna put blanco tequila, Jägermeister, and Chartreuse into a cocktail, but I'm not gonna list the ingredients." Problem is, confident as he was about the combination, he struggled with flavor

balance when presenting all three in a stirred format. Not ready to admit defeat, something inspired him to look toward the flip genre of cocktails, ones that use an entire egg to bind the ingredients and add creamy richness (don't worry, emulsifying the egg with the booze essentially "cooks out" any bacteria issues), and it worked.

He christened his drink "Death Flip" after an old-school daredevil skateboarding feat, but would never list the ingredients on his menu. "You don't want me to make this drink in a dark alley, ingredients unnamed," read the description. As an added schtick, he charged an as-yet-unheard-of AUS $19 for customers to accept the challenge. It somehow became a Melbourne drink sensation, despite Hysted-Adams not ever writing down what was in it.

At least for a few years.

• 1 oz (30 ml) blanco tequila
• ½ oz (15 ml) Jägermeister
• ½ oz (15 ml) Yellow Chartreuse
• ¼ oz (7 ml) rich syrup
• 1 whole egg

• Garnish: freshly grated nutmeg

Shake all ingredients with ice in a cocktail shaker until well chilled and frothy. Strain the ice out, then dry shake without ice for at least another 10 seconds to give it a creamier texture. Fine strain into a chilled coupe glass. Grate nutmeg over the top.

# BONE DRY MARTINI

⊕ 2011
⚐ LONDON, UK
⚇ RYAN CHETIYAWARDANA/
   TEAM WHITE LYAN

⌂ WHITE LYAN
◌ VODKA
🍸 NICK & NORA

London bar impresario Ryan Chetiyawardana, aka "Mr. Lyan," has been called the "mad scientist" of the cocktail world, pushing the limits of flavor combinations, ingredients, and techniques while playfully deconstructing the core foundations of classic cocktails. Before the Nitrate Manhattan at Dandelyan in 2017 and the Cereal Martini at Lyaness in 2019, one of the buzziest cocktails (in both the intoxicating and talked about senses of the word) in all of London was the Bone Dry Martini, invented in 2011 and featured prominently at White Lyan, which opened in 2013 in Hoxton.

The venue, which closed in 2017, was known for having no visible back bar. Instead, all the cocktails were served from pre-batched bottles and made from mostly in-house ingredients, right down to some of the spirits. The Bone Dry Martini, the final iteration of which was a team creation, was its star. It's made from a vodka that was distilled in-house, its acidic texture due to a tincture made from chicken bone that's broken down by phosphoric acid. "*Bone* dry," get it? Seems a lot of work for wordplay, but it was a hit.

The drink was created to demonstrate that a dry vodka Martini could have some oomph. Chetiyawardana says, "The drink celebrated the texture of our vodka, and how a great vodka Martini should have character, with a flinty minerality from the bone that dried it all out."

---

• 17 oz (500 ml) Lyan vodka (use a good rye or wheat-based vodka as substitute)
• 5 oz (150 g) Lyan water (distilled water)
• 2 dashes Bone Tincture

• Garnish: lemon distillate or lemon twist

Combine the vodka and water in a freezer-proof bottle big enough to hold the liquid. Freeze (the alcohol becomes cold and viscous, but not solid). Serve in a Nick & Nora glass with 2 dashes of bone tincture, then spray lemon distillate (or simply express the oils from a lemon peel) over the top.

For the Bone Tincture

• 1 chicken leg bone, cleaned after roasting whole
• 3½ oz (100 ml) food-grade phosphoric acid
• 1 g calcium salt
• 1 g Maldon sea salt
• 1 g food-grade magnesium salt

Roast an organic chicken thigh or leg bone until the meat falls off the bone and discard all the flesh and sinew. Pound the cleaned bone down as much as possible, then dissolve in food-grade phosphoric acid in a glass or nonreactive container. Add the salts once dissolved and place in an airtight container at room temperature for storage. Use within seven days.

# CHILIGUARO

🕐 2011
⚑ SAN JOSÉ, COSTA RICA
👤 MAURICIO AZOFEIFA
AND LUIS PABLO

⌂ BAR BAHAMAS
🍶 CACIQUE GUARO
🍸 SHOT

On the night of December 26, 2011 at Bar Bahamas in San José, Costa Rica, a customer ordered a Cacique Guaro with Tabasco, a classic way to serve the local firewater made from sugarcane as a spicy shot. Soon everyone at the bar wanted one. Realizing that an elaboration of the piquant combo could really take off, bar owners Mauricio Azofeifa and Luis Pablo enhanced the drink with tomato, lemon, salt, and pepper, adding the locally produced Lizano hot sauce for extra heat. They christened it Chiliguaro.

The fiery, boozy beverage soon ignited a national phenomenon. Chiliguaro became a signature not only at Bar Bahamas, but is now considered Costa Rica's national cocktail. Bars and restaurants all over the country serve them, or their own variations, often adjusting the heat and playing around with various juices and other spices.

Only two years after its conception, in June 2013, Azofeifa registered the name Chiliguaro and the bar's recipe, making it one of only a handful of cocktails—including the Dark 'n Stormy—with an official brand trademark. In 2015, The National Liquor Factory (FANAL) began producing their own bottled version, using similar ingredients, to be sold in grocery stores. However, the difference from the patented recipe was far too subtle to be considered much of one, and they notoriously lost a trademark dispute with Azofeifa a couple of years later.

It was reported in January 2020 that Bar Bahamas, now considered a tourist destination and with Pablo still at the helm, has been known to serve up to 3,000 Chiliguaros a night.

The recipe is one that is widely open to interpretation; this is one such interpretation, depending on heat level preference. It is typically prepared in larger format batches as opposed to a single shot.

Makes 6 to 7 shots

- 6½ oz (190 ml) Cacique Guaro
- 24½ oz (735 ml) tomato juice
- 4 oz (120 ml) fresh lemon juice
- 3 tbsp Tabasco
- 2 tbsp Lizano
- Pinch of salt
- Grated black pepper

- Garnish: spice mix, such as Tajín, for the rim (optional), lemon or lime wedge

Purée the ingredients in a blender until well combined and frothy. Refrigerate for at least 15 minutes. To serve, shake with ice and strain into shot glasses rimmed with spice mixture, if desired. Serve with a lemon or lime wedge.

# DRUNK UNCLE

🕐 2011
🏳 VICTORIA, CANADA
🧑 SHAWN SOOLE

🏠 CLIVE'S CLASSIC LOUNGE
🥃 WHISKY
🍸 COUPE

Canadian bartender Shawn Soole refers to the early 2000s as an "innocent time of discovery" when it comes to the introduction of certain cocktail modifiers that would become back bar essentials. He's referring to then "niche" liqueurs such as crème de violette, elderflower liqueur, and particularly amari and other bitters, such as Cynar, an Italian aperitif flavored with artichoke among its thirteen herbs and botanicals, that was then still uncommon in North America.

Introductions to these ingredients, of course, prompted cocktail experimentation, with mixed results. However, some of the stalwart signatures of the twenty-first century were born from this enterprising era, and Drunk Uncle is one of the greats from British Columbia, invented by Soole in 2011 at Clive's Classic Lounge in Victoria.

"This cocktail came out of my infatuation with the Negroni and that family of drinks, the Old Pal, Boulevardier, and so forth, as a younger bartender," says Soole. "Cynar had just hit the market in British Columbia and I was playing with it, so obviously, I applied it to my favorite family of cocktails."

Instead of going for the typical rye or bourbon whiskey base in the Old Pal style, which is made with white instead of red vermouth, Soole coaxes out the more roasty, chocolatey notes of Cynar by using smoky Scotch from Islay as the hero ingredient. A grapefruit twist instead of orange or lemon adds further aromatic structure.

Some of the most lasting signatures in history also happen to be the most uncomplicated, both in preparation and flavor profile. "I circle back to this drink [it's still on the menu at Clive's as of this writing] because it's a simple one to replicate but also reminds me that only ten years ago in Canada that the spirits that we take for granted now were especially amazing to get then."

- 1½ oz (45ml) Islay whisky (or other smoky style of Scotch)
- ¾ oz (22ml) Cynar
- ¾ oz (22ml) vermouth blanco

- Garnish: grapefruit twist

Stir all ingredients with ice until well chilled. Strain into a chilled coupe glass. Express the oils from a piece of grapefruit peel into the drink, skin side down, then twist and place in the glass.

# HOCUS POCUS

🕐 2011         ⌂ STARCHEFS PANEL
⚑ USA         ⏲ TEQUILA
𝔸 CHRISTY POPE         Y NICK & NORA

The Hanky Panky cocktail (page 78) was invented in 1925 by Ada Coleman, then head of the American Bar at the Savoy Hotel. The recipe, a combination of gin, sweet vermouth, and a touch of Fernet-Branca, sounds rather caustic. However, mix them together in the right measurements and it's truly magical.

Thus, it makes perfect sense that in 2011, bar consultant Christy Pope (then bartending at Milk & Honey in New York City) would name her update on the classic, Hocus Pocus. The drink was originally created for the StarChefs convention, for a presentation centered on female creativity in the mixology space. Her co-panellists were Audrey Saunders (then owner of Pegu Club in New York City) and Naomi Schimek (Spare Room and Harvard & Stone, Los Angeles).

For Hocus Pocus, Pope swapped the gin for tequila with a sprinkle of sherry. For added flavor alchemy, she replaced the more bracing Fernet-Branca with the richness of Bigallet China China Amer and other warm and spicy ingredients to form a sort of liquid Mexican mole mixture.

The flavors of Hocus Pocus melded so well together for the original presentation that Pope and her husband/business partner Chad Solomon decided to make it an opening menu signature of their Midnight Rambler bar in Dallas, Texas in 2014.

The recipe below is what was served at the bar—no spells are necessary to mix it yourself.

---

- ½ tsp (2.5 ml) Bigallet China China Amer
- ¾ tsp (3.7 ml) Tempus Fugit Cacao (or other chocolate liqueur)
- ½ tsp (2.5 ml) Ancho Reyes (spiced liqueur)
- ¼ tsp (1.2 ml) Combier Kummel (or other orange liqueur)
- 1¼ oz (38 ml) Ancho Chili-Infused Sherry
- 1½ oz (45 ml) tequila blanco
- 2 drops mineral saline (1 part Diamond Crystal Kosher salt: 9 parts mineral water)

- Garnish: whole star anise

Measure all ingredients into a frozen mixing glass, then add ice. Stir until properly chilled and diluted, then strain into a frozen Nick & Nora glass. Garnish with a whole star anise floating in the drink.

## For the Ancho Chili-Infused Sherry

In a nonreactive container, combine one 25 oz (750 ml) bottle of Lustau East India sherry and 1½ oz (45 g) stemmed, seeded, and coarsely chopped ancho chili peppers. Cover and let infuse at room temperature for 24 hours. Fine-strain and keep refrigerated.

# I AM VIRGINIA

🕐 2011
🏠 PX
⚑ ALEXANDRIA (VIRGINIA), USA
🜄 WHISKEY
👤 TODD THRASHER
🍸 ROCKS

The I Am Virginia cocktail exemplifies the state of Virginia and its local products, and has the distinction of being a signature for both a bar and a distillery tasting room. It was created as a collaboration between Todd Thrasher, head bartender of Alexandria's PX—which, in 2006, was one of the first craft cocktail bars in the Washington, D.C. area—and Scott Harris, general manager of Catoctin Creek Distilling Company in nearby Purcellville.

In 2011, the two local tastemakers visited New York City to take part in an event sponsored by the state of Virginia's agricultural organization (the people responsible for the iconic "Virginia is for Lovers" campaign) to showcase Virginia produce, meat, and beverage products at Chelsea Market. Concocted specifically for the event, Thrasher served I Am Virginia, a stirred, boozy number featuring a syrup

made from figs, which are native to the state, and Catoctin Creek's Roundstone Rye. "The flavors perfectly complemented each other in this Old Fashioned variant and press and guests from all over New York got their first exposure to Catoctin Creek through this wonderful drink," says Harris. It was such a hit that, once back home, I Am Virginia became one of the house drinks for both the Catoctin Creek tasting room and the PX bar.

As of this writing, Harris continues to operate Catoctin Creek with his wife Becky as master distiller. Although there is still Roundstone Rye and plenty of figs available to continue serving I Am Virginia in the distillery's tasting room and at local events, PX closed in 2019, when Thrasher founded Potomac Distilling Company at The Wharf in Washington, D.C.

- 2 oz (60 ml) Catoctin Creek Roundstone Rye 92 proof
- ½ oz (15 ml) Fig Syrup
- 1 to 2 dashes Angostura bitters

- Garnish: orange twist

Stir all ingredients together with ice until well chilled. Strain into a rocks glass with a large cube. Express the oils from a piece of orange peel into the drink, skin side down, then twist and place in the glass.

For the Fig Syrup

Chop a dozen or so figs and combine in a saucepan on low heat with 1 cup (200 g) sugar and 8 oz (240 ml) water. Simmer for about 30 minutes, watching the water and adding more if it gets low. Remove from the heat and strain through a sieve, pushing the figs with a wooden spoon to extract the juice. Store the syrup in the refrigerator for up to one month.

# KAME

🕐 2011
⚑ ANTIGUA, GUATEMALA
𝄞 MARIO ALARCÓN

⌂ ULEW COCKTAIL BAR
🍶 QUETZALTECA
🍸 ROCKS

Kame, created by bartender Mario Alarcón, put Antigua, Guatemala on the modern cocktail map. It was popularized at Ulew Cocktail Bar, an underground space accessed (à la New York City's PDT) through a phone booth in Antigua Brewing Company, and operates in the Milk & Honey tradition of eschewing formal cocktail menus. Instead, every bartender is fluent in classic cocktail recipes, but the bar is more famous for its own original recipes made with local fresh produce and other staple ingredients and flavors from Guatemalan culture ("Ulew" translates to "Earth" in Mayan Quiché). Kame was first conceived by Alarcón in 2011 but became one of the signature cocktails when the bar opened in 2018 and is considered a modern Guatemalan classic.

The drink is prepared with Quetzalteca (a type of regional sugarcane aguardiente), ground pepitas (pumpkin seeds), salt, and citrus juices—ingredients that are iconic to Guatemalan culture. "Older generations used to add this mixture to fruits, like the mango vendors set up in the corner of the park," says Alarcón. "Kame is culture, tradition, and heritage for our peoples. Kame is Guatemala in a glass!"

Kame's flavor profile has the classic sweet and sour notes of a shaken citrus cocktail, but the pepitas add an earthy layer, and the salt punches things up. Reflecting the zero alcohol cocktail trend starting in the late 2010s, Ulew also serves Kame as a mocktail option. "The flavor is not dependent on the alcohol," notes Alarcón.

Note: if Quetzalteca is not available, Alarcón suggests Kame can be prepared with white rum instead.

• 1½ oz (45 ml) Quetzalteca aguardiente or white rum
• 1 oz (30 ml) simple syrup
• 1 oz (30 ml) fresh lime juice
• 1 oz (30 ml) fresh orange juice
• Pinch of salt
• 1 tbsp pepitoria (ground, roasted pepitas/ pumpkin seeds)

• Garnish: orange twist

Add all ingredients to a cocktail shaker with ice and shake until well chilled and frothy, about 20 seconds. (If preparing without alcohol, omit the aguardiente/rum.) Strain into a rocks glass over fresh ice. Express the oils from a piece of orange peel into the drink, skin side down, then twist and place in the glass.

# MARGARITA AL PASTOR

🕑 2011
▷ MEXICO CITY, MEXICO
Å BENJAMIN PADRÓN NOVOA

⌂ LICORERÍA LIMANTOUR
◍ TEQUILA
Y ROCKS

Al pastor is a style of taco filled with slices of grilled pork shoulder that is spiced, prepared, and cooked on a vertical spit in much the same way as lamb for shawarma, introduced to Puebla, Mexico by Lebanese migrants. It's served in numerous variations throughout the country and beyond. The best examples have just the right amount of spicy, salty, and sour flavors set off with a garnish of tangy, sweet chunks of pineapple and aromatic cilantro (coriander). When it opened in 2011, Licorería Limantour led the way in Mexico City's unique and artistic cocktail scene by serving wondrous creations, such as founder Benjamin Padrón Novoa's take on the flavors of that famous taco style in cocktail form, Margarita Al Pastor.

Although it sounds carnivorous, vegetarians can fully make peace with this recipe, which features traditional Margarita ingredients—tequila, green lemon juice, and orange liqueur—shaken with a special "taco mix" that combines the flavors of just the garnish and salsa—pineapple juice, cilantro (coriander), basil, and mint—along with Serrano agave honey. The glass is rimmed with cilantro salt to add yet another salty-herbal dimension.

Margarita Al Pastor is recognized as a modern classic, and as much of an essential Margarita variation as the Tommy's and Spicy Margarita recipes from Julio Bermejo at Tommy's Mexican Restaurant in San Francisco, California (page 200). Not only is Licorería Limantour an obligatory Mexico City destination, consistently near the top of "best" lists for cocktail enthusiasts and the bar trade, Padrón Novoa has featured Margarita Al Pastor in numerous pop-ups around the world, alongside his other breakout recipes, such as the Mezcal Stalk (a similar twist using mezcal, served in a glass rimmed with worm salt).

---

- 2 oz (60 ml) tequila blanco
- ½ oz (15 ml) Cointreau or other orange liqueur
- ¾ oz (22 ml) fresh green lemon juice (can use a split of lime and lemon if none can be found)
- 1½ oz (45 ml) Taco Mix

- Garnish: cilantro (coriander) salt for the rim, pineapple wedge

Rim a double rocks glass with the cilantro (coriander) salt. Shake all ingredients with ice until well chilled and frothy. Strain into the prepared glass and garnish with the pineapple wedge.

For the Taco Mix

- 17 oz (500 ml) pineapple juice
- 7 oz (200 ml) water
- 1 oz (30 g) fresh cilantro (coriander)
- ¾ oz (20 g) each fresh spearmint and basil
- 5 oz (150 ml) Serrano Agave Honey

Mix all ingredients in a food processor and strain into a sealable container. It will keep in the refrigerator for up to a week.

For the Serrano Agave Honey

Slice 2 oz (60 g) Serrano chili peppers into strips and boil in 7 oz (200 ml) water for 25 minutes. Let cool for 20 minutes, then strain the water. Mix in 1 lb 7 oz (660 g) agave honey (or if none can be found use agave nectar).

# SHARPIE MUSTACHE

🕘 2011
⚐ NEW YORK CITY, USA
𝐀 CHRIS ELFORD

⌂ AMOR Y AMARGO
◑ GIN; RYE; AMARO
𝖄 FLASK OR NICK & NORA

This spicy gin concoction gets its name from the college prank of drawing a mustache with permanent marker on someone while they are sleeping. It was created in 2011 by bartender Chris Elford at Amor y Amargo, during its first year open in New York City. The East Village bar was the first in the Big Apple to specialize in all things bitter and stirred—nothing shaken, nothing made with juice; the only fresh citrus is used as garnish. Spanish for "love and bitter," the bar was originally opened as a temporary pop-up by Janet and Avery Glasser of Bittermens, and Ravi DeRossi of Death & Co, to introduce New Yorkers to the bitter side of cocktails. But it was so popular, a lease was signed to allow the pop-up to remain in the same location, now under the direction of Sother Teague. The Sharpie Mustache remains a fan favorite.

The drink is composed of the medium bitter Meletti amaro, earthy and aromatic gentian liqueur, dry gin, bonded rye, and spicy bitters. Not only can both gin and whiskey aficionados make peace with this cocktail, but it's also the easiest one to order at the bar because it's pre-batched in single-serve flasks—adorned, of course, with a mustache sticker—and kept in a tub of ice at the end of the bar. It's poured to order or can be taken to go. (It was obviously a big hit during lockdown.)

The Sharpie Mustache, which Elford has said is "dangerously drinkable," has since accompanied Elford to the West Coast, where he is now co-owner of Navy Strength, Here Today, and Trade Winds in Seattle, Washington.

- ½ oz (15 ml) Meletti amaro
- ½ oz (15 ml) Bonal gentian liqueur
- ½ oz (15 ml) London dry gin
- ½ oz (15 ml) bonded rye whiskey
- 2 dashes Bittermans Tiki bitters (or other spicy, aromatic bitters)

- Garnish: orange twist

Stir all ingredients with ice to chill and dilute. Strain into a 3½ oz (100 ml) flask (preferably one with a mustache sticker on it) to store. Keep chilled until ready to use.

Alternatively, if consuming immediately, strain into a Nick & Nora glass. Express the oils from a piece of orange peel into the drink, skin side down, then twist and place in the glass.

# AMARETTO SOUR (MORGENTHALER VARIATION)

🕐 2012
🏳 PORTLAND (OREGON), USA
👤 JEFFREY MORGENTHALER

🏠 CLYDE COMMON
🥃 AMARETTO; BOURBON
🍸 DOUBLE ROCKS

......................................................................................................

In 2012, a blog post entitled "I Make the Best Amaretto Sour in The World" was written by bartender Jeffrey Morgenthaler, who was then behind the bar at Clyde Common in Portland, Oregon. It seemed quite the vainglorious statement—was it even worth bragging about in the first place?

It turns out it was.

At the time, cocktails, particularly in the sweet liqueur and sour category—amaretto and Midori especially—were regarded by the connoisseurs as pedestrian holdovers from the late twentieth-century synthetic citrus mix era.

However, Morgenthaler set out to prove that amaretto, and ingredients like it, didn't deserve the snobbish acrimony. The recipes were flawed, but it wasn't the liqueur's fault.

He shared his theory that in traditional Amaretto Sour recipes, two things hindered its chance for greatness. The first that the sour mix itself is too sweet. The second was the game changer: "... amaretto isn't strong enough on its own to stand up to a bunch of other ingredients. It's weak. It needs help. And for this, I enlist the assistance of an old friend. One that knows amaretto's strengths and weaknesses." Here, he added cask-strength bourbon to the mix.

Boom.

It made the case for deliciously re-engineering a historically cloying drink. Not only did Morgenthaler make Amaretto Sours cool again, venues proudly added them to their menus and practically dared skeptical customers to order them.

This updated "disco era" classic opened the door for others like it. With a growing demand for more balanced and/or slightly more astringent flavor profiles, similar ingredients are now used to enhance recipes in sophisticated ways. What's next, rock and rye? Why, yes. Suddenly the old dusties have a purpose again.

......................................................................................................

- 1½ oz (45 ml) amaretto
- ¾ oz (22 ml) cask-strength bourbon
- 1 oz (30 ml) fresh lemon juice
- 1 tsp (5 ml) rich syrup
- 1 tbsp egg white (half a whole egg white), lightly beaten

- Garnish: lemon peel and brandied cherries (optional)

Combine all ingredients in a cocktail shaker and shake without ice, or (even better) use an immersion (stick) blender to combine and froth. Shake well with cracked ice. Strain over fresh ice in an old fashioned [sic] glass. Garnish with lemon peel and brandied cherries, if desired. Serve and grin with abandon as your friends freak out.

......................................................................................................

# FYNBOS

🕒 2012
⚐ JOHANNESBURG, SOUTH AFRICA
⚐ EUGENE THOMPSON

⌂ NEWS CAFE
◊ BRANDY
Y COUPE

Fynbos is an area of shrubland that covers the Western and Eastern Cape of South Africa, and includes several species of plants, among them rooibos, used for the popular tea hailed for its antioxidant benefits. The Fynbos cocktail was created in 2012 by bartender Eugene Thompson for a South African brandy competition; the front-of-house manager for News Cafe in Johannesburg took home the top R60,000 prize and the Fynbos was named Cocktail of the Year.

The purpose of the annual competition is to raise awareness of an industry that was deeply wounded by the international trade sanctions surrounding Apartheid, as well as to help shake off the poor reputation stemming from a time when most of the country's brandy was overproduced and cheap to make. The competition spotlights expressions of high quality in the category and the versatility of the spirit in various styles of cocktails, while also supporting talented local bartenders who use it in recipes that celebrate local ingredients. The Fynbos is made with an aged SA brandy to play off the inherently earthy, nutty flavor structure of locally sourced rooibos tea. At the time of the 2012 competition, ginger liqueur was a wildly popular ingredient, and here its spicy texture is boosted with honey syrup and orange bitters.

Since the win, Fynbos has been a mainstay at News Cafe, and a go-to recipe in the South African cocktail community. It has even been shared by the *Guardian* online newspaper as an example of a quintessential SA modern classic cocktail. Not only does Fynbos represent the flavors of the region and support local distillers, farmers, and producers, it's also simple to reproduce, with easily sourced ingredients and straightforward instructions—all the necessary components of a popular signature.

• 2 oz (60 ml) brandy
  (preferably South African)
• 1 oz (30 ml) brewed rooibos tea, cooled
• ½ oz (15 ml) ginger liqueur
• 1 tsp honey syrup (page 86)
• 2 dashes orange bitters

• Garnish: lemon peel

Stir all ingredients in a mixing glass with ice. Strain into a chilled coupe glass and garnish with lemon peel.

# SHAKY PETE

⊕ 2012
⚑ LONDON, UK
ᴀ PETE JEARY

⌂ HAWKSMOOR
◊ GIN
🍸 PINT

Warehouses and breweries have populated Hay's Wharf on the south bank of the Thames near London Bridge since the Middle Ages—the name followed in the mid-seventeenth century for Alexander Hay and his family, who set up most of the local businesses there. Sometime around 2012, while walking past one of the breweries and taphouses that still occupy the quay today, Pete Jeary, head bartender for Hawksmoor steakhouse, was inspired by a plaque detailing the history of the area, where goods, such as tea, and spices, such as ginger, were received after being shipped over the high seas.

The plaque and the sweet smell of the brewery lingering in the air inspired him to come up with a signature drink in a spicy shandy style that incorporates a house-made ginger syrup, gin, and local beer. Now, more than ten years later, Hawksmoor has several locations in London, and has expanded to other outposts in Manchester, Liverpool, Edinburgh, Dublin, and New York City; Shaky Pete is a staple on all of its menus. Each location also features a nonalcohol variation called Steady Pete.

The name comes from Hawksmoor co-founder Huw Gott, who joked that Jeary would get so nervous during cocktail competitions, his hands would "shake like the Waco kid."

- ¾ oz (45 ml) Ginger Syrup
- ¾ oz (45 ml) lemon juice
- 1 oz (30 ml) London dry gin
- 3½ fl oz (100 ml) premium ale (Hawksmoor uses London Pride), to top

Put the ginger syrup, lemon juice, and gin into a heavy-duty blender with a couple of ice cubes (the restaurant uses five, but because they are a different size than most standard cubes made at home, they suggest using two from a standard tray). Blend until it is liquidy but still retaining an airy froth. Pour the contents into an ice-cold beer mug or pint glass and top with beer.

### For the Ginger Syrup

Although it won't have quite the same fiery effect as the fresh ginger juice syrup made with restaurant-grade equipment at Hawksmoor, this method is still delicious. Make a 2:1 rich syrup with a piece of fresh ginger (about 3 inches/7.5 cm, roughly peeled with some skin on). Strain out the ginger and let cool before using. It will keep in the refrigerator for about 10 days.

# SPEAK LOW

🕐 **2012**
⚐ **NEW YORK CITY, USA**
👤 **SHINGO GOKAN**

⌂ **ANGEL'S SHARE**
🍶 **RUM**
🍸 **ROCKS**

........................................................................................

According to a May 2021 article for *50 Best*, when bartender Shingo Gokan moved from his native Japan to New York City around 2006, setting his sights on the groundbreaking second-story East Village speakeasy Angel's Share, the only style of American bartending that he recognized was flair, as demonstrated by actor Tom Cruise in the 1988 movie *Cocktail*. However, this over-the-top style of service seemed "too tough" to master, so to make his personal brand stand out, he decided his signature serve would incorporate elements of Japanese tea ceremony with comedic touches (particularly when crushing the ice) to liven it up, and his focus would be sherry. By 2012, that combination was evidently working for him. Not only had he become one of the most popular members of the Angel's Share bar team; he entered, and won, a Bacardí Legacy competition with his cocktail Speak Low, which incorporates two types of Bacardí rum

with matcha tea and Pedro Ximénez sherry, set off by yuzu zest.

By 2014, Speak Low was one of Angel's Share's most enduringly popular signatures by 2014, but Gokan moved on to open his own bar in Shanghai, China, which he named after the drink. It's endured as a signature at other bars in Shanghai, in Tokyo, and beyond, which Gokan either co-owns or has consulted with. Speak Low remained on Angel's Share's menu, even served as a bottled cocktail to-go during lockdown, until it closed its East Village location in 2022 and relocated to the West Village in 2023.

To make Speak Low, one needs a little practice to learn how to prepare traditional matcha tea, which must be whisked from its powder form with the white rum before mixing with the other ingredients.

........................................................................................

- 1 tsp matcha tea powder
- 1 oz (30 ml) Bacardí Superior white rum
- 1 oz (30 ml) Bacardí Reserva Ocho
- ½ oz (15 ml) Pedro Ximénez (PX) sherry

- Garnish: yuzu zest (if unavailable, use grapefruit)

In a small ceramic bowl, use a matcha tea brush to whisk the tea powder with the white rum until the powder dissolves and the mixture is slightly frothy. Add to a shaker along with the remaining ingredients and shake with ice until well chilled. Double strain into a rocks glass over a single block of ice, then zest yuzu over the top.

# CYNAR JULEP

◴ 2013
⚑ BUENOS AIRES, ARGENTINA
⚘ SANTIAGO LOMBARDI

⌂ FLORERÍA ATLÁNTICO
◊ CYNAR
Y JULEP TIN OR HIGHBALL

Argentinian palates tend to skew toward the bitter flavor spectrum when it comes to cocktails. Bitter liqueurs and aperitivi, such as Campari, varieties of Fernet (intensely bitter herbal liqueurs), and amaro, particularly Cynar, are as commonly consumed in Argentinian bars as whiskey is in other parts of the world. Fernet and Coke is considered the national cocktail of Argentina, but the Cynar Julep could be argued as a close second.

The Cynar Julep was created by bartender Santiago Lombardi at Florería Atlántico, which opened in Buenos Aires in 2013. The drink, along with charismatic bar manager Renato "Tato" Giovannoni, helped make it one of the city's top destination bars. Cynar gets its bracing vegetal and herbal notes from an infusion of artichoke with mint and other bitter herbs and botanicals. Swapping out the traditional bourbon in a Mint Julep for Cynar and a splash of gin makes complete sense from a flavor perspective, adding a counterpoint to the sugar syrup while matching the fresh mint—the two ingredients that make the cocktail a Julep in the first place—while adding an aromatic backbone to complement the lime and grapefruit juices.

The icy refresher is considered Argentina's most successful modern classic. It was such a hit at Florería Atlántico that, as other cocktail bars sprang up around the city and the country, Cynar Juleps were on every menu. For obvious reasons, it's especially popular in the blazing hot summer months.

The drink is prepared swizzle style, so be sure to have a swizzle stick and plenty of crushed ice on hand to prepare.

- 8 mint leaves
- ½ oz (15 ml) simple syrup
- ¼ oz (7 ml) fresh lime juice
- 1½ oz (45 ml) Cynar
- ½ oz (15 ml) London dry gin
- Fresh grapefruit juice, to top

- Garnish: mint sprig and grapefruit wheel

Lightly muddle the mint leaves with the simple syrup in a Julep tin or highball glass. Add the remaining ingredients along with crushed ice and quickly work a swizzle stick back and forth between the palms of the hands until the glass is frosted on the outside. Top with more crushed ice, then top with fresh grapefruit juice. Garnish with a mint sprig and grapefruit wheel.

# HEADLESS HORSEMAN

- ⏱ 2013
- ⚐ BROOKLYN, USA
- ⚇ RYAN LILOA

- ⌂ LEYENDA
- ⚗ CACHAÇA
- ♆ SKULL MUG OR HURRICANE

"His appetites for the marvelous, and the powers of digesting it, were equally extraordinary." Washington Irving, "The Legend of Sleepy Hollow" (1820)

When the leaves begin to turn in Carroll Gardens, Brooklyn, Leyenda—the Latin spirits-focused bar opened by Ivy Mix and her partners from Clover Club across the way on Smith Street in 2013—lights up the Headless Horsemen. The cocktail is inspired by the mythical figure of a rider on horseback who carries his own head under his arm, which dates to the Middle Ages but was popularized in Washington Irving's 1820 fictional short story "The Legend of Sleepy Hollow." The events of that fable, with the head famously interpreted as a pumpkin, take place only thirty-eight miles from the bar, in what is a real town in Westchester, New York. So it's only fitting that when Leyenda gets in the spirit for Día de

Muertos season, a spooky-themed cocktail takes up residence.

The drink somehow manages to be both frozen and flaming, elegantly showcasing the seasonal flavors of pumpkin spice, though not in a cloying way, and arrives in a skull mug with a lime shell filled with high-ABV rum and set aflame. It was created by resident tiki aficionado Ryan Liloa within the first year of the bar's opening, and the theatrical fan favorite—a balanced, frozen mixture of cachaça, allspice dram, pumpkin and cinnamon bark syrups, coconut cream, and fruit juices—is a constant from the early autumn months through the winter holidays, even during brunch service.

It's a potent mixture, though often shared by two or more guests Scorpion Bowl style. After all, sometimes it's tough to keep one's head on straight during the holiday season.

- 1½ oz (45 ml) aged cachaça
- ¾ oz (22 ml) fresh orange juice
- 1½ oz (45 ml) pumpkin syrup (1:1 syrup made with a cup of pumpkin purée, strained)
- ½ oz (15 ml) allspice dram liqueur
- ¾ oz (22 ml) cinnamon bark syrup (1:1 syrup made with 4 cinnamon sticks, strained)
- 1½ oz (45 ml) coconut blend (1:1 split coconut cream and coconut milk)
- ¾ oz (22 ml) fresh lime juice

- Garnish: hollowed-out lime disk filled with overproof 151 rum

Add all ingredients plus 1 cup of crushed ice to a blender and blend until smooth, 15 to 20 seconds. Pour into a ceramic mug (a skull mug is best!) or hurricane glass over a small amount of crushed ice. Set the lime disk over the drink and carefully fill with overproof rum, then light with a match.

# LAVENDER MULE

⊕ 2013  
⚐ SAN JUAN, PUERTO RICO  
人 LESLIE COFRESI  

⌂ LA FACTORÍA  
⚗ VODKA  
Ⴤ MULE MUG  

..................................................................................................

If the Piña Colada is the national cocktail of twentieth-century Puerto Rico, it can be argued that the Lavender Mule is its twenty-first-century counterpart. The cocktail was first created by Leslie Cofresi at La Factoría, San Juan's premier cocktail bar. Located in an unmarked building that is notoriously difficult to find at first, there is a main bar and five additional subterranean bars, each rocking a different shabby chic look, and each with their own separate menu and theme (one of them even sports a dance floor). Regardless, the Lavender Mule is considered the mascot of the entire establishment, which opened in 2013.

This elegant take on the classic Moscow Mule—vodka, ginger beer, lime—is made with vodka, lavender simple syrup, and lemon juice, but instead of topping with the traditional ginger beer, brewed ginger tea is shaken with the entire cocktail to provide that essential sharp bite of flavor. A dehydrated lemon wheel and sprig of lavender add the final, eye-catching touches.

"I can, with full confidence, say that this drink helped build cocktail culture in Puerto Rico," says bar consultant Natasha Sofia. As part of La Factoría's opening menu, the Lavender Mule was only meant to stay for a short time (the venues in the complex change menus on a weekly basis), but it has remained a constant by popular demand. In 2016, it was served at the World's 50 Best Bars awards ceremony. And thanks to the popularity of this drink, La Factoría has been on the list consistently ever since.

..................................................................................................

- ½ oz (15 ml) lemon juice
- ¾ oz (22 ml) brewed ginger tea, cooled
- ¾ oz (22 ml) Lavender Simple Syrup
- 1½ oz (45 ml) unflavored vodka (the bar uses Ketel One)

- Garnish: dehydrated lemon wheel, pesticide-free lavender sprig

Shake all ingredients vigorously with ice until well chilled and frothy. Strain into a copper mule mug or tall glass filled with fresh ice. Garnish.

For the Lavender Simple Syrup

- 8 oz (240 ml) water
- 1 cup (200 g) sugar
- 3 tbsp pesticide-free dehydrated lavender

Heat all ingredients in a small saucepan over low heat until the sugar dissolves, about 10 minutes. Strain into a sealable container and store in the refrigerator for up to 10 days.

# SALMONCITO

🕐 2013
⚐ MEXICO CITY, MEXICO
  KHRISTIAN DE LA TORRE

⌂ MAISON ARTEMISIA
◊ GIN
Y BULB OR STEMLESS WINE

Mexico City might be the last place one would expect to find a *fin de siècle*-inspired absinthe and wine bar, but Maison Artemisia is that place. Opened in 2012 by a group of French and Mexican friends, it is located above the natural wine bar Loup in the trendy Roma Norte neighborhood, decked out in velvet furnishings, candles, an upright piano, and yes, many a sugar cube dissolving over an absinthe spoon. However, the drink from the venue that made hearts all over Mexico City (and beyond) grow fonder, Salmoncito, is entirely absinthe-less, and originated by Khristian de la Torre in 2013.

Salmoncito is considered the Mexican Gin & Tonic (*Gin Tonic Mexa*) and consists of dry gin, fresh grapefruit juice, Campari, and tonic water. From Maison Artemisia, the drink followed de la Torre, heralded as one of CDMX's top bartenders, to Gin Gin, Café Taco Bar (as co-owner and head bartender), and was served at other venues, becoming one of the chicest drinks to order in town.

The English translation of "salmoncito" is "little salmon" and this this is in reference to the garnish: the grapefruit supreme should float and bob in the glass. If the proportions are mixed incorrectly without enough tonic, it will sink. Like receiving a Guinness with too thin a head of foam, apparently a sinking grapefruit supreme announces to discerning Mexicans that the ice in the bulb glass is too crushed, there is too much juice and not enough gin, Campari, and tonic used in the mix—and that the supreme had too much pith or probably wasn't carefully placed in the glass with tongs in the first place.

- 1½ oz (45 ml) London dry gin
- Splash of fresh grapefruit juice
- ¼ oz (7 ml) Campari
- Tonic water, to top

- Garnish: grapefruit supreme (section devoid of any pith or peel)

Build the ingredients in a bulb glass or stemless wine glass with large ice cubes. Stir with garnish tongs. Using the tongs, carefully add the "little salmon"—the grapefruit supreme garnish; this should float in the glass.

# BAMBOOZICLE

- C.2014
- NEW YORK CITY, USA
- NATASHA DAVID

- NITECAP
- SHERRY
- DOUBLE ROCKS

The classic Bamboo cocktail created by Louis Eppinger in the late nineteenth century is one of the darlings of the modern cocktail scene for its elegant yet austere mix of sherry, dry vermouth, and bitters. It presents like a stiff Martini, but because of its lower ABV, it drinks more like wine. Bartender and consultant Natasha David is such a fan of the cocktail that when she opened the low ABV-focused bar Nitecap in New York City's Lower East Side with the Death & Co team in 2014, one of its main draws was Bamboos on tap. Yet David writes in her 2022 book *Drink Lightly* that she had always wanted to find a way "to present the drink in a less serious format while still maintaining and honoring its core recipe." Half kidding, her husband, Jeremy Oertel, suggested going the slushy route.

What sounded like a joke suddenly seemed a stroke of brilliance. Bamboozicles—served all year long and garnished with mini umbrellas, edible flowers, and "disco dust"—became one of the star signatures of Nitecap until its closing in 2020.

David says that when she was formulating the recipe, she was inspired by the icons of frozen, blended cocktails—the Piña Colada, the frozen Margarita, and fruit-flavored Daiquiris. The base of her recipe remains dry Amontillado-style sherry with a split of white vermouth and dry vermouth, along with orange juice, strawberry purée, and a drop of banana rum. She notes that while the recipe calls for what sounds like a frighteningly large measure of simple syrup, it should be kept in mind that the drink doesn't taste clawingly sweet when combined with the tart fruit juices and the amount of ice necessary for the blended slushy effect.

- 1½ oz (45 ml) dry Amontillado sherry
- 1 oz (30 ml) simple syrup
- ¾ oz (22 ml) white vermouth
- ¾ oz (22 ml) dry vermouth
- ¾ oz (22 ml) fresh orange juice
- ½ oz (15 ml) strawberry purée
- ¼ oz (7 ml) banana rum
- ½ cup crushed ice

- Garnish: paper parasol, edible flower, disco dust, metal straw

Add all ingredients to a blender with the crushed ice. Blend on high until smooth, 15 to 20 seconds. Pour into a double rocks glass and garnish with a parasol, edible flower, disco dust, and straw.

# CHERRY BOUNCE SOUR

2014
HOUSTON, USA
ALBA HUERTA

JULEP
BOURBON
HIGHBALL

A bounce is the liquid cordial left over from the preservation of fruit, most famously cherries, when infused with brandy, sugar, and sweet spices. The infamous George Washington "I cannot tell a lie" cherry tree tale, ironically, may or may not be true, but what is true is that the first President of the United States and his wife Martha were huge cherry bounce fans, as were many early American colonists, particularly in the South. Cherry bounce became a staple in Southern kitchens, particularly when added to tall, frosty glasses of lemonade or iced tea (though most often sipped on its own).

Opened by Alba Huerta in Houston, Texas in 2014, Julep is a celebration of Southern ingredients and culinary traditions. One of the most famous, and still popular, of its early signatures is the Cherry Bounce Sour, a drink that lies between a traditional bounce and a boozy summertime soda fountain treat.

Bounces were traditionally prepared overseas with brandy as the main preservative, but many early American recipes used more readily available rye or bourbon, and since then the tradition has stuck. For the Cherry Bounce Sour, Huerta uses the liquid from a homemade bounce cordial made with 50% ABV bourbon, and gives it all a rigorous shake with lemon, sugar, egg white, and Angostura bitters in both the cocktail liquid and misted over the top as a garnish.

The cocktail is not only delicious, but is a treat for the eyes as well. Served in a highball glass, the liquid is a fetching dark pink capped with a foamy pillow, akin to the appearance of a Ramos Gin Fizz (page 48), but with slightly less strenuous a preparation.

- 1 ⅓ oz (40 ml) 50% ABV bourbon
- 1 oz (30 ml) homemade cherry bounce (Huerta's recipe is secret, but look for others online)
- ½ oz (15 ml) simple syrup made with turbinado sugar
- ¼ oz (7 ml) fresh lemon juice
- 1 dash Angostura bitters
- 1 egg white

- Garnish: Angostura mist, grated cinnamon, preserved bourbon cherry

Shake all ingredients without ice for about 10 seconds to emulsify. Add ice and shake vigorously for another 15 seconds or so until well chilled and very frothy. Strain into a highball glass over fresh ice. Mist with Angostura bitters, grate cinnamon over the top of the foam, and add a cherry.

# MARRERO DAIQUIRI

⏱ 2014
⚑ PARIS, FRANCE
𐐪 GUILLAUME LEBLANC

⌂ DIRTY DICK
🜹 RUM
🍸 HALF COCONUT SET
INTO A COUPE GLASS

When French bartender Guillaume Leblanc began working at the tropical-drinks-focused bar Dirty Dick in Paris, France, he was looking for a good excuse to create a cocktail with a coconut fat-washed rum. Fat-washing is a technique that enriches the flavors of a spirit with an oil or other protein (sesame, bacon, butter, etc.) to shuttle those flavors directly into the spirit. Leblanc's moment arrived when he entered a Don Q cocktail competition in 2014 and discovered that it was the 70th anniversary of the Piña Colada credited to Ramón "Monchito" Marrero Pérez and his team at the Caribe Hilton Hotel in San Juan, Puerto Rico (page 162). Leblanc's hybrid Colada and Daiquiri was intended to honor Marrero's memory as well as do justice to the Puerto Rican rum. It's "a Piña Colada in a coupe," or a "Daiquiri with the lightness of coconut water," as he describes it.

The Marrero Daiquiri finished second in the competition, but with its lavish presentation served in a half coconut vessel over an ice-filled coupe, it was a Dirty Dick menu staple for the next three years and one of the stars of Paris Cocktail Week 2015. The only change came about sometime later, when Leblanc's colleague at the bar, Cameron Cresswell, *zhuzhed* the impressive display even further by placing the stem of the glass in the crown of a fresh pineapple.

Leblanc notes that the organic coconut oil used in the infusion brings out the fresh coconut aromas without the need for heavy coconut cream. Instead of pineapple juice, he opts for fresh pineapple chunks to deliver the most authentic flavors of the fruit. The final touch is sugarcane syrup instead of simple syrup for a cleaner, slightly earthy sweetness.

---

• 1¾ oz (50 ml) Coconut Fat-Washed Don Q Crystal Rum
• ¾ oz (22 ml) fresh lime juice
• ½ oz (15 ml) sugarcane syrup
• 2 fresh pineapple cubes

• Garnish: hollowed-out half coconut as vessel, crown of pineapple, edible orchid

Plan to begin the fat-washing process at least a day ahead of serving the cocktail.

Set the stem of a coupe glass into the crown of the pineapple. Fill with ice and set aside. Shake all ingredients with ice for at least 20 seconds. Double strain into the half coconut and set atop the ice in the pineapple coupe. Garnish with the edible flower.

For the Coconut Fat-Washed Don Q Crystal Rum

Note: the liquid will be significantly reduced during the process

• 6¾ oz (200 ml) coconut oil
• 30 oz (900 ml) Don Q Crystal rum

Heat the oil to 115°F (45°C) and add to the rum. Stir, then let stand for 12 hours at room temperature before placing in the refrigerator for several hours. Strain the solids out of the rum without pressing it. Store in a sealed container in the refrigerator for up to 10 days.

# SUMMER MANHATTAN

🕘 **2014**
⚐ **BROOKLYN, USA**
👤 **MIKE VACHERESSE**

⌂ **TRAVEL BAR**
🍶 **RYE**
🍸 **COUPE**

There are people who swear off Manhattans—typically bourbon or rye mixed with sweet vermouth and bitters—for the entirety of the late spring to summer months, because it's thought to be too much of a wooly sweater (jumper) kind of drink. However, the Summer Manhattan from Travel Bar might change those perceptions.

Previously bartender at Gotham Bar & Grill and Masa in Manhattan, Mike Vacheresse opened Travel Bar, where he also serves as beverage manager, with business partner Joe Sweigart in 2014, at the edge of the Carroll Gardens section of Brooklyn, New York. "It's a neighborhood bar with a whiskey problem," Vacheresse likes to say. It boasts more than 480 whiskies in its collection (among an impressive range of other spirits) so, of course, at least one style of Manhattan cocktail must be on offer. They have four. A constant is the Summer Manhattan.

Vacheresse says he's not a fan of naming twists on classic things like, "Mike's New Hat," because those monikers don't adequately describe the base cocktail or what to expect when it's served. For a time, Summer Manhattan was originally known simply as "Manhattan No. 2." Heading into the spring/summer season of 2017, and recognizing how much lighter and more refreshing it is than the standard, he renamed it "Summer Manhattan." Now summer lasts forever at Travel Bar.

Instead of the heavier ratio of the classic, this take is mixed with Old Overholt Rye—a more neutral, less spicy, and grainy expression—Dubonnet Rouge (in recent years, reformulated to be drier and more aromatic), and orange bitters. Though either citrus twist or cocktail cherry is technically the correct garnish for a classic Manhattan, Vacheresse goes for lemon here. "It gave me the right not to use a syrupy cherry," he says of complementing the juicier flavor profile.

- 2 oz (60 ml) Old Overholt 86 proof rye (previously 80 proof)
- 1 oz (30 ml) Dubonnet Rouge
- 3 dashes Regan's No. 6 orange bitters

- Garnish: lemon twist

Stir all ingredients with ice until well chilled. Strain into a chilled coupe glass. Express the oils from a piece of lemon peel into the drink, skin side down, then twist and place in the glass.

# CRYSTAL RAMOS GIN FIZZ

- ⏱ 2015
- ⚐ SINGAPORE
- ☌ AKI EGUCHI

- ⌂ JIGGER & PONY
- ⚗ GIN
- ⍦ TULIP

The Ramos Gin Fizz (page 48) is one of the most beloved, and one of the most hated, classic cocktails. It's loved because it's a creamy, frothy treat, but hated because it's so strenuous to shake—and loathed particularly if ordered when a bar is at high capacity.

In 2015, Aki Eguchi, bar director of Jigger & Pony group in Singapore, sought to reformulate the classic New Orleans signature into one that was both lighter in appearance and sensation. He came up with the Crystal Ramos Gin Fizz, which became an instant classic at the organization's namesake bar and brought worldwide attention.

A traditional Ramos Gin Fizz famously consists of gin, lemon and lime juices, orange blossom water, and heavy (double) cream that is shaken vigorously for a prolonged time, then strained over chilled soda water. Eguchi reverse-engineered the recipe by first clarifying the cream component as a clear gin milk punch with a peridot hue from green tea. He then creates the fizz effect by using a carbonator, and a special technique for the garnish of "orange blossom bubbles." The result is a stunning showstopper of a cocktail with the essential sweet, sour, aromatic flavor elements of a classic Ramos, yet without the fattiness of the cream.

Serves 2

- 1½ oz (45 ml) dry gin
- 6¾ oz (200 ml) Clarified Gin Milk Punch

- Garnish: Orange Blossom Bubbles

In a carbonator bottle, combine the gin, clarified gin milk punch, and ¾ cup (180 ml) water, and carbonate (using a soda siphon). Pour into a large tulip glass. Add a large ice cube or rectangular block of ice. Garnish with orange blossom bubbles.

### For the Clarified Gin Milk Punch

Combine 10 oz (300 ml) brewed green tea, 12 oz (355 ml) Tanqueray gin, ¾ cup (150 g) sugar, 4 oz (120 ml) white rum, 2¾ oz (80 ml) spiced rum, 1½ oz (45 ml) dark rum, 1½ oz (45 ml) absinthe, 10 oz (300 ml) fresh lemon juice, 9 pieces of ½ x 2-inch (1 x 5 cm) orange peel, 4 pieces of ½ x 2-inch (1 x 5 cm) lemon peel, 9 cloves, 1 piece star anise, and 1 cinnamon stick in a large bowl.

Stir to dissolve the sugar. Cover and refrigerate for at least 12 hours. Strain over a large bowl usin a sieve, reserving the spiced liquid. Heat 5 oz (150 ml) whole (full-fat) milk in a pan over medium heat until it reaches 140°F (60°C), then combine with the spiced liquid infusion. Stir and refrigerate for another 12 hours. Strain the liquid through cheesecloth (muslin) into a large bowl. According to volume, set aside 1 g agar agar for every 3¾ oz (105 ml) liquid. In a pan, combine the agar agar with one-third of the liquid. Slowly heat the mixture to 131°F (55°C), then add the remaining liquid to the pan. Stir. Refrigerate for 3 hours. Strain through a coffee filter before using. It will keep in the refrigerator for a few days.

### For the Orange Blossom Bubbles

Combine 8 oz (240 ml) water, 1½ oz (45 ml) orange blossom water, 1.25 g Versawhip, and 0.5 g xanthan gum in a bowl. Using a handheld blender, blend ingredients. Use a hand air pump to create bubbles.

# GREEN EYES

⏱ 2015  
⚑ PORTLAND (MAINE), USA  
👤 BRIANA AND ANDREW VOLK  

⌂ PORTLAND HUNT + ALPINE CLUB  
🍸 GIN  
🍸 DOUBLE ROCKS

Husband and wife team Briana and Andrew Volk opened the Scandinavian culture-inspired bar/restaurant Portland Hunt + Alpine Club in Portland, Maine in 2013, a few years after meeting on the other coast's Portland, Oregon, when Andrew was behind the bar at Clyde Common. That tenure occurred during a time when the early twentieth-century Last Word cocktail (page 72)—gin, Chartreuse, maraschino, lime—was having its second wind, particularly on the West Coast. Hunt + Alpine's Last Word variation, Green Eyes, eschews the typical "word" play (Final Word, Oh My Word, etc.) and instead takes the form of a frothy egg white concoction that is inspired by the sea foam of the nearby coastal waters. The couple say in their 2018 book *Northern Hospitality With The Portland Hunt + Alpine Club* that it's a "sister of the sea."

To accompany dishes such as smoked trout, deviled eggs, fresh oysters, and various open-faced sandwiches on homemade breads, Green Eyes has been one of the "most ordered and photographed" drinks since the early days of the bar/restaurant. Apparently, a local couple even chose to hold their wedding reception there, because of their love of that particular cocktail. It is also the drink the venue uses as a gateway to the beguiling wonders of Chartreuse liqueur, a spirit made by monks in the French mountains using a secret blend of herbs and spices, here boosted by the aromatics of gin, and balanced by the sweetness of rich simple syrup.

The venue says it batches the egg whites by the dozen ahead of cocktail prep by whisking them to break down the proteins, then transferring them to a squeeze bottle, which they recommend if preparing Green Eyes for a crowd. Note: be prepared for an arm workout!

- 1½ oz (45 ml) London dry gin
- ¾ oz (22 ml) Green Chartreuse
- ¾ oz (22 ml) fresh lime juice
- ½ oz (15 ml) rich syrup
- 1 tbsp egg white (half a whole egg white)

- Garnish: lime wheel and cocktail cherry

Shake all ingredients with ice for 30 to 40 seconds. Transfer to one side of the shaker tin and fine strain into the other. Discard the ice. Shake again without ice for another 10 seconds (this ensures the drink doesn't separate in the glass). Strain into a double rocks glass filled with fresh ice. Garnish with a lime wheel and cocktail cherry.

# HOT GIN & TONIC

⏱ 2015
⚐ LONDON, UK
👤 JARED BROWN AND EOIN KENNY

⌂ HAM YARD HOTEL
🍶 GIN
🍸 HEATPROOF GLASS MUG

....................................................................................

The Hot Gin & Tonic is exactly as it sounds, the ever-popular cocktail-hour refresher retrofitted into toddy form. It debuted at London's Ham Yard Hotel in 2015 for a Sipsmith Gin winter seasonal takeover menu and is the brainchild of master distiller/drink historian Jared Brown and the hotel's bar manager, Eoin Kenny.

Brown says the concept came about as a dare. At the time, the Hot Gin & Tonic followed a series of "classic gin cocktail, but make it hot" challenge recipes that in previous seasons included steamy versions of Negronis (made with red berry tea), Martinis (served with a fried, breaded olive on the side), and Espresso Martinis (page 190), which Brown says was just a cheeky jab in memory of his dear, departed friend, the barman Dick Bradsell (inventor of the original), as it was essentially just an Irish Coffee made with gin. But could a Hot G&T even be done? Would people be into it?

Not only could it be done, but it also seems it always should have been. Hot G&T became a winter staple at the Ham Yard and took off at other Sipsmith outdoor pop-ups, especially during the cold months of 2020 and 2021, when events could only be held outside because of the COVID-19 pandemic. Brown says the drink has become an integral part of the Sipsmith distillery tour tasting room, where at least thirty-five are served a night, three to four nights a week.

The original recipe was prepared with a tonic syrup as both the essential aromatic quinine component and the sweetener. Later versions call for less tonic and a touch of simple syrup, though the sweetener can be modified according to preference.

....................................................................................

- 2 oz (60 ml) Sipsmith London dry gin
- ½ oz (15 ml) tonic syrup (several brands are available online)*
- 1 tsp (5 ml) simple syrup*
- Boiled water, to top

- Garnish: orange twist

Combine the gin and syrups in a heatproof mug or toddy glass. Add hot water and stir until the syrups dissolve. Garnish with an orange twist.

*Note: if more tonic flavor is desired, omit the simple syrup and add another teaspoon or so of tonic syrup.

# SAKURA MARTINI

- 2015
- NEW YORK CITY, USA
- KENTA GOTO

- BAR GOTO
- SAKE
- COUPE

When Pegu Club alum Kenta Goto opened his *izakaya* (a traditional Japanese bar with small dishes and cocktails), Bar Goto, in New York City's Lower East Side in 2015, along with his take on a Calpico Fizz, the Far East Side sour, and bar bites, such as okonomiyaki, he wanted to present a house Martini that represented his hometown of Tokyo in both its ingredients and presentation. The Sakura Martini deftly ticks all those boxes.

It's made in the proportions of a reverse Martini, with dry sake forming the base, a smaller amount of dry gin, with a dash of maraschino liqueur. As a simple yet striking flourish, peeping up from the bottom of the coupe is a soft pink Sakura cherry blossom, Japan's national flower, that's been salted as a preservative. Goto has said that he always wanted to find a way to incorporate it into

a cocktail. As of this writing, his team serves dozens of Sakura Martinis a day. The flavor combination sounds like it would be too fruity and floral for a Martini, but mixed in the right proportions, the drink is perfectly balanced with delicate aromatics.

In early 2020, Goto opened a second, larger location in Park Slope, Brooklyn: Bar Goto Niban (meaning "second"). Although it soon had to close for the COVID-19 lockdown, the bar offered home delivery of its magically addictive spicy miso wings, croquettes, and other bar bites Goto fans were craving. One could also order a mini bottle of the Sakura Martini, enough for two, complete with two of the cherry blossom garnishes, adding a little pink cheer to an otherwise bleak time. They survived the trip nicely, too.

- 2½ oz (75 ml) dry sake
- 1 oz (30 ml) dry gin
- 1 dash maraschino liqueur

- Garnish: preserved Sakura cherry blossom (available at specialty stores and online)

Combine all ingredients in a mixing glass. Stir with ice until well chilled. Strain into a chilled coupe glass. Carefully place the cherry blossom in the glass.

# LEEWARD NEGRONI

⏲ 2016
⚐ SAN FRANCISCO, USA
🜨 KEVIN DIEDRICH

⌂ PACIFIC COCKTAIL HAVEN
🍸 GIN
🍸 ROCKS

When San Francisco bartender Kevin Diedrich was introduced to pandan during his travels in Southeast Asia, it was love at first taste. Though somewhat grassy, the plant also lends a rich flavor—a cross between macadamia nuttiness and vanilla—to dishes and cocktails. At Pacific Cocktail Haven in San Francisco, where he has been both a partner and general manager since 2016, Diedrich has incorporated pandan in a salted pandan syrup and an oleo saccharum. For the Leeward Negroni, a crowd favorite that has been on the menu since the early days and lasted through two locations (the original burned down in 2021, but the bar opened in the Union Square neighborhood a year later), he uses it in a cordial.

The pandan cordial in the Leeward Negroni is the perfect foil for another star ingredient: coconut fat-washed Campari. Unlike most Negronis, which are traditionally composed of equal parts, Diedrich opts for a more generous measure of the coconut Campari, which is boosted by Sipsmith VJOP Gin and tiki bitters.

During lockdown, the Leeward Negroni was a popular cocktail kit offered by Shaker & Spoon. Although the gin was sold separately, the home mixology kit included mini bottles of pandan elixir and instructions for the coconut fat-washed Campari (sure beats sourdough!). To make the cocktail from scratch, Diedrich recommends that fresh pandan leaves, sold at Asian grocery stores and online, are best for the syrup and garnish, as frozen leaves tend to be too grassy and lack the desired buttery, nutty-vanilla notes that really tie the drink together.

---

• Bittermen's Tiki bitters, to rinse glass
• 1 oz (30 ml) coconut fat-washed Campari
• ½ oz (15 ml) Sipsmith VJOP Gin
• ¾ oz (45 ml) Pandan Cordial

• Garnish: pandan leaf

Rinse a rocks glass with the Tiki bitters, discard the excess, and set aside. Stir the rest of the ingredients in a mixing glass with ice until well chilled. Strain into the prepared rocks glass over a large ice cube. Garnish with a pandan leaf.

## For the Coconut Fat-Washed Campari

• 3 oz (90 ml) coconut oil
• 8 oz (240 ml) Campari

Heat the coconut oil in a saucepan until it liquefies. Pour into a plastic or glass container with the Campari and let sit at room temperature for at least 24 hours. Transfer to the freezer and freeze until solids form (about an hour). Strain out the solids and store in a cool, dry place, tightly covered, for up to 10 days.

## Pandan Cordial

• 3 fresh pandan leaves
• 4 oz (120 ml) Everclear grain alcohol
• 6 oz (180 ml) simple syrup

Tie the pandan leaves in a knot and place in an airtight container with the Everclear. Let infuse for 48 hours, then strain out the leaves. Combine with the simple syrup. Store in the refrigerator for up to 10 days.

# PARASOL

⊕ 2016
⌂ GLADY'S
⚑ BROOKLYN, USA
🍶 RUM
ⵣ SHANNON MUSTIPHER
ⵗ COUPE

Parasol is a sleek, modern take on a Banana Daiquiri, created by Shannon Mustipher in 2016. As the beverage director of the Glady's Caribbean restaurant in Crown Heights, Brooklyn, Mustipher made it a mission to cast Daiquiris in an elegant, food-friendly light, eschewing the slushie machine and sugary accoutrements while celebrating the simple beauty of a traditional stripped-down recipe with fresh lime juice, a hint of sugar, and good-quality rum. According to Mustipher in an essay for *Flaviar*, the components of the signature Parasol cocktail unfurled by happenstance during a post-shift visit to her local, King Tai Bar.

The owner of local jam company BRINS was also at the bar and handed Mustipher a jar of banana jam, a new flavor. Mustipher immediately handed it to the bartender, requesting it be mixed with aged white rum, pineapple juice, and lime juice. The result, she says, "was pure heaven: bright, fruity but not overly sweet, silky with a full mouthfeel that did not come off as cloying, familiar and yet slightly novel."

Mustipher says that while cocktail research and development and thorough knowledge of ingredients and flavors is key to cocktail creation success, "sometimes you need to leave the door open for a happy accident to take place." A tweaked Parasol with banana syrup instead of the jam was a stalwart at Glady's until it closed in 2020, and remains one of Mustipher's signatures.

For the Parasol recipe in her 2019 book *Tiki: Modern Tropical Cocktails*, Mustipher suggests that if no banana syrup is on hand, use a high-quality banana liqueur such as Tempus Fugit Crème de Banane or Giffard Banane du Brésil.

---

• 2 oz (60 ml) white rum
  (it's best with clarified aged rum)
  or high-quality spiced rum
• ¾ oz (22 ml) banana syrup
  (or substitute with banana liqueur)
• ½ oz (15 ml) pineapple juice
• ¾ oz (22 ml) fresh lime juice

• Garnish: grated nutmeg

Shake all ingredients with ice until well chilled and frothy. Strain into a chilled coupe glass. Finely dust grated nutmeg over the top.

# PERFECT PEAR

🕐 2016  
⚑ BERLIN, GERMANY  
🜨 KEITH CORWIN  

⌂ THELONIOUS BAR  
🜔 GENEVER  
🍸 COUPE  

By the time Thelonious Bar opened in 2014 in Berlin's trendy Neukölln neighborhood, the modern German cocktail scene had settled into its own groove. As with most major cities, high-end bars with whimsical concoctions were popular with the masses all over the city, but there is also a less showy, more relaxed vibe in certain venues around town. Thelonious falls into this latter category, and as the name suggests, it's the sort of mellow, jazzy spot where one would want to stop by and sip something equally chill.

Keith Corwin relocated to Berlin from the US following his marriage to a city native, and after a few months bartending at Thelonious, he joked with his regulars that he was going to create a "modern classic" for the bar. Though it's set on a street that draws an international crowd and known for its well-presented classics and variations on those themes, the staff are also welcomed to experiment, and co-owner/head bartender Laura Maria

Marsueschke soon encouraged Corwin to mix things up for a new menu.

Being a fan of the equal-parts measurement genre of classics such as the Negroni (page 82) and Corpse Reviver No. 2 (page 124), Corwin wanted to work with that template. He was enthralled with bitter-yet-fruity Amaro Montenegro liqueur and genever and wanted to incorporate them. He then turned to a German pear liqueur to balance the flavors out, with a hit of crème de cacao for subtle richness. To keep the mix from getting too flabby, it's balanced with fresh lemon juice. The result is essentially a more autumnal, earthy variation on the 20th Century (page 134).

Marsueschke was so impressed, she still serves Perfect Pear at Thelonious Bar every autumn. While the ingredients can be found at any time of year, somehow the cocktail is especially delicious on a brisk autumn evening. Around midnight, of course.

- ¾ oz (22 ml) Bols genever
- ¾ oz (22 ml) Schladerer Williams Pear (or other pear brandy)
- ¾ oz (22 ml) Amaro Montenegro
- ¾ oz (22 ml) white crème de cacao
- ¾ oz (22 ml) fresh lemon juice

- Garnish: dried pear, rolled onto a cocktail pick

Shake all ingredients with ice until well chilled. Strain into a coupe glass and balance the pick over the glass.

# BLACK NEGRONI

🕐 **2017**
⚑ **HONG KONG, CHINA**
👤 **YURIKO NAGANUMA**

⌂ **BAR DE LUXE**
🥃 **GIN**
🍸 **ROCKS**

.................................................................................................

Bar High Five in Tokyo, headed by Hidetsugu Ueno, is considered one of the best bars in the world. Its first Hong Kong outpost, Bar De Luxe, opened in 2017 on the thirteenth floor of the men's tailoring and grooming emporium Attire House on Wyndham Street. Its head bartender is Yuriko Naganuma, who trained under Takao Mori of Tokyo's Mori bar before going on to shadow Hidetsugu in Melbourne and Tokyo. One of the standout cocktails featured on her menu is the Black Negroni.

Laser-focused flavor combinations and striking aesthetic details are the focus of Naganuma's menu. Made with a combination of gin, Carpano Antica Formula, and Fernet-Branca liqueur, palate-wise, the Black Negroni lies between a traditional Negroni (page 82) made with aperitivo liqueur, and a Hanky Panky (page 78), which is made using the same ingredients in a different ratio of measurements. In the Black Negroni, not only do the individual elements harmonize beautifully in the glass once they mix, the cocktail is also particularly fetching to look at against the chic design of the venue, which includes a sleek walnut bar top and modern leather armchairs, overlooking a plate glass window with city views. Taking the drink's setting into full consideration, those visual details make perfect sense given Naganuma's background as a photographer who prefers conventional film to digital, according to a 2018 interview in *The Drinks Business*.

Since it first appeared on the menu, the Bar De Luxe version of the Black Negroni (there are others that replace the Fernet-Branca with coffee liqueur) has traveled the world as one of the most popular variations in the equal parts gin-vermouth-liqueur pantheon.

.................................................................................................

- 1 oz (30 ml) dry gin (the bar uses Bulldog London Dry)
- 1 oz (30 ml) Carpano Antica Formula sweet vermouth
- 1 oz (30 ml) Fernet-Branca

- Garnish: orange twist

Mix all ingredients with ice (preferably two large cubes) in a rocks glass until well chilled. Express the oils from a piece of orange peel over the drink, skin side down, then twist and add to the glass.

.................................................................................................

# FLYING DUTCHMEN

🕑 2017
⚐ AMSTERDAM, NETHERLANDS
👤 TESS POSTHUMUS
   AND TIMO JANSE

⌂ FLYING DUTCHMEN
🍸 GENEVER
🍷 COUPE

In 2017, after an almost ten-year collaboration behind the bar at the speakeasy Door 74 in Amsterdam, bartenders Tess Posthumus and Timo Janse opened Flying Dutchmen in the heart of the city, focusing on neoclassic cocktails as well as providing a center for drinks education to the industry.

As with many Europeans, Dutch people are increasingly more tuned in to food and drink provenance, and Posthumus and Janse believe there is a direct connection between food and drink culture when it comes to where and how ingredients are sourced.

For the bar's signature namesake cocktail, which has been on the menu since its opening, the team manages to effectively pour all these ideas and principles into a single glass.

"This cocktail is a real crowd pleaser," says Posthumus. "All ingredients represent our bar and Dutch (drinking) history. For example, the basis is the traditional spirit of the Netherlands, genever, and the orange bitters give a nod to the Dutch Royal family and their traditional drink for 'royal celebrations': oranje bitter. The orange flower water hints at our famous export product: flowers [tulips]. Speculaas is a spice mix that originates from the ancient spice routes, and the addition of gum arabic is a classic way of making syrup, which provides a wonderfully full mouthfeel and adds to the viscosity of the cocktail. The result of all this is a fresh concoction that evolves into warming spice notes."

- 1½ oz (45 ml) Bols Barrel Aged genever
- 1 oz (30 ml) fresh lemon juice
- ½ oz (15 ml) Speculaas-Gum Syrup
- 2 dashes Regan's Orange Bitters
- 1 dash orange blossom water

- Garnish: orange peel twist, edible flower

Add all ingredients to a cocktail shaker filled with cubed ice. Shake hard and strain into a chilled coupe glass. Garnish with an orange twist and edible flower.

For the Speculaas-Gum Syrup

- 1¼ oz (35 g) gum arabic
- 5 cups (1 kg) sugar
- ¾ oz (25 g) cinnamon sticks (broken)
- ⅓ oz (10 g) cloves
- 5 g each chopped nutmeg, white pepper, green cardamom, and chopped, peeled fresh ginger
- 17 oz (500 ml) water

Mix the gum arabic with 1 cup (200 g) sugar. Add 12 oz (350 ml) water and heat, without boiling, until the gum and sugar have dissolved. Strain and set aside. This is your gum syrup mix.

Toast the spices in a large pan. Add 5 oz (150 ml) water and 1¾ cups (350 g) sugar and heat, without boiling, until the sugar has dissolved. This is your spiced syrup mix.

Add the spiced syrup mix to the gum syrup mix. Heat again and add the remaining sugar. Let it dissolve, then let cool to room temperature. Fine strain and store in a sterilized glass bottle in the refrigerator for up to 3 months.

# HIT ME BABY ONE MAI TAI

🕘 **2017**
⚑ **LOS ANGELES, USA**
🅰 **BRYNN SMITH**

⌂ **SOTTO**
🝒 **RUM**
🍸 **DOUBLE ROCKS**

.................................................................................................

If she isn't already wearing one of her dozen or so Britney Spears T-shirts when you first meet her, it takes less than five minutes upon doing so to learn that LA-based bartender Brynn Smith is one of the world's biggest fans of the pop singer. Hit Me Baby One Mai Tai is a Mai Tai variation that Smith first developed in 2017, during her nearly eight-year run as the bar manager of Sotto restaurant in West Los Angeles, before its closing in 2019. She had been searching for a way to honor her idol on a new menu, and a co-worker came up with the name based on the hit single "Hit Me Baby One More Time."

Smith says, "I was inspired to make a Mai Tai because Britney loves Hawaii, and during her conservatorship she considered it a place of solitude, one of the only places she was allowed to visit." For her take, Smith took a springier fruit-forward approach to the tropical classic, incorporating muddled strawberries. The addition of Aperol provides a Paper Plane-like element of subtle bitterness to balance out the orgeat and fruit sweetness. Together with the strawberry, the ingredients also lend a very much on-brand sunset pink hue.

In 2021, Hit Me Baby One Mai Tai was featured in MTV's *Lifestyles of the Biggest Standoms*, in which Smith was profiled for her extensive private Britney collection. Oh baby, baby, how was Smith supposed to know that perhaps the Aperol was a foreshadowing? Says Smith, who hopes to serve the drink to the star one day, "During her conservatorship, she [Britney] was not allowed alcohol and she actually recently had Aperol in a spritz for the first time in 2022 and loved it."

.................................................................................................

- 2 strawberries
- 1 oz (30 ml) fresh lime juice
- ¾ oz (22 ml) orgeat
- 1 oz (30 ml) dark rum
  (Smith uses Angostura 5 Year)
- 1 oz (30 ml) Aperol

- Garnish: mint sprig, rose petal (to form a bouquet)

Add the strawberries to a cocktail shaker and gently muddle. Add all remaining ingredients and shake hard for at least 5 seconds. Double strain over crushed or nugget ice into a double rocks glass. Garnish with a "bouquet" of mint and rose petal.

# MODERNIST FALAFEL

🕐 2017
🏳 BEIRUT, LEBANON
👤 JAD BALLOUT

🏠 CENTRAL STATION BOUTIQUE BAR
🍶 VODKA
🍸 ROCKS

One of the few things shared throughout the Middle East is a common cuisine: falafel. Whether in Egypt, Palestine, Saudi Arabia, Iran, Jordan, Israel, or just about anywhere in that part of the world, versions of fried chickpea fritters are eaten everywhere, from private homes, street carts, and casual cafés to fine dining establishments. In Beirut, Lebanon, not only is falafel a staple of the local diet, but it is also available in *mashroob* ("drink" in Arabic) form at Central Station Boutique Bar, which has made several of the "top" lists of the world since it opened in that city's trendy Mar Mikhael neighborhood in 2010.

Invented in 2017, Modernist Falafel is the brainchild of Central Station's bar manager Jad Ballout. When he joined the team, he was more interested in culinary pursuits, however he soon realized that cocktail recipe creation

shares similar traits. "I joined the bar where I started to learn more about bartending and realized that I can play with ingredients and do some cooking to create drinks," Ballout says in a 2015 interview with *Tales of the Cocktail Foundation*. "What I loved the most was creating recipes and mixing ingredients together like chefs do in the kitchen, and at the same time, meeting people and sharing my creations."

As the name suggests, Modernist Falafel is made with the spices that go into a falafel mix, which is used as a homemade vodka infusion, then added to Mastika (a Greek spirit seasoned with resin from mastic trees), Chartreuse, lemon, and basil. The effect is reminiscent of a Southside (page 106), but with more aromatic and spicy characteristics.

---

• 3 basil leaves
• 1 oz (30 ml) Vodka Falafel
• 1 tsp (5 ml) Skinos Mastika
• 1 tsp (5 ml) Green Chartreuse
• ½ oz (15 ml) fresh lemon juice
• ½ oz (15 ml) simple syrup

• Garnish: Green Herbal Oil and slice of pickled turnip

Muddle the basil in the bottom of a shaker. Add the remaining ingredients and shake with ice until well chilled. Double strain into a rocks glass over fresh ice. Drop 2 to 3 drops of the herbal oil over the drink and add the turnip to the side of the glass.

For the Vodka Falafel

• 17 oz (500 ml) unflavored vodka
• ⅓ oz (10 g) falafel spice mix

Infuse the falafel mix in the vodka in a covered plastic container at room temperature for 2 hours or more. The bar uses a rotary evaporator to redistill from here, but the flavors will still come through from a simple infusion. Strain through cheesecloth (muslin) and store in a bottle or sealed container for up to a month.

For the Green Herbal Oil

• ¾ oz (20 g) fresh parsley leaves
• ⅓ oz (10 g) fresh coriander (cilantro) leaves
• 3½ oz (100 g) olive oil

Add all ingredients to a high-speed blender and blend at medium-high speed for 30 seconds. Store in an airtight container in a cool, dark place for up to 10 days.

# PETRONIO

🕐 2017
⚐ CARTAGENA, COLOMBIA
👤 ALQUÍMICO BAR STAFF

⌂ ALQUÍMICO
🍸 TEQUILA
🍸 DOUBLE ROCKS

Petronio Álvarez Pacific Music Festival, "El Petronio," is an annual event held in August in Santiago de Cali, Colombia in honor of revered musician and poet Patricio Romano Petronio Álvarez Quintero, who died in 1966. The weeklong festival has taken place for nearly three decades and is a celebration of Afro-Colombian cultural heritage, featuring musical performances, poetry readings, dance, food, and drink from a diverse range of Colombian Pacific communities. In Alquímico bar in Cartagena, El Petronio festival is celebrated with a signature cocktail that was created in 2017 and has remained on the menu ever since.

Alquímico project manager Irene Díaz says Petronio is not attributed to a single member of the bar staff. Like El Petronio festival itself, it combines influences and flavors from different cultural backgrounds that represent the team.

Petronio features tequila mixed with a purée of the local fruit lulo, vanilla liqueur (heirloom vanilla beans are a national product), orange juice, lemon juice, and the local Colombian cane spirit, viche. "Viche is the distillate of the Colombian Pacific, made from sugarcane when it is still fresh. One of the most outstanding factors in its preparation is that sugarcane grows between the sea, the river, and the jungle characteristic of the Colombian Pacific," says Díaz. As with certain mezcals in Mexico for Day of the Dead and other special occasions, she explains that viche "is carried out by communities and accompanies families in the most important moments of their lives." The spirit also represents cultural resistance. It has only been commercially legal in Colombia since 2022.

- 1½ oz (45 ml) tequila reposado (the bar uses Olmeca Altos)
- ½ oz (15 ml) viche dona sofi
- ¼ oz (7 ml) vanilla liqueur
- 1 oz (30 ml) lulo purée
- ½ oz (15 ml) fresh orange juice
- ½ oz (15 ml) fresh lime juice

Shake all ingredients with ice until well chilled and frothy. Strain into a double rocks glass with fresh ice.

# RHUBARB & CUSTARD

◴ C.2017

⚐ LONDON, UK

ⴷ MIA JOHANSSON AND
BOBBY HIDDLESTON

⌂ SWIFT BAR

◊ CALVADOS

🍸 ROCKS

Swift Bar was opened on bustling Old Compton Street in the heart of London's Soho in 2016 by Mia Johansson and Bobby Hiddleston, in partnership with Rosie Stimpson and Edmund Weil from the ultra-successful Nightjar. The venue is a two-story operation with separate menus. A bright yet inviting European Art Déco café-like atmosphere welcomes the crowd upstairs with mostly shaken concoctions, highballs, spritzes, wine, and beer, and their ever-popular Irish Coffee variation served with light bar snacks. Below is a dark, cozy, subterranean cocktail den, featuring a regularly changing, themed menu (in summer 2022 it was "Legends," with playful recipes honoring everyone from the Queen Mother to Ernest Hemingway to Snoop Dogg to Carmen Miranda). Yet one of the offerings that returns by popular demand every year in the late spring is Rhubarb & Custard, a calvados-based milk punch using fresh rhubarb juice, lemon, custard, and vanilla bitters.

"The drink fits Swift very well because it is ultimately a very simple drink, and with very familiar flavours, but presented in an interesting way," says Hiddleston. "It is very reminiscent, particularly with British people, of a specific Rhubarb & Custard-flavoured boiled sweet [rhubarb and custard crunch] that everyone had growing up, so there is a strong nostalgic element to it."

The drink was conceived by both Johansson and Hiddleston for an event sometime around the opening of the bar, and it was so well received that they bring it back as soon as rhubarb is in season in the UK. Hiddleston says, "We even bottled it during lockdown, and it was a fan favourite!"

Serves 4

- 4¾ oz (140 ml) calvados
- 4¾ oz (140 ml) simple syrup
- 3½ oz (100 ml) fresh custard
- ⅓ oz (10 ml) vanilla bitters
- 1¾ oz (50 ml) fresh rhubarb juice
- 1¾ oz (50 ml) fresh lemon juice

Add all ingredients to a large bowl or plastic container ("rhubarb & lemon last," says Hiddleston). Let sit airing out long enough to allow the mixture to split, then strain in batches through coffee filters (you might need more than one). Bottle the liquid and refrigerate. When ready to serve, simply pour over ice into a rocks glass and finish with a squeeze of lemon peel.

# YUZU COLADA

2017

TOKYO, JAPAN

ROGERIO IGARASHI VAZ

BAR TRENCH

MEZCAL

COUPE

Yuzu Colada is a lighter, more citrusy take on the Puerto Rican classic Piña Colada (page 162), a rich, sweet, frozen drink which is traditionally prepared with rum, coconut cream, heavy (double) cream, and pineapple juice. This zippy Japanese variation was debuted at Tokyo's Bar Trench in 2017 and is one of the signatures of the bar's co-founder, Rogerio Igarashi Vaz.

Vaz, who was born in Brazil, moved to Japan permanently in 2000 (his mother is Japanese). His first job in hospitality was in Tokyo at the Mexican spirits-focused bar, Agave, before he worked his way up to becoming a partner in the entirely cocktail-focused Bar Trench. The Yuzu Colada is a nod to his time at Agave, where he learned to appreciate agave spirits. It is prepared with mezcal instead of the requisite rum, and mixed with white cacao liqueur instead

of coconut, then gets a refreshing boost from sparkling sake and a homemade yuzu sorbet.

Though it sounds light and summery, the Yuzu Colada is a signature of Bar Trench's winter menu. "Winter is the season for yuzu, a beautiful Japanese citrus," says Vaz. "If you can't make it to the Caribbean or Mexico, we have something to comfort you, Yuzu Colada, but without all those colorful paper umbrellas." He describes the flavor profile as a "a smoky and citrusy holiday [in the vacation sense of the word] inspired drink."

Most Piña Coladas are prepared in the blender. Vaz says the Yuzu Colada can be prepared in either a blender or simply shaken, since the yuzu sorbet already provides that thick, frosty element to the cocktail.

- ¾ oz (20 ml) joven mezcal
- ⅓ oz (10 ml) fresh lemon juice
- ⅓ oz (10 ml) white crème de cacao liqueur
- 1 oz (30 ml) sparkling sake
- 1 scoop yuzu sorbet

- Garnish: candied dehydrated lemon wheel (lemon chip)

Option 1: blend all ingredients in a blender until smooth. Pour into a large coupe glass and garnish.

Option 2: shake all ingredients with 2 small ice cubes until well mixed. Pour into a large coupe glass and garnish.

# AKI PALOMA

⏱ 2018
⚑ NEW YORK CITY, USA
A MASA URUSHIDO

⌂ KATANA KITTEN
◊ TEQUILA
Y HIGHBALL

Palomas, a Mexican highball tradition combining tequila and grapefruit, are most often associated with spring and summer—a juicy thirst-quencher for a hot day. Similarly refreshing, whisky highballs are considered one of the pillars of Japanese cocktail service. In Japan, the highball is a ritual that is not merely about adding soda water to whisky —the glass must be frosty, the bubbles in the soda water strong yet not too gassy, the ice as clear as possible and well formed, always added to the glass with tongs. Created by Masa Urushido, co-owner of Katana Kitten in New York City, the Aki Paloma is an autumn version of a Paloma ("aki" in Japanese refers to "autumn")—one that celebrates the ingredients and flavors of a Paloma but reflects the craft of refined Japanese highball service— that debuted in 2018 and returns seasonally.

In his 2021 book *The Art of the Japanese Cocktail*, co-written with Michael Anstendig, Urushido says the aroma of hojicha, green tea that is roasted in porcelain pans over charcoal heat, stimulates sense memories of burning autumn leaves. As a play on that theme for the Aki Paloma, jasmine tea leaves are toasted for a syrup that is prepared with the perfumy zest of pomelo fruit. Along with ruby red grapefruit, he adds yuzu for an extra tangy kick. Combined with a roasty blanco tequila, served cold and frosty in a crowded bar under red lights surrounded by Japanese posters of American movies, the flavors come together to inspire thoughts of cozying up under a warm blanket near a fireplace.

- 1½ oz (45 ml) 100% agave tequila blanco (the bar uses Olmeca Altos Plata)
- ¾ oz (22 ml) ruby red grapefruit juice
- ¼ oz (8 ml) yuzu juice
- ¾ oz (22 ml) Toasted Jasmine-Pomelo Syrup
- Soda water, chilled, to top

- Garnish: Smoked Pomelo Salt

Combine all ingredients except the soda water in a highball glass with ice (preferably one long ice spear). Stir, then top with chilled soda water. Garnish with a sprinkle of pomelo salt.

### For the Toasted Jasmine-Pomelo Syrup

- Rind of ¼ pomelo fruit, cut into strips
- 1 cup (200 g) sugar
- 1½ tbsp loose jasmine tea leaves
- 8 oz (240 ml) water

In a small bowl, muddle the rind with the sugar and let stand for 30 minutes to form an oleo saccharum. Lightly toast the jasmine tea leaves in a pan over medium-low heat, keeping the pan in motion, about 4 minutes. Let cool. In another pan, combine the water, oleo, and tea leaves. Simmer over medium heat, stirring to dissolve the sugar. Let cool, then strain through cheesecloth (muslin) into an airtight container. Will keep in the refrigerator for up to one month.

### For the Smoked Pomelo Salt

1 pomelo, dehydrated (using a dehydrator, or store-bought), pulverized to a powder
¼ cup (68 g) smoked Maldon sea salt
¼ cup (68 g) Maldon sea salt

Combine the pomelo powder with the salts in an airtight container. Store for up to one year.

# BIG TROUBLE IN OAXACA

- ⏲ 2018
- ⚑ ROME, ITALY
- ☌ LIVIO MORENA

- ⌂ DRINK KONG
- ◊ TEQUILA; MIDORI
- ⍦ TUMBLER OR ROCKS

........................................................................

Set in a quaint, out-of-the-way town square in Rome, Italy, Drink Kong is the sort of bar that reminds people that drinking is supposed to be fun. Inside, it's a chic, modern, wraparound venue with an aesthetic that's a futuristic mashup of late 1970s and 80s arcade kitsch sprinkled with *Blade Runner*-esque Japanese influences along with King Kong design themes (the Kong reportedly because of the resemblance to hulking, bearded co-owner Patrick Pistolesi, who opened the bar in 2018 with the Jerry Thomas Speakeasy team)—even the ice is stamped with the bar's Kong-esque logo.

For its opening menu, bar manager Livio Morena created Big Trouble in Oaxaca. As the perfect reflection of the bar itself, the cocktail combines retro 80s neon cheekiness (Midori) with crowd-pleasing yet sophisticated ingredients such as tequila, ancho

chili and pineapple liqueurs, and lemon sour, all wrapped in a nostalgic nod to period pop culture; the name references the 1986 action-comedy *Big Trouble in Little China*, starring actor Kurt Russell.

Pistolesi says that one of the main reasons they used electric-green Midori melon liqueur in the cocktail was because in 2018 it just seemed so dated and weird that it might be the perfect way to attract attention to the bar and also show love for Japanese culture. It worked. Although the bar's thematic menu changes seasonally, Pistolesi says Big Trouble in Oaxaca has been one of Drink Kong's bestsellers since the beginning, helping to garner massive international awards in its first year.

"No chains will ever hold that," as they say in the 1933 original movie.

........................................................................

- 1½ oz (45 ml) tequila blanco
- ¾ oz (22 ml) pineapple liqueur
- ½ oz (15 ml) Midori liqueur
- ½ oz (15 ml) green ancho chili liqueur
- 1 oz (30 ml) fresh lemon juice
- ½ oz (15 g) sugar

Shake all ingredients with ice. Strain into a short tumbler or rocks glass over a large ice cube (at the bar it is stamped with the Drink Kong logo).

# FREYDIS

⏲ **2018**
⚐ **NEW YORK CITY, USA**
⚲ **SELMA SLABIAK**

⌂ **MOTHER OF PEARL**
⚗ **RUM**
🍸 **HURRICANE OR PEARL DIVER**

The classic Mai Tai is a deceptively simple cocktail that can be used as a template for many other flavor combinations. It was originally credited to Victor J. Bergeron, aka Trader Vic, in 1944, but now almost any working cocktail bartender knows how to make one, often with personal signature tweaks.

Mai Tais were a particular specialty at the now-closed Mother of Pearl tiki bar in New York City. It was already a favorite haunt of Copenhagen native Selma Slabiak when she was hired to work there in 2018. Encouraged to come up with her own recipe for the menu and feeling homesick for Nordic flavors, she settled on the Mai Tai as a base, and began to experiment.

Slabiak says various snacks she craved could be shipped from home by family and friends. However, what she was really yearning for were the frozen ice pops of her youth, particularly Kung Fu, which is a lemonade popsicle topped with a root beer-flavored section, all covered with a licorice-chocolate coating—slightly astringent, yet harmonious. In the Freydis, aquavit represents Scandinavia, and brings a needed anise-like nuance, while the peach ties it all together and brings a mid-summer feel.

"The cocktail is named after Freydis," explains Slabiak. "She was the sister of Leif Erickson, and the first Scandinavian woman to make it to America, or 'Vinland' as they called it in the old Norse tongue. She is a woman I related to because of our travels from the North to America in the name of adventure."

The drink became Slabiak's signature, served at Mother of Pearl, Donna Cocktail Club in Brooklyn, and now at her traveling Scandinavian cocktail pop-up, Selma's Bar.

---

- ¾ oz (22 ml) El Dorado 3-year rum
- ¾ oz (22 ml) Krogstad aquavit
- ¾ oz (22 ml) fresh lime juice
- ½ oz (15 ml) L'Orgeat almond liqueur (or homemade orgeat)
- ¼ oz (7 ml) Orchard peach liqueur

- Garnish: fresh mint sprig, edible orchid (optional)

Whip shake all ingredients without ice. Serve over crushed ice in a hurricane or pearl diver glass. Garnish with fresh mint and orchid, or whatever tickles your fancy.

# GRASSHOPPER GIBSON

🕐 2018
⚐ MEXICO CITY, MEXICO
👤 ISMAEL MARTÍNEZ

⌂ HANKY PANKY
🝯 SOTOL
🍸 MARTINI

Anyone expecting this drink to be a variation on the creamy dessert cocktail known as the Grasshopper is in for a bit of a shock. Quite the opposite: the Grasshopper Gibson is a unique take on the Gibson cocktail, which is made from gin, white vermouth, and its star garnish, the pickled onion. This showstopping sotol variation is served with dried grasshoppers along with the onion and a chunk of Parmigiano, and was created by Ismael Martínez, head bartender of Hanky Panky in Mexico City.

The bar is known for its creative twists on classics, and the Grasshopper Gibson is no exception. Martínez, who goes by the nickname "Pollo," says he wanted to come up with a house Martini concept that would please the palate of foreign visitors, who are the core of

the bar's clientele. But it was also necessary for the drink to be a vehicle for experiencing regional Mexican flavors and delicacies.

Grasshoppers (*chapulines*) can be found in many local markets around the country, and are a common ingredients in traditional cuisine. Dried whole grasshoppers are consumed as snacks and as main ingredients in tacos. "Every ingredient—the grasshopper, the Parmigiano, the onion—gets the cocktail's taste close to that of a traditional Oaxacan tlayuda [crunchy tortilla snack topped with beans, meat, cheese, and salsa]," he says.

The bar makes the drink with house-made cocktail onions, though one can sub store-bought. However, *chapulines* are an essential part of the experience.

- 2 oz (60 ml) Flor del Desierto sotol
- 1/3 oz (10 ml) vermouth mix (equal parts dry + bianco)
- 3 barspoons pickled onion juice (see below)

- Garnish: dried grasshopper, pickled cambray onion (store-bought or see below), Parmigiano

Stir all ingredients with ice and double strain into a chilled Martini glass. Serve with *chapuline*, onion, and Parmigiano on a pick or skewer over the drink.

## For the Onion and Onion Juice

- 3½ oz (100 g) salt-and-pepper-seasoned cambray onions
- 2 g cumin seeds
- 2 g dried rosemary
- 2 g dried thyme

- 8 oz (240 ml) equal parts cider, apple, and rice vinegars
- 1 oz (30 g) sugar
- 2¾ oz (80 ml) Amontillado sherry
- 1¼ oz (40 ml) orange liqueur
- 3½ oz (100 ml) Calvados
- 2 g sea salt

In a medium saucepan large enough to hold all the liquids, slow cook the first five ingredients over low heat for 5 minutes to make a reduction of the vinegars. Add the sugar, Amontillado sherry, orange liqueur, Calvados, and sea salt. Stir until dissolved. Remove from the heat. Mix the onions and the vinegar reduction while still warm and store, refrigerated, in a glass container for at least 24 hours before using.

# GRASSHOPPER PIE

2018
KUALA LUMPUR, MALAYSIA
DAVID HANS

THREE X CO
VODKA
NICK & NORA OR NOSING

The traditional Grasshopper is a creamy cocktail flavored with mint that is typically served as a dessert drink. Originating in the early twentieth century as a pousse-café—a layered drink—consisting of equal parts cream, crème de menthe, and crème de cacao, the combination was eventually streamlined into a shaken ice cream-like drink in 1920s New Orleans, likely at Tujague's, where it is still the bar's most popular cocktail. By the Swinging Sixties, "grasshopper" was its own chocolate-mint genre of dessert, boozy or not (most often the former). Having made a comeback as a sort of retro kitsch cocktail in the 2010s, the Grasshopper Pie at Three X Co in Kuala Lumpur, Malaysia is one of the most notable signature Grasshopper iterations served around the world.

Three X Co's unique take on the Grasshopper is inspired by local Malaysian food culture. Bartender David Hans created this variation in 2018, borrowing some of the classic cocktail's flavor profile, but it also takes inspiration from the traditional Hokkien snack, apam balik—a sweet pancake turnover sold in the local night markets—which he says was a childhood favorite. "Our Grasshopper Pie uses the core ingredient of apam balik—*jagung* [sweet corn]—as well as nuts, egg yolk, mint, and vodka to create this dessert cocktail," he explains. He mentions that the "pie" part of the name is a play on the word "*kuih*," the Malaysian word for a bite-sized dessert. "It's just like eating the *kuih* after your dinner, but as a cocktail."

• 1 oz (30 ml) peanut oil sous vide vodka*
• ¾ oz (22 ml) sweet corn juice (blend corn and water 1:1)
• ½ oz (15 ml) Frangelico liqueur
• ⅓ oz (10 ml) white crème de menthe liqueur
• 1 egg yolk

• Garnish: lemon wedge and matcha powder for the rim

Coat a Nick & Nora or nosing glass with matcha powder by rubbing the rim with the lemon wedge, then dipping it in a saucer of matcha powder. Set aside. Shake the remaining ingredients with ice until well chilled. Strain into the rimmed glass.

*Hans uses a peanut oil-infused vodka made in a sous-vide machine. To mimic that flavor, take a ½ cup (100 g) roasted peanuts and infuse them in a bottle of vodka for a few hours, then strain into another bottle with an airtight cap. Store in a cool, dry place for up to 6 months.

# HILLS AND VALLEYS

| | | | |
|---|---|---|---|
| 🕐 | 2018 | ⌂ | DEVIL'S DARLING |
| ⚑ | LONDON, UK | 🝙 | TOKAJI HÁRSLEVELU |
| 👤 | GERGŐ MURÁTH | 🍸 | COUPE |

........................................................................................

Cocktails mixed with ingredients made from fermented grapes are common—think vermouth, which starts as wine made from grapes; or sparkling wine cocktails, such as Mimosas or Negroni Sbagliato (page 184); or wine-based liqueurs, such as certain amari expressions. However, rarely is a cocktail composed of more than a couple of fermented grape ingredients. Hills and Valleys, created by Gergő Muráth, uses four of them.

Muráth, now a bar consultant, conceived of his signature Hills and Valleys in 2018 while behind the bar at Devil's Darling in London to showcase the different ways grapes could be featured in cocktails. It's made with semi-sweet Tokaji Hárslevelu, an aromatic white wine from his native Hungary, along with Chilean pisco (grape-based brandy), Riesling-based vermouth, and verjus cordial mixed with pear eau-de-vie and balanced by tartaric acid capillaire.

The ingredients are measured according to the Fibonacci Spiral, a 1:1:2:3:5:8 sequence—also known as the "golden ratio," "extreme and mean ratio," or "divine proportion"—that has been used by artists, architects, and other visionaries (Michelangelo, Salvador Dalí, the makers of Aston Martin, etc.), because it is thought to have the most aesthetically pleasing results. So why not try it with flavors?

Muráth admits some of the ingredients might be tough to source, but the Hills and Valleys concept can be adapted. The Tokaji is not the fully sweet dessert wine most of us are familiar with. If a substitute is needed, he suggests off-dry Riesling from Alsace or Mosel, or Austrian Grüner Veltliner. He also says any good-quality pear eau-de-vie will work in the recipe if the Hungarian one is unavailable.

........................................................................................

- 1 ⅓ oz (40 ml) Tokaji Hárslevelu
- Generous ¾ oz (25 ml) Chilean pisco (El Gobernador preferred)
- ½ oz (15 ml) Belsazar Riesling vermouth, or similar
- ⅓ oz (10 ml) Ferdinand's verjus cordial
- 1 tsp Tarpa Poire William eau-de-vie
- 1 tsp Tartaric Acid Capillaire

- Garnish: side of frozen white grapes

Stir all ingredients with ice until well chilled. Strain into a chilled coupe glass and serve with a saucer of frozen white grapes.

For the Tartaric Acid Capillaire

- 17 oz (500 ml) sugar syrup
- 1 oz (30 ml) tartaric acid
- ¾ oz (25 ml) orange blossom water

Mix all ingredients together, transfer to a sealable container, and store in the refrigerator for up to 10 days.

........................................................................................

# JEJU NEGRONI

🕐 2018
⚐ SEOUL, SOUTH KOREA
👤 LIM BYUNG-JIN

⌂ BAR CHAM
🝪 SOJU
🍸 ROCKS

Bar Cham is situated in a back alley near Gwanghwamun Square in Jongno-gu, one of the oldest and most storied areas of Seoul, South Korea. *Cham* means "oak" in Korean, and the aptly appointed bar features sleek wood designs in what is known as "hanok" style, referring to its location within a traditional dwelling. The bar specializes in Korean spirits and the use of local ingredients in new twists on classic recipes. One of Bar Cham's star signatures that helped it land on several "top" lists of Asian bars is the Jeju Negroni, created by bar manager Lim Byung-jin in 2018.

The drink borrows the traditional equal parts formula for a Negroni—gin, sweet vermouth, and Campari or other aperitivo. Here, in place of the gin, it's made with a tangerine- and Solomon's seal root-infused local rice spirit.

"We use soju named 'Gosorisul' traditionally produced on Jeju Island," explains Lim. "The term '*gosori*' is a word in Jeju island's dialect that means '*sojut-gori*,' a tiny clay pot for distillation." He says the tangerine (gam-gyul) is also grown on the volcanic island of Jeju, and Solomon's seal root is one of the ingredients Koreans consume as a light tea.

"We like to combine traditional soju with local products, and represent Korean culture," Lim says. "Compared to gin, traditional soju gives a mild and round mouthfeel from the rice, as well as light and fruity aromas. Infusing dehydrated tangerine peels and Solomon's seal root adds rich cacao flavor into the soju." It's a simple technique with effective results. The Jeju Negroni is a richer and bolder style than the classic gin recipe.

---

- 1 oz (30 ml) Solomon's Seal Root & Tangerine-Infused Gosorisul
- 1 oz (30 ml) sweet vermouth
- 1 oz (30 ml) Campari

Add all ingredients to a rocks glass over ice. Stir to combine, chill, and allow the ice to slightly dilute.

For the Solomon's Seal Root
& Tangerine-Infused Gosorisul

- ½ cup (100 g) dried tangerine peel
- 1 tbsp dried Solomon's seal root (available online)
- 25 oz (750 ml) bottle Gosorisul

Add the tangerine and root to the gin in a container with tight-fitting lid. Leave to infuse for at least 2 hours or overnight. Strain through a mesh strainer and cheesecloth (muslin) into a clean bottle.

# LECHE DE TIGRE MARTINI

| | | | |
|---|---|---|---|
| 🕐 | 2018 | ⌂ | BEBEDERO |
| ⚑ | PUNTARENAS, COSTA RICA | 🍶 | GIN |
| 👤 | LIZ FURLONG | 🍸 | MARTINI |

The Leche de Tigre Martini was invented in 2018 by Canadian-born bartender Liz Furlong at Bebedero in Puntarenas, Costa Rica. It's based on the Latin American delicacy caldosa, a variation on white fish ceviche, which in Costa Rica is traditionally served with picaritas (barbecue corn chips). Along with Latin American gin and dry vermouth, it's prepared with a clarified leche de tigre (caldosa) mix made from white fish, celery, cilantro (coriander), lime juice, ginger, and honey. The picaritas are served alongside the drink. Although Bebedero closed during the COVID-19 pandemic, Furlong's signature recipe lives on at the bars Cata on Playa Tamarindo and El Curandero in San José. The Leche de Tigre is considered one of the modern classics of Costa Rica.

Furlong explains that in Costa Rica, caldosa refers to a soup, which is why she refers to this drink as "Leche de Tigre." The picaritas are the local touch.

The cocktail also reflects the difference in the regional palate compared with the rest of Latin America. Furlong describes Costa Rican ceviche as "generally a little less acidic with a balance of lime or orange. You might even find people add ginger ale to their ceviche broth."

To represent these flavors in the drink, Furlong blends citrus mix along with the classic caldosa flavors of red bell pepper, onion, celery, cilantro (coriander), ginger, chili, and honey in a blender, then strains it. And yes, there is fish.

- 2 oz (60 ml) Xibal gin (or use another Latin American dry gin)
- ½ oz (15 ml) dry vermouth (ideally also hailing from Latin America)
- ½ oz (15 ml) Leche de Tigre Mix

- Garnish: red bell pepper curls and a side of picaritas (optional, if available)

Stir all ingredients with ice until well chilled. Strain into a Martini glass and garnish with the red pepper curls and picaritas, if you can find them.

### For the Leche de Tigre Mix

- 4 oz (115 g) sea bass, or another firm white fish (Furlong notes: "usually you use the scraps after making ceviche for this part")
- 5 oz (150 g) red bell pepper, seeded
- 5 oz (150 g) red onion, peeled
- 7 oz (200 g) celery
- 4 g cilantro (coriander)

- 14 oz (415 ml) Mesino lime (aka Persian lime) juice
- 10 oz (300 ml) Mandarin lime (aka Rangpur lime) juice, or use lemon juice
- ¾ oz (20 g) peeled fresh ginger
- 3 oz (60 ml) honey
- 1 Panamanian chili, seeded and finely chopped
- Salt, to taste (at least 2 good pinches)

Add all ingredients except the chili and salt to a blender and blend until smooth. Add a little cold water and blend for 2 minutes until smooth, adding more water if needed. Add the chili and salt to taste (the mix should be spicy and salty). Strain through cheesecloth (muslin) and store in the refrigerator for up to a day, or in the freezer for up to 2 months.

# PAHADI LEMONADE

C. 2018
NEW DELHI, INDIA
YANGDUP LAMA

SIDECAR
GIN, VODKA, OR RUM
DOUBLE ROCKS OR HIGHBALL

Sidecar, in Greater Kailash, New Delhi is one of the most famous bars in India and consistently ranks in "top bars" lists. It was opened in 2018 by Yangdup Lama and Minakshi Singh, who are also the team behind the successful Cocktails & Dreams. Sidecar is split into two levels. The bottom floor functions as an all-day bookstore café with a selection of locally produced teas and coffees. The upper floor is a self-described "bartender's dream," serving modern and classic cocktails that are made in-house using a wide variety of ingredients, with seasonal and eco-friendly concerns in mind. Pahadi Lemonade is one of Lama's signatures and exemplifies the theme of translating Indian culinary traditions into cocktails.

Its star ingredient is pickled lime. "Pickling, also known as *achar*, is an old Indian practice of preserving vegetables and other ingredients," explains Lama. "Pickles can be sweet, tangy, or salty and are served with most meals, a great complement for most traditional food in the Indian sub-continent."

The Pahadi Lemonade is also a nod to the tradition of serbet, refreshing citrus drinks prepared in summertime. The cocktail is sweetened with wild honey from the Himalayas.

At Sidecar, salt-pickled lime is made in-house and kept at the back bar, along with the other homemade tinctures, infusions, bitters, and grogs. Customers are given the option to choose their preferred base for the drink—gin, vodka, or light rum—which is added to the preserved lime and other ingredients, then topped off with soda water.

- 2 oz (60 ml) gin, vodka, or light rum
- 1 tbsp salt pickled lime (homemade or store-bought)
- ¾ oz (20 ml) wild honey (Sidecar uses one made in the Himalayas)
- Soda water, to top

- Garnish: candied lime wheel

Shake all ingredients except the soda water with ice until well chilled. Strain into a double rocks or highball glass over fresh ice. Top with the soda water and garnish with a candied lime wheel.

# PALOMA DE LA CASA

⏲ 2018
⚐ GUADALAJARA, MEXICO
☖ EL GALLO ALTANERO
🍸 ALAN MULVIHILL, AMELIA
BOOT, AND TEAM

⌂ EL GALLO ALTANERO
🍶 TEQUILA
🍸 HIGHBALL

El Gallo Altanero is one of the most famous contemporary cocktail bars in Guadalajara, Mexico and has been named in the World's 50 Best Bars. It is accessed through Café Fitzroy, a bright, traditional-looking adobe-plastered coffee shop. But ascend a narrow set of stairs, and a fetching, dimly lit bar set off by a glowing stained-glass rendering of an agave plant awaits. It is like climbing to an agave shrine, and the reward for the effort comes in the form of delicious drinks. The cocktail menu changes regularly, but one of the signatures that has remained a constant since 2018 is Paloma de la Casa.

For the drink, the bar team led by Alan Mulvihill and Amelia Boot reinvented the Paloma—the classic Mexican highball made with tequila or mezcal and grapefruit soda, or soda with fresh grapefruit juice—for a modern clientele. Instead of grapefruit juice or flavored soda, it is made with a special ingredient derived from lime and grapefruit oleo out of the scraps of fruit used for making other cocktails. Using the whole fruit showcases the bar's commitment to sustainability while paying homage to the classic Mexican staple. Since the bar is in Jalisco, the heart of tequila country, the cocktail is made with tequila (the bar uses Tromba Blanco 44).

Paloma de la Casa has represented El Gallo Altanero on the cocktail circuit—served at various pop-ups around the world and drinks conventions such as New Orleans' Tales of the Cocktail.

---

- 1½ oz (45 ml) tequila blanco (the bar uses Tromba Blanco 44)
- 2½ oz (75 ml) Batch Grapefruit
- Sparkling mineral water, to top

- Garnish: Tajín spice and lime wedge for the rim, dehydrated grapefruit wheel

Rim a highball glass with Tajín (available in most supermarkets or online) by rubbing it with a lime wedge then dipping it into a saucer containing a thin coating of the spice. Set aside. Shake the tequila and Batch Grapefruit with ice until well chilled. Strain into the rimmed glass filled with fresh ice. Top with mineral water.

For the Batch Grapefruit

Note: you will need to prepare the oleo a couple of days ahead. Cover a pile of the discarded citrus peel (about 3½ oz/100 g) with enough sugar to cover. Let sit in a plastic container or sealed jar at room temperature for 2 to 3 days. Strain out and discard the skins.

- 4 oz (120 ml) lime oleo
- 8 oz (240 ml) grapefruit oleo
- 22 oz (640 ml fresh grapefruit juice

Combine the ingredients together and store in the refrigerator in a sealed container for up to 5 days.

# BAHIA BEACH

🕐 2019
⚑ BERLIN, GERMANY
𝗔 FIONA BRUCE CASTRO

⌂ MONKEY BAR
🝪 RUM
🍸 HIGHBALL

Although the bar opens at midday, the drinks service really gets into full swing at Monkey Bar starting around dusk till the wee hours. Located on the rooftop terrace of the 25hours Hotel Bikini Berlin, above the Berlin Zoo (yes, overlooking the monkeys), it's considered one of the busiest bars in the city. But fast shouldn't mean sub-par. In 2019, Spanish-born staff bartender Fiona Bruce Castro was called upon to design the bar's first conceptual menu, which included a lasting signature, Bahia Beach.

The clientele are mostly tourists, who, according to Castro, often order drinks by color or potency: "I want the red one . . ." or "I want the strongest one . . ." etc. But Castro really wanted the drinks to stand out beyond the typical "party cocktail" palate, so customers would remember the flavor, not just the color. "Our goal was to please the crowd but also sneak in other spirit categories that they wouldn't

usually order, maintaining the balance and keeping it delish," she says. "We made drinks with calvados, cognac, amari . . . you name it." She says drinks like Bahia Beach—a nonblender Piña Colada-esque number that combines two kinds of rum, coconut water, lime juice, orgeat, saline solution, and the syrup from a jar of pre-served amarena cherries—were a hit.

Drinks from that conceptual menu sold over 200 a night, on top of other well-worn classics. Castro left the bar in December 2021, but because of its well-balanced structure of festive tropical flavors, the cocktail has since landed on other menus around town, including Tucker Brunch, Orania.Bar, and various pop-ups.

Castro says Bahia Beach can be tweaked according to whatever ingredients are on hand, using alternate fruit juices or subbing the amarena syrup with others.

- 1 ⅓ oz (40 ml) aged Jamaican rum
- ¾ oz (20 ml) unaged overproof Jamaican rum
- 1¾ oz (50 ml) coconut water
- ¾ oz (25 ml) lime juice
- ⅓ oz (10 ml) orgeat
- ⅓ oz (10 ml) amarena syrup (from a jar of amarena cherries)
- 2 dashes saline solution

- Garnish: amarena cherry and mint sprig

Shake all ingredients with ice until well chilled and frothy. Double strain into a tall glass filled with fresh ice. Garnish with an amarena cherry and mint sprig.

# CACAO SBAGLIATO

🕐 2019
⚑ BOGOTÁ, COLOMBIA
👤 ERIN ROSE

⌂ SORELLA
◊ VERMOUTH
🍸 WINE OR SPRITZ

········································································································

When American ex-pat bartender Erin Rose opened the Italian restaurant/bar Sorella in Bogotá, Colombia, her approach was to create a menu featuring what she refers to as "aperitivo tropical," that is, aperitivi (cocktails such as Negronis and Americanos) with native South American flourishes. "I was looking to use local products from Colombia and also highlight that many amari and fortified wines in general that we think of as 'European' wouldn't exist without ingredients taken from South America," says Rose. She lists "cochinilla that was Campari's colorant until the early 2000s, the cascarilla bark still featured in various amari, including Campari [now], and the cinchona bark, native to the Andes, which of course gave rise to a whole class of kinas, such as Lillet and Dubonnet, as well as tonic water." In this vein, her signature 2019 Cacao Sbagliato for Sorella has become a Colombian modern classic.

Although *sbagliato* is Italian for "mistake," Rose's take on the sparkling aperitivo—traditionally prepared with sweet vermouth, Campari, and Prosecco—has very deliberate intentions with its use of vanilla and cacao nibs. "The vermouths available in Colombia are limited and I wanted to re-create the chocolate and vanilla notes of vermouths I had loved in other countries, like Carpano Antica, using ingredients from here," Rose explains. She mentions that Colombia has twenty-three different native species of vanilla and various species of ancestral cacaos. "Sbagliato was a way to support local producers cultivating cacao and vanilla while still staying in a traditionally Italian cocktail profile to assure a good fit with the food."

Rose says she prefers to treat the Sbagliato like the "hip cousin to the spritz," served in a wine glass with a splash of soda.

········································································································

- 1½ oz (45 ml) Cacao vermouth
- ½ oz (15 ml) Campari
- 1 oz (30 ml) Prosecco (or other dry sparkling wine)
- 1 oz (30 ml) soda water, to top

- Garnish: orange wheel

Add the vermouth and Campari to a wine or spritz glass. Add ice and stir until chilled. Add the Prosecco and top with soda. Stir briefly to mix. Garnish with an orange wheel.

### For the Cacao Vermouth

- 5 oz (150 ml) Dubonnet rouge
- 5 oz (150 ml) sweet vermouth
- 1 tsp cacao nibs
- ⅛ vanilla bean (pod), split

Mix all ingredients together in a container with a tight-fitting lid, then leave for 2 to 3 days at room temperature before straining. Store in the refrigerator for up to a month.

# DONNER, PARTY OF TWO

- 🕐 2019
- ⚐ USA/UK
- ⚲ CHOCKIE TOM

- ⌂ DOOMMERSIVE POP-UP
- ⚱ TEQUILA
- ⍦ COOKIE JAR

........................................................................................

This is one of the rare examples of a large format cocktail that is specifically designed to be shared between two people. Its creator is hospitality consultant and educator Chockie Tom of Doommersive (formerly Doom Tiki), a traveling cocktail pop-up that focuses on cultural education and awareness, which she co-founded between New York City and the UK in 2019 in collaboration with rum personas Austin Hartman and (her now husband) Gergő Muráth.

The drink is a response to the gruesome story of the Donner Party, a wagon train of pioneers who were en route to California from the Midwest when they became stranded in the Sierra Nevadas in the winter of 1846–47. They famously became so desperate for food that they turned to cannibalism. However, rarely mentioned are the lasting impacts of that winter on the indigenous tribes who lived in the area.

"The inspiration for this drink started with looking for a large cocktail vessel. I settled on a wagon-shaped cookie jar, inspired by the reclamation of the term 'wagon burner'," explains Tom. The acorn liqueur is a nod to her Pomo family from California, who historically consumed and traded acorns. The cornflake orgeat represents dried flakes of corn that were historically given as government commodities. Bow & Arrow's Scenic West Hazy IPA, made by the first female-owned Indigenous brewery, adds body and a citrusy kick. Lastly, she says of the garnish, "I couldn't pass up a flaming lime shell with arrow-shaped swizzles."

........................................................................................

Serves 2

- 2 oz (60 ml) tequila blanco (Tom uses El Tesoro)
- 1½ oz (45 ml) aged light rum (Tom uses Cruzan)
- 1 oz (30 ml) Licor de Bellota
- 2 oz (60 ml) Cornflake Orgeat
- 1½ oz (45 ml) fresh lime juice
- 3 oz (90 ml) Bow & Arrow Scenic West Hazy IPA

- Garnish: 6 dashes Better Bitters Cali almond bitters, 2 arrow swizzle sticks, hollowed out lime shell filled with ultraproof rum, set alight

Combine all ingredients except the IPA in a cocktail shaker with ice and give it a hearty shake. Strain into an upcycled cookie jar filled with crushed ice. Top with IPA. Garnish with the bitters, swizzle sticks, and lime shell.

For the Cornflake Orgeat

In a blender or food processor, pulverize ¾ cup (18 g) cornflakes until super fine. Add to 8 oz (240 ml) prepared classic orgeat (store-bought or homemade) and shake well before using.

........................................................................................

# INDIANO

🕐 2019
⚐ BARCELONA, SPAIN
👤 MOE ALJAFF

⌂ TWO SCHMUCKS
🍸 WHITE RUM
🍸 HIGHBALL OR DOUBLE ROCKS

One of the age-old questions is whether one can open a dive bar on purpose, or if "dive" just happens through time, character, and spilled beer. Another is whether a dive bar is even allowed to serve good cocktails. Two Schmucks, housed in a former taco joint in the historic El Raval district of Barcelona, Spain, is one of the rare exceptions to both of those questions, billing itself as a "five-star dive bar" while promoting "good drinks and good vibes." The business saw a change in ownership in 2022, but Indiano is a 2019 signature from one of the bar's original founders, Moe Aljaff.

Spain is known for its exceptionally sweltering summers and, to help endure them, its gin and tonic ("gin tonic") culture. Indiano is technically a variation on the tonic highball, however it eschews the ubiquitous *copa de* *balon* glass and the floating horticultural extravaganzas as garnish. Here, the gin is swapped out for white rum, which is mixed with coffee, sweet sherry, and Fernet-Branca Menta (the minty variation of the bitter liqueur). Therefore, it's more of a caffeinated bridge between a rum tonic and a Mojito, a drink Aljaff told *Mixology Magazine* in 2018 was "highly underrated."

Along with other Mojito variations, it's one of a few rum cocktails from early Two Schmucks menus that has endured. And, of course, the use of Pedro Ximénez sherry is a nod to Spain's native fortified wine. The use of this sweet style eliminates the need for further sweetening agents in the drink and plays well off the brightness of the rum, while adding nutty richness to the bitter earthiness of the coffee.

- ¾ oz (40 ml) white rum
- ⅓ oz (10 ml) Pedro Ximénez (PX) sherry
- 1 tsp (5 ml) Fernet-Branca Menta
- 1 oz (35 ml) chilled brewed coffee, or cold brew
- 2 drops saline solution
- 3 oz (90 ml) tonic water

- Garnish: mint sprig

Shake all ingredients except the tonic water with ice until well chilled and frothy. Add the tonic water, then fine strain all into a highball glass or double rocks glass over fresh ice. Garnish with a mint sprig.

# KYIV SOUR

🕑 2019
⚑ KYIV, UKRAINE
🧍 DMYTRO SHOVKOPLIAS

⌂ PAROVOZ SPEAKEASY
🍶 WHISKY
🍸 ROCKS

Parovoz Speakeasy is located on the ground floor of what was once one of the oldest movie houses in Kyiv, Ukraine. However, the name has little to do with the silver screen—*Parovoz* translates to "locomotive," referring to its long, narrow interior. Here, modern cocktails are served in a setting that's a nod to the grand style of early twentieth-century nightlife.

Although Parovoz opened in 2012, one of its most beloved recipes wasn't found on the menu until 2019. The Kyiv Sour, created by bartender and co-owner Dmytro "Dima" Shovkoplias, is a take on the New York Sour—a bourbon or rye whiskey sour with a float of red wine—using iconic local ingredients in place of traditional ones as a celebration of Ukrainian heritage. It's sweetened with a syrup made

from chestnuts, the symbol of the capital city. In lieu of the wine float, homemade bitters made from cranberries and beets (beetroot), two ingredients found in much of the local cuisine, are sprayed over the foam in the glass at the end. And instead of American whiskey, Shovkoplias swaps in Scotch blended with grain whisky for the base as a nod to Ukraine's most important agricultural export.

In spring 2022, Parovoz Speakeasy celebrated its 20th anniversary, just a couple of weeks after Russia launched its first strikes in the country. As of this writing, Kyiv has not been captured, and the bar has remained open, serving Kyiv Sours and other libations, albeit with more limited hours.

• 1¾ oz (50 ml) Naked Grouse Scotch whisky
• ¾ oz (22 ml) fresh lemon juice
• ¾ oz (22 ml) chestnut syrup (a simple syrup made with 1 part chestnut purée and 1 part gum arabic)
• 3 drops Easy Foam or Fee Foam (bottled non-egg-white foam alternatives)

• Garnish: spray of cranberry & beet (beetroot) bitters over the top, beet (beetroot) chip

Shake all ingredients with ice until well chilled and foamy. Strain into a rocks glass over ice chunks. Spray the bitters over the top and add the beet (beetroot) chip.

# MIDNIGHT RAMBLER

- 🕐 2019
- ⚐ DALLAS, USA
- ⚇ CHRISTY POPE
  AND CHAD SOLOMON

- ⌂ · MIDNIGHT RAMBLER
- 🍾 BOURBON
- 🍸 DOUBLE ROCKS

When husband and wife bar team Christy Pope and Chad Solomon opened Midnight Rambler in Dallas, Texas in 2014, it was a new era in the cocktail world—but it was missing something. Wildly creative as cocktail names can be, gone were the days of simply naming a house cocktail after, well, the house.

In May 2019, when devising the autumn menu that would be called Deep Cuts II, Solomon was inspired by famous house-named signature drinks, such as the Pegu Club, Sazerac, Clover Club, etc. He decided Midnight Rambler should have a Midnight Rambler cocktail, and put a lot of thought into the recipe process.

He decided, "The drink should be reflective of the time, place, and Midnight Rambler creators [Chad Solomon and Christy Pope], and the bar that Midnight Rambler has evolved to be thus far over its first five years."

The drink Solomon concocted features flavors and products that he considered to be reflective of the bar, its home locale of Dallas, and the local cuisine that incorporates Mexican ingredients. These influences are all presented in a common style of serve at MR, what he refers to as the "Fancy Cocktail."

As for adapting the recipe at home, he says he purposely came up with separate recipes so one could be easily made outside of the bar, too. Here are both.

Bar version

- ½ tsp rich Demerara syrup
- 2½ tsp (12.5 ml) Ancho Reyes liqueur
- 2 oz (60 ml) Balcones TX Pot Still bourbon
- 1 dash Bittermens xocolatl mole bitters
- 1 dash Angostura bitters
- 2 drops mineral saline

- Garnish: Rio Star grapefruit (pink grapefruit) twist

Measure all the ingredients into a mixing glass, then add ice. Stir until chilled and just shy of full dilution, then strain over a large rock into a double rocks glass. Express the grapefruit twist over the top of the drink, and add to the drink to garnish.

Home version

- ½ oz (15 ml) Ancho Reyes/Demerara Blend*
- 2 oz (60 ml) Balcones TX Pot Still bourbon

- Garnish: Rio Star grapefruit (pink grapefruit) twist

Prepare as opposite.

* Ancho Reyes/Demerara Blend is 1 part 2:1 Demerara syrup and 5 parts Ancho Reyes.

# MILKICILLIN

⏲ 2019
⚐ BUENOS AIRES, ARGENTINA
🜨 SEBASTIÁN ATIENZA

⌂ TRES MONOS
🜂 WHISKY
🍸 ROCKS

One of the most famous modern classic cocktails is the Penicillin (page 234)—a mixture of unpeated blended Scotch, lemon, ginger syrup, and a float of Islay peated Scotch—created in 2005 by Sam Ross at Milk & Honey in New York City. The cocktail itself is a riff on another Milk & Honey neoclassic, the Gold Rush (page 218). Milkicillin, invented in 2019 by Sebastián Atienza at Tres Monos in Buenos Aires, Argentina continues the Gold Rush evolution by mashing up the Penicillin with a milk punch.

"When building a new cocktail, in Tres Monos we usually mix different classics to create new flavors," says Charly Aguinsky, owner of Tres Monos. "In the case of the Milkicillin, we combine a Penicillin and a Milk Punch, so the process is a bit more complex than the classic Penicillin, but the outcome is a smoother, more delicate cocktail." The punch uses both green tea and ginger tea for further dimension. Aguinsky says the Milkicillin is one of the most popular drinks at the bar, and because of its bright and restorative flavor profile, since its inception has been a favorite all year round.

The milk punch component is quite labor intensive and must be prepared at least a day ahead of time, but it's well worth the effort. The recipe is enough to make fifteen to twenty cocktails, which makes it an ideal candidate for parties and holiday gatherings. However, if there is no immediate need for that many Milkicillins in one sitting, the mix will keep in the refrigerator for at least ten days and would be delicious on its own with a spritz of soda water. Just remember there is whisky already in it!

---

- 3 oz (90 ml) Milkicillin Clarified Milk Punch
- 1 barspoon peated Scotch whisky (to float)

- Garnish: lemon wheel

Pour the Milkicillin mix into a rocks glass over one large cube. Float the peated Scotch whisky over the top. Add a lemon wheel to garnish.

For the Milkicillin Clarified Milk Punch

- 8 green tea bags and 8 ginger tea bags
- 41 oz (1.16 liters) boiling water
- 15 x 1-inch (2.5 cm) pieces whole ginger, peeled and sliced
- 2½ cups (500 g) sugar
- 8¼ oz (250 ml) honey
- ¾ oz (20 g) whole cloves
- ¾ oz (20 g) dried coriander
- 6 g cardamom pods

- 15 pieces each lemon and orange peel, cut into 1-inch (2.5 cm) strips
- 35 oz (1 liter) unpeated Scotch whisky
- 28 oz (800 ml) whole (full-fat) milk
- 41 oz (1.16 liters) fresh lemon juice

Brew the green and ginger teas in the water and let cool. Mash the ginger in a large bowl. In a large plastic container, add the sugar and honey with the ginger mixture and incorporate to form a molasses-like mixture. Add the spices, citrus skins, and the tea blend and let macerate, stirring the molasses until dissolved. Then add the whisky, cover with plastic wrap (cling film), and let rest for an hour. Once the time has elapsed, warm the milk and add it to the mix with the lemon juice. Filter the mixture into a separate container. The liquid should be clear.

# MYSTERY SOLVER

- 2019
- DENVER, USA
- ALEX JUMP
- DEATH & CO
- WHISKEY
- ROCKS

Bartender Alex Jump grew up snacking on Coca-Cola and peanuts, as many do when they're from Chattanooga, Tennessee. That might not sound so unusual, except in that part of the world, the nuts and soda aren't consumed side by side as a pairing, per se. Explains Jump, "It's traditional to take a bag of peanuts and pour them into your bottle of Coca-Cola, so you've got a snack and a drink all in one while keeping one free hand for whatever task you've got going on." It was this flavor profile that inspired the first iteration of Mystery Solver, conceived in 2015 behind the bar at Chattanooga's Main Street Meats, a combination bar and butcher shop.

The first version was simply a Coke with 2 oz (60 ml) poured out and replaced with Chattanooga whiskey and topped with salted peanuts. When Alex made the move to Denver, Colorado to help open the new (and much higher elevation) location of New York City's

Death & Co in 2017, Mystery Solver stayed in her back pocket. However, as cute as the presentation was (it's still on the menu at Main Street Meats), the swank Ramble Hotel Lobby bar called for a more refined offering than a Coke bottle filled with nuts and whiskey.

For the autumn/winter 2019 menu, Jump, then Death & Co bar manager and Speed Rack cancer charity bartending competition winner, revised her signature cocktail to celebrate the classic childhood tastes of peanut butter and jelly. She infuses rye whiskey with peanut butter, complemented by American Single Malt, berry liqueur, cane syrup, and bitters, served Old Fashioned style.

Although she's now mostly found on the other side of the bar as a consultant, Jump says Mystery Solver, with its comforting hug-in-a-glass flavor profile, is still a favorite go-to.

---

- 1.25 oz (45 ml) Peanut Butter-Infused Rye Whiskey
- ½ oz (15 ml) American single malt (Jump uses Westward)
- ¼ oz (7 ml) Giffard Framboise liqueur
- 1 tsp cane syrup
- 1 dash Angostura bitters
- 1 dash orange bitters

- Garnish: orange twist

Stir all ingredients with ice in a mixing glass. Strain into a rocks glass over fresh ice (a large cube is best). Express the oils from a piece of orange peel into the drink, skin side down, then twist and place in the glass.

For the Peanut Butter-Infused Rye Whiskey

Note: scale down as needed

- 25 oz (750ml) bonded rye whiskey (Jump uses Rittenhouse)
- ¾ oz (20 g) smooth peanut butter

Combine the rye and peanut butter in a blender and blend until well mixed. Pour into a plastic storage container, cover, and store in the freezer overnight (the alcohol will keep it from being frozen solid). Strain through a coffee filter, then keep refrigerated for up to 10 days.

# SELVA

🕐 2019
⚑ OAXACA CITY, MEXICO
🨂 ALEXANDRA PURCARU

⌂ SELVA
🍶 MEZCAL
🍸 COUPE

Selva is the house drink at the award-winning cocktail bar of the same name in Oaxaca City, Mexico, invented in 2019 by its head bartender, Alexandra Purcaru. Each drink on the menu celebrates a different regional cuisine, plant, or community and Selva is emblematic of the bar's philosophy. "Our drinks are an ode to the diversity of Oaxaca," says Purcaru. "We strive for synergy between innovation and tradition, and we use local ingredients, kitchen techniques, and Mexican distillates to create gourmet cocktails."

Selva is the liquid cocktail version of one of the dishes found on the menu at the venue's sister restaurant next door, and like the drinks served at Selva bar, the offerings exemplify Oaxacan cuisine and native ingredients. "The inspiration came from a popular dish, Hoja Santa, served at Los Danzantes Restaurant next door. Hoja santa is a bright green leaf the shape of an elephant ear. The dish is a whole hoja santa leaf filled with Oaxacan cheese, goat cheese, and tomatillo baked together at low temperature," says Purcaru. The cocktail consists of hoja santa leaf, mezcal, Ancho Reyes green poblano liqueur, agave honey, lemon juice, and juniper tincture.

Purcaru explains the flavor of hoja santa as "a mix of pepper, eucalyptus, tarragon, licorice, mint, anise. It's literally a 'sacred leaf', also known as yerba santa, hierba santa, Mexican pepperleaf, root beer plant, and sacred pepper."

If one is unable to sip the cocktail at the source, Purcaru says the cocktail's flavor is meant to be transportive. "My goal with the Selva cocktail was not to make a copy of the dish but to re-create the sensations I had the first time I tried hoja santa. It's literally a jungle in a glass with expansive layers of flavor."

- 1 fresh hoja santa leaf
- 1½ oz (45 ml) Mezcal Alipus Santa Ana
- ½ oz (15 ml) Ancho Reyes Verde
- ¼ oz (7 ml) agave honey
- ½ oz (15 ml) fresh lemon juice
- 2 dashes juniper tincture

- Garnish: spheres of grilled Oaxaca cheese and basil leaves threaded through a cocktail pick

Remove the midrib from a fresh hoja santa leaf. In a blender, combine the prepared hoja santa and the rest of the ingredients and blend until well mixed. Transfer the ingredients to a shaker tin with ice. Shake until the shaker feels cold to the touch. Double strain into a chilled coupe. Place the cocktail pick containing the garnish over the glass.

# CAPTAIN ALICE

○ 2020
⚑ NEW YORK CITY, USA
👤 LUCKY MICHAELS

⌂ N/A
🍸 MEZCAL
🍸 DOUBLE ROCKS

Captain Alice was created by Lucky Michaels, the first trans woman to be recognized by the culinary nonprofit James Beard Foundation, at its Talent Beyond Walls event for International Women's Day in early 2020. The cocktail was created as a tribute to the legacy of all women in leadership roles, and features Ilegal Joven mezcal, bitters, Aperol, and cold brew coffee, which honors early twentieth-century business owner Alice Foote MacDougall.

MacDougall was the first woman in New York City to export her own coffee beans and set up her own wholesale coffee roasting business, initially as a storefront in Grand Central Station in 1919. With so many requests from potential customers to taste the products before making purchases, she set out chairs and tables to operate as both a café and coffee retail outlet and renamed it The Little Coffee Shop, which also famously served waffles. She eventually opened four more locations.

In the Captain Alice cocktail, the cold brew tie-in to MacDougall's memory adds an earthy, roasted kick, yet like a well-made Espresso Martini (page 190), the proportions of the coffee element serve as a complement to the other ingredients instead of overwhelming them with bitterness. "This well-balanced cocktail was designed to mix up your palate," says Michaels, who is as of this writing one of the lead bartenders at the prestigious Gage & Tollner restaurant in downtown Brooklyn. "It's smoky, spicy, and has a sour pucker."

To continue the sweet-and-sour theme, she finishes this artful concoction by adding a slice of refreshingly sweet grilled mandarin orange coated in blue agave syrup that's been lightly coated with citric acid.

- 2 oz (60 ml) Ilegal Joven mezcal
- ½ oz (15 ml) cold brew coffee
- ¾ oz (22 ml) Hella bitters
- ½ oz (15 ml) Aperol
- ½ oz (15 ml) lemon juice
- 2 dashes Angostura bitters

- Garnish: grilled mandarin orange slice coated with blue agave syrup and powdered citric acid

Prepare the garnish by grilling a slice of mandarin orange until browned, then brush with blue agave syrup. Set aside. Shake all ingredients with ice until well chilled. Strain into a double rocks glass over fresh ice. Lightly dust the mandarin slice with powdered citric acid, then skewer it on a cocktail pick and set over the glass.

# GIPPSLAND ICED TEA

🕐 2020
⚐ MELBOURNE, AUSTRALIA
👤 MATTHEW JENSEN

⌂ FARMER'S DAUGHTERS
🍶 WHISKY
🍸 STEMLESS WINE

.................................................................................

While there have been a handful of farm-to-table themed restaurants since at least the mid-twentieth century, the 2000s is when the concept of provenanced-based food and drink truly became a worldwide phenomenon. Farmer's Daughters is a tri-level culinary complex in Melbourne, Australia that includes a rooftop bar, a main restaurant that surrounds a kitchen with an open "campfire"-esque design, and a takeout deli, all with a focus on the seasonal produce and products unique to the Gippsland district of Victoria. This region stretches from Melbourne all the way to the New South Wales border and is rich with farmland, vineyards, beaches, lakes, mountains, and forests. The mostly all-Gippsland represented drinks menu is inspired by the local winemakers, brewers, and distillers that dot the map. Since Farmer's Daughters inception in 2020, the Gippsland Iced Tea has been one of the venue's biggest sellers, created by beverage director Matthew Jensen.

The food-friendly drink is the modern Melbourne cuisine and drink scene represented in a glass. It's based around Starward Two-Fold whisky, a modern local brand that has enjoyed much international success. This expression is distilled from both wheat and malted barley and matured in Shiraz and Cabernet wine casks from local producers, speaking to Jensen's training as a sommelier. The whisky is combined with orange and lemon myrtle tea from Outback Chef, and Marionette orange curaçao, both local producers, as well as a homemade "faux lime," aka lime cordial.

The whisky is available in many regions worldwide, though the tea might be harder to source. If none can be found, try swapping it out for blood orange tea made with rooibos.

.................................................................................

- 1 oz (30 ml) Starward Two-Fold Australian whisky
- 2½ oz (75 ml) iced tea brewed using Outback Chef orange and lemon myrtle tea
- ½ oz (15 ml) Marionette orange curaçao
- 1 oz (30 ml) faux lime/lime cordial (homemade or store-bought)
- ½ oz (15 ml) simple syrup

Shake all ingredients with ice until well chilled. Strain into a stemless wine glass over fresh ice.

# THE HEISENBERG

🕑 2020                           ⌂ TESOURO
⚐ GOA, INDIA                    🝙 FENI
🙎 ARIJIT BOSE                   🍸 DOUBLE ROCKS

·······································································································

It was simply bad luck that Tesouro opened in 2020 in Colvá in South Goa, India, just as the COVID-19 pandemic hit. However, the team, led by Donovan Vaz, Arijit Bose, and Pankaj Balachandran, found a means of survival, and even delivered to-go cocktails on bikes during peak monsoon season, according to an article in *50 Best Stories* (the bar ranks in Asia's top 50). Once the team could open to the public again, a casual yet finely tuned level of hospitality, and cocktails such as The Heisenberg, grabbed the global bar scene's attention.

In many ways the blue-hued cocktail symbolizes the theme of perseverance in tough times, yet, like its inspiration, it comes with unexpected twists. Although other Heisenberg iterations exist—one created at Experimental Cocktail Club in New York City, another at Mark's Bar in London—Bose, who created Tesouro's variation, explains the inspiration, which, unlike the others, is particularly story-specific in presentation:

"The drink is an ode to one of my favourite shows, *Breaking Bad*, where a down-on-his-luck chemistry professor with the help of an ex-student creates a morally questionable product called 'Blue Sky'. The code name for the character Walter White [Bryan Cranston] was 'Heisenberg,' where the drink gets its name, and it's served with blue ice." (Don't worry. It's only frozen blue curaçao, citrus, and water.)

The Heisenberg's base ingredient is Cazulo coconut feni, a local Goan spirit that is reminiscent of mezcal, and which shares similar traditional roots. *Cazulo* means "firefly" in the local Konkani Goan language, and this spirit comes from a 300-year-old distillery.

Bose reminds us that cocktails should be delicious, but there's room for creativity and a little cheekiness. "The drink is often meant to make us realize not to take ourselves too seriously behind the bar and have fun with guests," he says.

·······································································································

- ¾ oz (22 ml) Cazulo coconut feni
- ¾ oz (22 ml) vermouth blanc
- ¾ oz (22 ml) Skinos Mastiha
- ½ oz (15 ml) fresh lemon juice
- Tonic water, to top
  (the bar uses East Imperial)
- 2 dashes absinthe
- Blue Ice, to serve

Shake all ingredients except the tonic and absinthe with regular ice until well chilled. Strain over blue ice into a double rocks glass. Top with tonic and add 2 dashes of absinthe.

For the Blue Ice

Combine equal parts blue curaçao, water, and fresh lemon juice. Add to an ice mold with 1-inch (2.5 cm) cubes. Freeze until ready to use.

·······································································································

# LAS PIÑAS

🕐 2020
⚑ ALBUQUERQUE, USA
👤 BAR TEAM

🏠 LOS CONEJOS
🍶 MEZCAL
🍸 ROCKS

Las Piñas is a gingery, tropical concoction that debuted on the opening menu for Los Conejos, an agave spirits-focused bar that opened in 2020 as the sister bar to the buzzy Copper Lounge in Albuquerque, New Mexico. Due to COVID-19 pandemic lockdown restrictions, and in the interest of public safety, the cozy and intimate Copper Lounge was unable to operate under its normal service conditions, however Los Conejos could accommodate outdoor seating. Las Piñas was an instant fan favorite and has remained on the menu ever since.

Although it opened as a "pandemic baby," Los Conejos wasn't just a desperate, slapdash pivot, but something that could grow into an integral part of the expanding Albuquerque cocktail culture once indoor service safely returned, explains general manager Giovanni Martinez. "We wanted to create a modern-day Mexican cocktail bar, not a 'Mexican themed' bar but an actual cocktail bar that would fit right into the cocktail scenes in modern-day Mexico City, Oaxaca City, or Merida." It features a well-curated list of mezcal, tequila, raicilla, sotol, and bacanora, offers educational spirits flights, and has a dedicated section on the menu for sophisticated Michelada (Mexican beer shandy) variations. He says it was important not to perpetuate common cultural stereotypes. "No sombreros or pictures of Pancho Villa, etc."

Martinez says, "This drink is still one of our favorites and is a super approachable yet adventurous step into mezcal." It's built around Ilegal Joven mezcal, a mildly smoky, vegetal expression that compliments the aromatic vermouth, tropical pineapple, spicy honey ginger syrup, and tangy lemon. Think of it as a Mexican riff on the Penicillin (page 234).

- 1½ oz (45 ml) Ilegal Joven mezcal
- ½ oz (15 ml) blanc vermouth (the bar uses Routin)
- ¾ oz (22 ml) Honey Ginger Syrup
- ¾ oz (22 ml) lemon juice
- ¾ oz (22 ml) pineapple juice

- Garnish: half pineapple wheel and pineapple frond

Shake all ingredients with ice until well chilled and frothy. Strain into a large rocks glass over ice. Garnish with a half pineapple wheel and pineapple frond.

For the Honey Ginger Syrup

- 8 oz (240 ml) water
- 8 oz (240 ml) honey
- 6-inch (15 cm) piece fresh ginger, peeled and cut into pieces

Heat all ingredients in a saucepan over low heat until the honey is dissolved, about 5 minutes. Remove from the heat. For a spicier flavor profile, store in the refrigerator overnight, then strain out the ginger before using (though it can be used immediately once cooled, if in a hurry).

# MARVIN'S GARDEN

- ⏲ **2020**
- ⚑ **SEATTLE, USA**
- ☌ **LINDSAY MATTESON**

- ⌂ **THE WALRUS AND THE CARPENTER**
- ⚱ **GIN**
- ⏣ **ROCKS**

The Marvin's Garden cocktail, a floral gin sour, is named for a quiet garden across the street from Bergen Place Park in the Ballard district of Seattle, Washington. Those familiar with the game of Monopoly might think there is a connection to the destination Marvin Garden on the US game board, but the space was named for Marvin Sjoberg, a beloved resident of the Ballard neighborhood who was bestowed with the title "Honorary Mayor" in 1977. The cocktail celebrating this quiet oasis and storied history was created in 2020 by Lindsay Matteson at The Walrus and the Carpenter, which is located near the park. The cocktail has remained on the menu ever since.

Marvin's Garden is made from London dry gin, Dolin Blanc vermouth, lemon, honey syrup, and Italicus Rosolio di Bergamotto liqueur, which for a time was enjoying the same attention from bartenders as the go-to "it" floral ingredient that St-Germain had been a decade earlier. A dash of Scrappy's lavender bitters ties the flavors together. Alhough it sounds like it would be intensely floral, the gin adds enough backbone to counterbalance these ingredients, and provides its own botanical texture, while the acidity of the lemon and sweetness of the honey add body.

"I wanted to incorporate the flavors of an English garden setting in a single cocktail," says Matteson of her concept. "It's got the flavors of an afternoon tea deconstructed in a drink." The Walrus and the Carpenter is focused mainly on fresh oysters and seafood, and the lightness of Marvin's Garden beautifully complements these dishes, as well as the seasonal vegetable offerings on the menu. It would also pair well with creamy styles of cheese.

- 1½ oz (45 ml) London dry gin
- ¼ oz (7 ml) Dolin Blanc vermouth
- ¼ oz (7 ml) Italicus Rosolio di Bergamotto
- ¾ oz (22 ml) fresh lemon juice
- ½ oz (15 ml) rich honey syrup (page 86)
- 1 dash Scrappy's lavender bitters

- Garnish: sprig of fresh thyme

Shake all ingredients with ice until well chilled. Strain over fresh ice into a rocks glass. Garnish with a sprig of thyme.

# MOSSY LANE

🕐 2020  
⚐ CHAOSHAN, CHINA  
👤 AYA LU  

⌂ SANYOU  
🍶 BAIJU  
🍸 COUPE

When the Hope Group—the hospitality team behind the successful jazzy speakeasy Hope & Sesame in Guangzhou, China—opened bar SanYou in the city's then newly developed shopping area in summer 2020, their goal was to shine a light on the diversity of baiju. The native Chinese spirit is the most consumed in the world, however it is also the most misunderstood. Outside of China, and with a limited range available in most markets, it's often associated with "firewater" and pungent characteristics of sulfur and decaying vegetables (or worse).

In China, there are twelve categories of baiju, and the bar boasts more than 270 bottles. The venue is split into two sections: Le Comptoir (counter bar) is a casual, high-volume drinkery, while the SanYou bar is operated by multiple bartenders who engage with clientele at counter seating for baiju tastings and arrive at the most suitable drink to prepare. Bartender Aya Lu's Mossy Lane is one of the signatures.

"Spring happens to be the ripening season of Chaoshan," says Lu. Long periods of rain saturate everything. "It drips from the green tiles, and it splashes on the moss. This is such a beautiful and soothing picture. I decided to make a cocktail for this moment."

Mossy Lane is an aromatic sour made with fen jiu, a delicate and subtly floral style of baiju, that she infuses with green olives then sets off with Lillet Blanc, Palo Cortado sherry, star fruit and licorice syrup, lemon juice, and soothing agarwood spray. Begin the recipe at least thirty-six hours ahead to make the olive infusion. If fen jiu is not available, try preparing with a good rye-based vodka, though it lacks quite the same complexity.

---

- 1 oz (30 ml) Green Olive-Infused Fen Jiu
- ½ oz (15 ml) Lillet Blanc
- ½ oz (15 ml) Palo Cortado sherry
- ½ oz (15 ml) homemade star fruit and licorice syrup (prepare simple syrup with a sliced star fruit and a couple of pieces of dried licorice root, cool and strain before using)
- ⅓ oz (10 ml) lemon juice
- 1 spritz agarwood spray (made from ingestible agarwood tea, available online)

Shake all ingredients except the spray with ice until well chilled. Strain into a coupe glass. Spritz agarwood spray over the drink.

### For the Green Olive-Infused Fen Jiu

- 1 x 4.9 oz (140 g) jar mild green olives (such as Castelvetrano)
- 25 oz (750 ml) bottle fen jiu baiju or unflavored rye vodka
- 1 tbsp lemon juice

Combine all ingredients in a jar with a tight-fitting lid. Let steep for 24 to 36 hours at room temperature, agitating the contents now and then. Strain before using. Store at room temperature and use within a few weeks.

# PAPAYA HIGH

🕒 C.2020　　　　　　　　⌂ HOPE & SESAME
⚑ SHENZHEN, CHINA　　　◊ RUM
👤 ANDREW HO　　　　　　Y HIGHBALL

When Hope & Sesame opened in 2016 behind a Cantonese café in Guangzhou, in China's DongshanKou enclave, it was certainly not the first speakeasy-style bar to join the contemporary cocktail scene. However, the sleek, modern venue that splits into a separate bar for live jazz performances is anything but stodgy. The drinks are prepared using sous vide infusions, vacuum redistillation techniques, and clarified punches, along with local spirits and ingredients. One of the popular signatures at the second Shenzhen location opened in 2020 is Papaya High, concocted by co-founder Andrew Ho.

The cocktail is based on a traditional Cantonese dish, tong-sui, a sweet soup or custard dessert course. "Sweet soup is one of the most popular afternoon tea choices in Guangdong," says Ho. "One dish is famous for having papaya in it. We wanted to create something that could remind of the Cantonese signature, but at the same time, be more refreshing and perhaps have a kick to it."

Papaya High is *very* Hope & Sesame, featuring a house redistilled papaya rum, lime oleo saccharum, citric acid solution, and black pepper soda. Ho says the flavor combination is a play on the common perception of "sweet," and how that flavor profile can also be refreshing and palate-cleansing.

This is one of those cocktails that will taste and look best at the source. However, the papaya rum flavor can be mimicked via traditional infusion by steeping dried papaya in white rum for a couple of days and straining out. Add a little cracked Szechuan peppercorn to tonic water for the soda, to capture the essence of the bar's black pepper soda.

---

- 1½ oz (45 ml) papaya redistilled rum
- ½ oz (15 ml) Lime Oleo with Crystal Sugar
- 1 tsp citric acid solution
- 2½ oz (70 ml) black pepper soda

- Garnish: basil leaf

Add the rum, oleo, and citric acid solution to a highball glass with ice and stir. Top with black pepper soda. Add a basil leaf to the side of the glass.

### For the Lime Oleo with Crystal Sugar

- Peel of 5 limes
- Granulated sugar

Place the lime peels (use the pulp for juice or other purposes) in a nonreactive bowl. Add enough sugar to cover evenly. Let sit at room temperature for 2 to 3 hours. Strain out and discard the peels and collect the syrup in an airtight container.

# PRESIDENTIAL GIFT

🕒 2020
⚑ WASHINGTON, D.C., USA
🜨 RYAN CHETIYAWARDANA/
 TEAM SILVER LYAN

⌂ SILVER LYAN
🜪 WHISKY
🍸 COUPE

After a few successful pop-ups in the United States, British cocktail iconoclast Ryan Chetiyawardana, aka "Mr Lyan," opened his first US brick and mortar bar in 2020: Silver Lyan, in Washington, D.C. He is the founder of some of London's most avant-garde hot spots of the 2010s—White Lyan, Dandelyan, Lyaness, and Cub—all known for molecularly mixed interpretations of classics using ingredients that can only be described as "way far out" (Moby Dick Sazerac with sperm whale ambergris, anyone?), and mostly pre-batched and bottled. For Silver Lyan in D.C., the menu had to be as impressively offbeat as the others, yet he wanted to play into the history of the region. One of the most notable signatures is the Presidential Gift.

The drink, which Chetiyawardana says is a team effort, is a reference to the variety of diplomatic gifts that are bestowed on sitting US presidents. The rule is the gift can be kept by them only if it costs $375 or less. Therefore, the drink is priced at $375, but, according to Chetiyawardana, it "celebrates wonderful, rare ingredients, rather than simply baller ones."

It's presented in a Steuben crystal glass from a decanter ("measured on scales, White Lyan style," he says) and is made from rare single cask Aberfeldy whisky (a nod to the type that would have been favored by Scottish-born nineteenth-century steel magnate Andrew Carnegie when he was "buttering up sitting dignitaries with whisky from his homeland"), applejacked bitters (a reference to one of the original Colonial native spirits), and a raw honey sourced from bees that forage on the Congressional Cemetery.

Re-creating the recipe with exact ingredients will be pricey, but the flavors can be achieved with substitutes.

---

- 2 ⅓ oz (70 ml) Aberfeldy 22-year single cask whisky (or use other nonpeated Scottish single malt)
- ⅓ oz (12 ml) D.C. Honey Water
- ½ oz (15 ml) filtered water
- 3 dashes Applejacked Bitters

Stir all ingredients with ice to quickly dilute, then strain into a glass bottle. Store in the refrigerator to cool. Serve in a chilled coupe glass (cut crystal to be fancy) that has been stored in the freezer.

### For the D.C. Honey Water

The syrup used at Silver Lyan is made with honey from the Congressional Cemetery in D.C. which won second place in a North American honey competition in 2019. However, other local honey will do the trick. Heat together 2 parts honey to 1 part water until the honey dissolves. Leave to cool.

### For the Applejacked Bitters

Combine equal parts Angostura bitters and high ABV cider. Add to an airtight, freezable container and freeze for 12 hours. Strain out the frozen solids. Store in a glass bottle in a cool, dark place.

# RUST + BONE

🕐 2020
⚑ TORONTO, CANADA
🧑 SANDY DE ALMEIDA

⌂ DRAKE HOTEL
🍶 BOURBON
🍸 ROCKS

Rust + Bone is a stirred, boozy concoction that features bourbon infused with cedarwood and was created by bartender Sandy De Almeida in 2020 for the Drake Hotel bar in Toronto, Canada. De Almeida was a beloved member of that city's bar community until her tragic death in 2022. This was the recipe that bars around the city served in her memory at the time of her passing, and the drink has lived on as a defining classic of the Toronto cocktail scene.

Gord Hannah, the Drake's beverage manager and De Almeida's co-worker, says Rust + Bone, named for a 2012 Jacques Audiard movie, is a true representation of her character as both a friend and bartender. She was known to engage clientele on all manner of discussions about books, film, visual art, history, and cocktail culture, for which she had an "encyclopedic knowledge."

Hannah notes that Rust + Bone contains all of De Almeida's cocktail "must haves": 1. A piece of art that showcases the base spirit; 2. KISS (Keep It Simple Stupid); 3. Every ingredient down to the garnish must have a purpose; 4. Tools and technique matter.

De Almeida was also known as a talented tattoo artist and perfumer, and the aromas from the cedar infusion mixed with Amaro Nono, Bénédictine, and Angostura bitters all showcase her knowledge and understanding of combining aromatic ingredients without overdoing it.

Hannah says a favorite saying of De Almeida's was, "Cocktails should taste like cocktails... why would I want an apple pie cocktail if I could just have a f***ing piece of apple pie?"

---

- 2 oz (60 ml) Cedar-Infused Bourbon
  (the Drake uses Four Roses)
- ½ oz (15 ml) Amaro Nono
- ¼ oz (7 ml) Bénédictine D.O.M. liqueur
- 2 dashes Angostura bitters

- Garnish: good-quality maraschino cherries, such as Luxardo

Stir all ingredients until well chilled. Strain into a rocks glass over fresh ice (the bar uses Kold draft). Garnish.

For the Cedar-Infused Bourbon

Add ½ oz (15 g) food-grade cedar leaf to 25 oz (750 ml) bourbon in a container. Leave to infuse in a cool, dry environment for 4 hours. Fine strain, bottle, and refrigerate.

# TRAMONTO

- 2020
- DUBAI, UAE
- DARIO SCHIAVONI
- BULGARI BAR, IL RISTORANTE–NIKO ROMITO
- GIN
- HIGHBALL

In the twenty-first century, Dubai, capital city of the United Arab Emirates, has emerged as a major destination for dining and cocktails. As a city that hosts thousands of international travelers, it has become known not only for its sophisticated Middle Eastern fare, but also for its top-notch cuisines from other countries—Japan, France, Spain, etc.—and as *The New York Times* reported in December 2022, Dubai has more restaurants per capita than New York City. Tramonto is one of the signature cocktails created in 2020 by Italian-born bartender Dario Schiavoni for the Bulgari Bar, located in the two Michelin-star Il Ristorante–Niko Romito in the Bulgari Resort.

*Tramonto* is Italian for "sunset," and like the Tequila Sunrise (page 120), the cocktail features red-hued components that settle through the tall glass like a changing sky. Unlike that drink, however, Tramonto features ingredients with no added sugars, which answers a call for lighter drinks with fewer calories that still have the feel of a proper cocktail. The luxury bar adds an artful flourish by painting a feathery swoop of white chocolate along one side of the glass.

"Dubai is a vibrant and fashionable city where everyone is looking to lead a healthy lifestyle in a very hot place," says Schiavoni. "So the idea is to have a refreshing drink that can please everyone, but they won't have regrets the next day."

Although The Botanist gin serves as the base for the drink, Schiavoni says they give customers the option of ordering Tramonto without any additional alcohol (there is some in the pineapple and raspberry cordial to keep it from fermenting). The cordial can also be enjoyed on its own splashed with soda or tonic.

- 1 oz (30 ml) dry gin (the bar uses The Botanist)
- 1½ oz (45 ml) Pineapple and Raspberry Cordial
- 1 tsp fresh lime juice
- Perrier, or other sparkling water, to top

- Garnish: white chocolate, melted and brushed on one side of a highball glass in an upward swoop

Prepare the glass by melting a few white chocolate pieces and, using a pastry or other food brush, dip into the chocolate and brush a few strokes upward on one side of the glass. Set aside. Shake all ingredients except the Perrier with ice until well chilled. Strain into a highball glass over fresh ice. Top with Perrier.

For the Pineapple and Raspberry Cordial

- 1 lb 2 oz (500 g) fresh pineapple chunks
- 1 lb 2 oz (500 g) fresh raspberries
- 5 oz (150 ml) dry gin

Juice the fresh fruit and heat the juices in a saucepan over medium heat for 12 minutes. Let cool. Filter with a super bag or fine strainer into another container. Add the gin to avoid any fermentation, then bottle. It will keep in the refrigerator for up to 10 days.

# TTEOKBOKKI

🕐 2020
⚐ SEOUL, SOUTH KOREA
👤 MASON PARK

⌂ ALICE CHEONGDAM
🍶 SOJU
🍸 ROCKS

Tteokbokki is a traditional Korean comfort dish made from garae-tteok, cylindrical cakes made of rice noodles, served either with spicy gochujang sauce, or more commonly a sweet honey and ganjang (soy sauce) based topping. Alice Cheongdam is an upscale cocktail den with details inspired by Lewis Carroll's *Alice in Wonderland*, accessed through a hidden door in the back of a flower shop in the Gangnam district in Seoul, South Korea. Named one of Asia's 50 Best Bars, the venue specializes in whimsical, though accessible adults-only concoctions based on elements of childhood treats, and is known to hold events such as hot dog and cocktail pairings. The Tteokbokki cocktail celebrates the flavors of the popular snack in liquid form and has been a signature since 2020.

"If there is Italian pasta, think of Korea as having tteokbokki," says the drink's creator, co-head bartender Mason Park. He explains that the less spicy version of the dish is often served to children, and that it's been his favorite food since he was a child. "The chewy texture, the spiciness of red pepper, and the sweetness of jocheong—honey made of rice—are fantastic."

Park says, "I wanted to experience this popular Korean food as a cocktail, and this is the recipe I found the most appropriate way." To accomplish the flavor profile, the bar prepares clarified punch mixed from Korean soju, pineapple juice, V8 juice, lemon, milk, and bottled sweet tteokbokki sauce, pepper, and sweetened with cane syrup.

At Alice, the drink is presented with a piece of tteokbokki and sweet sauce as a garnish. To replicate, prepared tteokbokki and bottled sauce can be purchased at Asian markets, though there are also numerous recipes online.

• 3 oz (90 ml) Clarified Tteokbokki Punch

Pour the punch into a rocks glass over a large ice cube and stir to chill. Serve with tteokbokki and sauce in a dish on the side.

### For the Clarified Tteokbokki Punch

Note: scale down as needed

• 41 oz (1.2 liters) traditional soju
• 41 oz (1.2 liters) fresh pineapple juice
• 4 x 5½ oz (163 ml) cans V8 vegetable juice
• 27 oz (800 ml) whole milk
• 27 oz (800 ml) tteokbokki sauce (sweet)
• 10 oz (300 ml) sugarcane syrup
• A little ground pepper
• 10 oz (300 ml) fresh lemon juice

Combine all the ingredients except the lemon juice in a nonreactive container. Pour the lemon juice carefully using a barspoon, then slowly stir into the mix. Cover and let the mixture rest at room temperature for 2 hours. Strain through a coffee filter or cheesecloth (muslin). It will keep in the refrigerator for up to 5 days.

# DOLE WHIP

🕐 2021  
⚑ NEW YORK CITY, USA  
👤 HARRISON SNOW AND  
    BROTHER CLEVE

⌂ LULLABY  
🍶 RUM  
🍸 CERAMIC COFFEE CUP

The frozen Dole Whip was one of the first Instagram-famous cocktails of post-COVID-19 pandemic New York City when it debuted in 2021. It's inspired by the booze-less pineapple-flavored Disneyland ice cream treat and is served in a ceramic version of the iconic "We Are Happy To Serve You" coffee cup, a team effort from bar manager Harrison Snow and Boston-based bartender/musician/tiki enthusiast Brother Cleve, who opened Lullaby in the former Nitecap space in New York City's Lower East Side. After being cooped up for months during lockdown, the Dole Whip was the antidote for the monotonies of quarantine, and instantly connected with the city's cocktail imbibers eager for new adventures and a drastic change from homemade Negronis and ready-to-drinks (RTDs).

According to Snow, Cleve had been obsessed for years with coming up with a boozy version of the Dole Whip, with its colada-like flavors minus the rum. By sheer coincidence, Snow had been brainstorming ideas for a signature frozen cocktail for Lullaby, at a time when it seemed every bar in the city was trying to out-slush the other with blender drinks.

Sadly, Cleve passed away suddenly in 2022, however his fun-loving spirit and appreciation for good rum and wild flavor combinations lives on in the Dole Whip.

Note: Lullaby makes its own ice cream for the drink, but suggests using pineapple sorbet as a stand-in.

- 1 to 2 scoops plus 3 tbsp pineapple sorbet
- 1 oz (30 ml) spiced rum
- ½ oz (15 ml) sherry blend
  (1:1 split Oloroso and Pedro Ximenez)
- ½ oz (15 ml) fresh lime juice
- ½ oz (15 ml) coconut mix
  (1:1 split Coco López cream of
  coconut and Thai coconut milk)
- ¼ oz (7 ml) Jamaican rum
- ¼ oz (7 ml) Fernet-Branca
- 3 drops saline solution

- Garnish: toasted coconut, mint sprig

Place 1 to 2 scoops of pineapple sorbet in a serving cup. Add the 3 tablespoons of sorbet to a cocktail shaker along with the remaining ingredients and 3 ice cubes. Shake vigorously and strain over the sorbet in the cup, then sprinkle with toasted coconut and add mint sprig.

# EDICION LIMITADA

🕐 2021
⚑ NASSAU, BAHAMAS
🧑 CRISTAL CULMER

⌂ CINKO BAR, ASIAN LATINO GRILL
  AT GRAND HYATT BAHA MAR
🝪 SAKE; TEQUILA
🍸 DOUBLE ROCKS

In the bleakest period of the COVID-19 pandemic, between March 2020 and summer 2021, when it was mostly impossible to travel more than a few miles from home, many of us did what we could to mentally satiate our sense of wanderlust. Some took advantage of extra down time by temporarily decking out a room at home to mimic foreign backdrops with various props, perhaps matching the set design by preparing elaborate, thematic meals, or at least took a Zoom cooking class to learn a new cuisine or cooking technique. Some simply attempted a cerebral escape with a good book and/or movie set in a faraway land. Still others, craving a vacation from pre-mixed ready-to-drinks (RTDs) or cans of wine, turned to home bartending, seeking out esoteric ingredients and learning to mix up more ambitious recipes.

Luckily, by mid-2021, the tourist industry began to recover. This cocktail was created by bartender Cristal Culmer in December of that year for the grand opening of the Cinko Bar in the Asian Latino Grill at Grand Hyatt Baha Mar in Nassau. The opening also coincided with the Bahamas reopening to international tourists.

Edicion Limitada personifies travel and adventure in a glass by featuring an exhilarating mix of Asian, Latin American, and tropical island ingredients—and (bonus) it's prepared live in an exquisite island setting! It's no wonder the striking color palette and vibrant edible flower garnish is a huge hit with guests. Thus, though the name would suggest otherwise, its popularity has solidified its place as a regular fixture on the cocktail menu.

- 2 oz (60 ml) dry sake
- 1 oz (30 ml) Monin yuzu fruit purée
- 1½ oz (45 ml) tequila blanco
- 1 oz (30 ml) passion fruit purée
  (fresh or store-bought)
- 4 drops Angostura bitters

- Garnish: edible flower (such as commercially available Dendrobium orchids)

Shake all ingredients with ice. Strain into a double rocks glass filled with fresh, crushed ice. Garnish with an edible flower.

# HER NAME IS RIO (CHERRY ICE CREAM SMILE)

- 2021
- NEW ORLEANS, USA
- ABIGAIL GULLO
- N/A
- CACHAÇA
- COCKTAIL

"If I'm on vacation and I'm drinking a fruity, refreshing drink, I actually think of *Rio*… I want something that's refreshing, light, citrusy," says Annie Zaleski, author *of Duran Duran's Rio (33 1/3, 156)* in a 2021 article by this author for *Forbes*. "I don't think of beer or wine, not even rosé. It must be a fancy, tropical cocktail."

It may be hard for some diehard fans from the 1980s to fathom, but in 2022 the British rock band Duran Duran celebrated the 40th anniversary of their groundbreaking second record, which included the massive global hits "Hungry Like the Wolf," "Save a Prayer," "The Chauffeur," and the crisp, transportive title track, "Rio."

Abigail Gullo is a New Orleans-based bartender and cocktail consultant who has been a fan of the band since the early days. Her signature drink from 2021 is a tribute to the song and the splashy music video featuring the handsome young band dressed in flashy silk suits designed by Antony Price, as they woo a gorgeous model decked out in body paint (and not much else) aboard a yacht. This refresher is exactly what Zaleski had in mind. It's made from cachaça, the national spirit of Brazil, with muddled cherries that speak to the lyric "Cherry ice cream smile." Gullo garnishes the drink with the Patrick Nagel illustration in homage to the album cover, printed in edible ink on rice paper. To paraphrase the song, you'll suppose it's very nice.

- 2 to 3 fresh cherries, stemmed and pitted
- 1½ oz (45 ml) sweet tea syrup (commercially available, or make simple syrup from brewed tea instead of water)
- Juice of 1 lime
- 1 egg white
- 1 oz (30 ml) cachaça

- Garnish: edible Nagel print on rice paper (optional)

Muddle the cherries in a mixing tin with the sweet tea syrup. Add the lime, egg white, and cachaça. Dry shake without ice, then add ice and shake hard. Double strain into a chilled cocktail glass. Step to the left. Flick to the right. Garnish with edible Nagel print on rice paper, if desired.

# PLETOK

🕐 2021
⚑ JAKARTA, INDONESIA
A ALBERT YACOB

⌂ HELLO MR. FOX
🍶 VODKA
🍸 ROCKS

Bir pletok is a carbonated nonalcoholic beverage originated by the Betawi people of Jakarta, Indonesia. Its Western equivalent would be root beer, though this *bir* is made with various spices (clove, cardamom, etc.), ginger, secang (sappanwood), pandan, lemongrass, and other native roots. In 1962, Indonesia's first president, Bapak Soekarno, commissioned Hamami Mamiek, head bartender at the Hotel Indonesia (now Kempinski Jakarta) to invent a cocktail in honor of the country's hosting of the Asian games. Thus, an alcoholic Bir Pletok, now considered the signature cocktail of Indonesia, was concocted of vodka, Cointreau, lime juice, and sugar topped with Anker beer. In 2021, the drink was updated by Albert Yacob at Jakarta's premier cocktail den, Hello Mr. Fox.

Yacob took many of the spices used for the nonalcoholic bir pletok and amplified them with sarsaparilla to make a spicy soda in-house. This is mixed with vodka, Fernet-Branca, and lemon juice and topped with a beer-Cointreau foam (a nod to the classic cocktail), over which the bar's fox logo is etched in secang powder using a stencil. "We combined two concepts," explains Yacob. "It's like a mashup between traditional bir pletok plus the classic cocktail plus Moscow Mule plus Fernet Con Coca [Argentina's national drink] plus root beer."

Of course, the best place to drink Pletok is at Hello Mr. Fox (especially if you want the full fox stencil effect). Directions for the pletok soda are included below, but if that's too much trouble to replicate, you can get a sense of what this cocktail tastes like by preparing it with a bottled nonalcoholic bir pletok or good-quality root beer, or, failing that, cola.

---

- 1⅓ oz (40 ml) vodka
- ¼ oz (7 ml) Fernet-Branca
- ¼ oz (7 ml) fresh lemon juice
- 3 oz (90 ml) Pletok Soda, chilled (or use bottled soda)
- Vanilla Cointreau Foam, to top

- Garnish: secang powder set in foam via fox stencil (optional)

Build the ingredients in a rocks glass. Top with foam. If garnishing, place a fox stencil over the foam and sprinkle with secang powder.

### For the Pletok Soda

- 17 oz (500 ml) clarified sarsaparilla
- ½ oz (15 g) secang (sappanwood) powder
- 1¾ oz (50 g) fresh, peeled ginger
- ½ oz (15 g) lemongrass

- 4 cloves and 4 star anise
- ¾ oz (20 ml) vanilla syrup

Heat all the ingredients in a saucepan for 20 minutes over medium heat. Remove from the heat and let sit for at least an hour. Strain and allow to cool completely. Charge with $CO_2$.

### For the Vanilla Cointreau Foam

- 3½ oz (100 ml) Cointreau
- 11 oz (330 ml) beer (use Anker, or similar)
- 1 oz (30 ml) vanilla syrup
- 3½ oz (100 ml) heavy (double) cream
- 6 g gelatin sheets

Warm all ingredients over low heat until the gelatin has dissolved. Allow to cool then charge with a cream charger.

# PALM TREE

🕐 2022
⚐ PHNOM PENH, CAMBODIA
👤 ALFIE AMAYO

⌂ SEEKERS SPIRITS
🝂 GIN
🍸 ROCKS

Founded in Phnom Penh in 2018, Seekers Spirits is the first distillery to produce premium gin in Cambodia. The dry gin is distilled from cassava root and made with eleven botanicals foraged from the banks of the Mekong River, including pandan, Khmer (Thai) basil, Battambang green oranges, Asian lime leaf, and palm seed. Its head distiller is London spirits veteran Alfie Amayo, who co-created the Palm Tree cocktail for the tasting room in 2022.

"One of the things that I challenged my team with our latest menu is to be more mindful of our sustainability efforts," says Amayo. He adds that Cambodia has been slower to adopt the concept of sustainability in the service industry, but the brand works with local farmers to deliver products without plastic, using natural coverings such as banana leaves.

The tasting room menu makes use of the more than sixty different herbs and spices grown in the distillery's garden. "I am proud of this cocktail because not only is it delicious, but it also showcases how far my team have come in their knowledge and flavour creation. They've created a refined and complex drink with so much depth of flavour and a clear objective towards sustainability."

Palm Tree is a variation on the classic clarified milk punch, and Amayo mentions that the team even uses the whey left over from the filtering process to make a cheese garnish to be eaten alongside the drink. Obviously optional if preparing at home, but definitely encouraged! The palm tree cocktail mix makes enough for a crowd.

---

• 2¾ oz (80 ml) Bottled Palm Tree Cocktail Mix

• Garnish: orange twist

Pour the cocktail mix into a chilled rocks glass over a large ice cube. Express the oils from a piece of orange peel over the drink, skin side down, then twist and place in the glass.

### Bottled Palm Tree Cocktail Mix

• 7 oz (210 ml) Seekers Mekong dry gin
• 4 oz (120 ml) coconut water (ideally fresh)
• 2 oz (60 ml) Star Anise and Pandan Syrup
• 4 oz (120 ml) fresh pineapple juice
• 1½ oz (45 ml) fresh lime juice
• 4 oz (120 ml) whole (full-fat) milk

Combine all ingredients except the milk in a pitcher (jug). Add the milk to a second pitcher. Slowly add the contents of the first pitcher to the milk (not the other way round). Stir gently and let sit at room temperature for about 30 minutes. The lime juice will cause the milk to curdle. Strain the mixture through a coffee filter. Discard the first 1¾ oz (50 ml) and collect the rest (about 1 to 2 hours). Pour the cocktail into a bottle.

### For the Star Anise and Pandan Syrup

• 5 star anise pods
• 10 pandan leaves (best if fresh)
• 14 oz (400 ml) water
• 2 cups (400 g) sugar

Add the star anise pods and pandan leaves to a saucepan with the sugar and water. Stir over low heat until all the sugar has dissolved. Let sit for a few hours to cool. Once cool, strain out the solids. Pour into a bottle. This syrup will keep for up to 8 weeks in the refrigerator.

# PEACH TATIN

⊘ 2022
⚑ LONDON, UK
⚇ JOSH POWELL

⌂ THE NATURAL PHILOSOPHER
◊ GIN
⛾ HEATPROOF ROCKS OR GLASS MUG

In the first quarter of the twenty-first century, the culinary world was not the only sector to make sizeable shifts toward plant-based consumption. Many cocktail bars are also using fewer dairy- or meat-based ingredients and looking toward more environmentally sustainable service practices. The Natural Philosopher bar in London's Hackney neighborhood is owned and run by Welsh-born Josh Powell, who mixes a tight, well-curated selection of spirits and wines with ethically sourced, fresh ingredients against a modern fern bar chic backdrop. Cocktails have simple names—Pear, Hibiscus, Darjeeling, etc.—but the preparation involves intricate syrups, infusions, and other elements resembling fine dining. One of the most striking examples is the Peach Tatin, created in 2022.

It's a vegan evolution of what began as a fat-washed chorizo and cranberry Old Fashioned, once championed by the late British bar talent Gary "Gaz" Regan. Peach Tatin is a warm, peachy, liquefied take on the classic French tarte tatin pastry. The result is a sumptuous, but not unctuous, drink that deftly knits together elements of a hot toddy with an Old Fashioned using G'Vine, a grape-based French gin, G'Vine peach liqueur, Sūpāsawā (bottled and clarified sour mix alternative), saline solution, and a caramelized peach and oat syrup. At the bar, Powell uses an intricate technique of caramelizing the peach purée in an oat syrup using sous vide and other restaurant-grade equipment, plus the crumble mix is homemade. Here, the recipe is simplified for the home mixologist.

Serves 8

- 7 oz (200 ml) G'Vine French grape gin
- 4 oz (120 ml) G'Vine June peach and summer fruit gin liqueur
- 2¾ oz (80 ml) Sūpāsawā
- 1 oz (30 ml) 10% saline solution
- 8 oz (240 ml) Caramelized Peach & Oat Syrup

- Garnish: sliced peach dipped in Lotus Biscoff spread and Biscoff crumbles

Combine all ingredients in a large bowl or pitcher (jug), then transfer to a bottle. Make the garnish by slicing a peach and thoroughly blotting the slices dry with a paper towel. Heat a little Biscoff spread in a microwave for 5 to 10 seconds, then dip one end of each slice in. Crush a few Biscoff cookies and spread in a thin layer in a saucer. Dip the same end of the peaches in to lightly coat with crumble. Set aside.

To warm the drink, add 12 cups (3 liters) of boiled water to a pan. Stand the bottled cocktail mixture in the pan. Bring to a light simmer, being sure to carefully agitate the bottle every now and again to mix the contents. When it's warm enough (about 140°F/60°C), pour 3 oz (90 ml) into 8 heatproof rocks glasses. Add the dipped peach slices to the side of the glass.

For the Caramelized Peach & Oat Syrup

- 8 oz (240 ml) oat milk
- ½ cup (100 g) brown sugar
- ⅔ cup (140 g) white sugar
- 8 oz (240 g) peach purée (homemade or store-bought)

Add the oat milk and sugars to a large pot and place on low heat to dissolve the sugars. Let cool before adding the peach purée. Stir and bottle. This will keep in a sealed container in the refrigerator for up to a month.

# TWIN CITIES

⊕ 2022
⚑ NEW YORK CITY, USA
ᚼ IAN ALEXANDER

⌂ DEAD RABBIT
⬧ WHISKEY
Ⴘ NICK & NORA

Opened on the New York City Financial District waterfront in February 2013 by Sean Muldoon and Jack McGarry, who previously ran the award-winning bar in the Merchant Hotel in Belfast, Northern Ireland, the Dead Rabbit has been one of the most famously successful bars of the modern cocktail era. It's split into two levels. The lower floor is the Tap Room, an upscale, yet casual pub-style vibe with fresh Guinness and beers on draft, a massive selection of Irish whiskey and other spirits, modern pub food, highballs and other cocktails, and occasional live music. This is also where guests wait for their turn to visit the upstairs Parlor, where Victorian-era charm meets cocktail innovation.

In 2022, following an extensive service and menu overhaul in the wake of the COVID-19 pandemic, Muldoon and McGarry split when Muldoon left NYC to open Hazel & Apple in

Charleston, South Carolina with former DR beverage director Jillian Vose. A new Dead Rabbit era had begun, and Twin Cities was one of the first signatures.

The drink's creator is head bartender Ian Alexander, who wanted a lighter-style Manhattan variation that stands up to what he describes as the "richness and depth of Teeling Irish Whiskey," which he uses instead of the traditional bourbon or rye. He infuses the whiskey with fig leaves.

He says, "The fig leaves work really well with the vanilla and toasted coconut flavors from the ex-bourbon barrels [that the whiskey is matured in] and the apricot helps to accentuate the nutty tones in the whiskey. The cocktail is a riff on a Manhattan, but it is a bit juicier and more unctuous with the addition of cognac, fig leaf, and verjus."

- 1½ oz (45 ml) Fig Leaf-Infused Teeling Small Batch Irish Whiskey
- ½ oz (15 ml) Pierre Ferrand 1840 cognac
- 1 oz (30 ml) Cocchi Vermouth di Torino
- ¼ oz (7 ml) Giffard Abricot liqueur
- ½ teaspoon verjus blanc
- 2 dashes Angostura cacao bitters

Stir all ingredients with ice until well chilled. Strain into an ice-cold Nick & Nora glass.

For the Fig Leaf-Infused Teeling Small Batch Irish Whiskey

- 25 oz (750 ml) Teeling Small Batch Irish whiskey
- ½ oz (15 g) fresh fig leaves
- ½ oz (15 g) dried fig leaves

Combine all ingredients in a container with a tight-fitting lid. Let steep at room temperature for 2 hours, then fine strain and store in a bottle.

# PHAIDON 100

🕑 2023
⚐ LONDON, UK
👤 AGOSTINO PERRONE

⌂ N/A
🍶 GIN
🍸 COUPE

Phaidon 100 is a signature cocktail designed in 2023 by Agostino "Ago" Perrone, Director of Mixology at London's Connaught Hotel, in celebration of the 100th anniversary of Phaidon Press. The chic, Negroni-esque, gin-based drink combines elements of style and layers of flavor, which collectively represent the company's roots, as well as its creative journey with its publications focusing on visual arts and culinary themes.

Phaidon was founded in Vienna, Austria in 1923 by Dr. Béla Horovitz, Frederick "Fritz" Ungar, and Ludwig Goldscheider. The company's name references Phaedo, a Greek philosopher and pupil of Socrates, and is a nod to the love of classical culture shared by Horovitz, Ungar, and Goldscheider. The business partners set out to publish what is still the company's signature offering—affordable books with elegant and polished designs. At the start of World War II,

Phaidon relocated to the UK and set up its offices in London. Today, with its headquarters in both London and New York, offices in Paris and Berlin, and with dedicated representatives all around the world, Phaidon has grown to be an international company with a truly global reach.

"Phaidon 100 is a cocktail that blends memories of a legendary journey with the vibrancy and bliss of present and future times," explains Perrone. "Championing the creative arts and the iconic style that sets Phaidon apart, for its one hundredth anniversary, the recipe brings together references to Vienna with chocolate, along with the allure of other countries—a nod to London through gin and the Martini cocktail style, and Italy through vermouth, bitter, vinegar, and bergamot. Absinthe adds that electric and hard-to-describe vibe of New York. It's a timeless classic re-imagined through the lens of an ever-evolving heritage."

- 5 dashes absinthe (French-style preferred)
- 1½ oz (45 ml) London dry gin
- 1 oz (30 ml) Sweet Vermouth, Bitter Liqueur, Cocoa Husk & Bergamot Oil Mix
- 2.5 ml (½ barspoon) balsamic vinegar

- Garnish: triangle of white chocolate, spritz of Podere Santa Bianca green mandarin essential oil

Swirl the absinthe in a frozen coupe glass to coat. Set aside. Stir the rest of the ingredients in a mixing glass over crystal clear ice and pour into the frozen glass. Garnish with a triangle of white chocolate perched on the side of the glass and spritz with mandarin oil.

For the Sweet Vermouth, Bitter Liqueur, Cocoa Husk & Bergamot Oil Mix

- 8¼ oz (250 ml) each: Martini Rubino Riserva Speciale Rosso; Punt E Mes; Campari; and Galliano L'Aperitivo
- 5.5 g cocoa husk
- 1 drop bergamot essential oil

Put all the ingredients except the bergamot essential oil in a sous vide bag and heat at 60°C (140°F) for 45 minutes.* Strain everything through a coffee paper filter into a bottle. Once the liquid has cooled, add 1 drop of bergamot essential oil.

* Alternatively, infuse the ingredients for 6 hours in a container at room temperature.

# GLOSSARY

## BAR EQUIPMENT

If you plan to make cocktails at home on a regular basis, it is worth investing in some of these quintessential bar tools, as they will really make a difference to the outcome of your drinks.

Cocktail shaker
A Boston shaker, composed of one glass and one metal tin—or two metal tins (one larger)—that together form a tight seal when put together with the openings facing each other in order to shake.

Jiggers
One or more jiggers that measure ¼ oz (7 ml), ½ oz (15 ml), ¾ oz (22 ml), 1 oz (30 ml), and 2 oz (60 ml). Many are available two-sided with different units of measure on each side.

Strainer
A Hawthorne strainer with a metal coil is used to strain shaken drinks from the larger metal shaking tin. It is a good all-purpose tool to start with. A Julep strainer with perforated holes is used to strain stirred liquids from a mixing glass.

Barspoon
A long-handled spoon used both to stir drinks and to measure very small amounts of liquid. A typical barspoon measures ½ teaspoon, which is the equivalent of $\frac{1}{12}$ oz (2.5 ml).

Large ice cube trays
A tray for 1½–2 inch (4–5 cm) square ice cubes for drinks served on the rocks. Smaller cubes of 1 inch (2.5 cm) square are used for shaken preparations and serving tall drinks.

## KITCHEN BASICS

Additional useful items to keep on hand include a set of measuring spoons and measuring cups for making syrups, a "Y" (swivel) vegetable peeler for garnishes (twists), a sharp paring knife, a small cutting board, and, if possible, a blender.

Mixing glass
A tall glass with a wide, flat bottom and pouring spout used to mix stirred drinks.

Muddler
A blunt wooden, metal, or plastic cylinder used to muddle—or mash—fruits, herbs, and spices in a mixing glass or cocktail shaker in order to release their flavors.

Fine strainer
A small, fine-mesh strainer used to remove solids from shaken cocktails made with fresh herbs or fruit.

Swizzle stick
A long stick with one forked end used to mix cocktails served over crushed ice. Also called a *lélé*.

Glassware is more than just aesthetic. The shape of the glass impacts the olfactory experience of a drink. A stemmed glass minimizes contact between your warm hands and the cold liquid. Here are a few recommendations on what to have on hand for optimal success. Coupes, rocks, and highball glasses are the most essential.

Coupe
A stemmed glass with a shallow, rounded bowl. Used for cocktails that are shaken or stirred and served up, such as the Daiquiri. Larger sizes are best for drinks that include egg to accommodate the extra volume.
5–8 oz (150–240 ml)

Rocks
Also known as an "Old Fashioned" glass, a straight-sided or slightly tapered short glass, preferably with a heavy bottom. Used for cocktails built in the glass or served over ice, such as the Amaretto Sour. Double Rocks refers to those double the size to accommodate highballs and other "taller" (fizzy) drinks.
10–12 oz (300–360 ml)

Highball
Also known as "Collins" glass, is a versatile, straight-sided tall glass used for long drinks including the Mojito.
10–12 oz (300–360 ml)

Flute
A classic champagne flute is a tall, slender glass used for sparkling cocktails.
6–8 oz (180–240 ml)

Nick & Nora
A stemmed glass with a smaller bowl used for stirred drinks served up, such as the Bamboo.
5 oz (150 ml)

Martini
A stemmed glass with a conical ("V") shape, used for stirred cocktails such as Martinis but sometimes also shaken ones such as the Cosmopolitan.
5–6 oz (150–180 ml)

Heatproof mug
A ceramic or glass mug with a handle used for hot drinks including Toddies and Irish Coffee.
10 oz (300 ml)

Hurricane
A footed, tall, flared glass used for many Tiki drinks, such as the Blue Hawaii and the Singapore Sling.
12 oz (360 ml)

Pint glass
A classic tall glass for beer cocktails, such as the Black Velvet.
16 oz (480 ml)

Shot glass
Used for shots and occasionally serving a spirit or chaser on the side of a larger cocktail, such as the Lemon Drop.
1–2 oz (30–60 ml)

Snifter
A short-stemmed glass with a large bowl that can be used for larger format served over crushed ice or for brandy cocktails.
6–10 oz (180–300 ml)

Wine glass
Used for drink served on the rocks where a stem is preferred, such as the Dried Fruit Sangria.
8–12 oz (240–360 ml)

Building drinks
When mixing a drink, start with the least expensive ingredients first—typically syrups and juices—so that in case a mistake is made with the measurements, there is no need to throw away the expensive ingredients. Bitters are also almost always added first, unless specified otherwise. For example, when making a Margarita, first measure the lime juice, then the Cointreau, and finally the tequila.

Chilling glasses
To ensure that your drinks stay cold, chill your glasses (particularly coupes and Martini glasses) before serving. You can store them in the freezer, or fill them with some ice and cold water while you make your cocktail and discard before straining the drink into them. Chilling is particularly important for sparkling cocktails, where you do not stir the Champagne over ice.

Shaking and stirring
Shaking or stirring cocktails with ice before serving, chills, aerates, and dilutes the drink. Depending on the recipe, different techniques are employed to accomplish this result. Ideally, use 1-inch (2.5 cm) square cubes, or cracked ice from larger pieces. If you only have very small cubes or fragments, stir or shake for less time to avoid overdiluting the drink. Shaken drinks should result in ones that are cold and frothy, shaken for at least 15 seconds before straining. For a stirred drink, the mixing glass should be cold to the touch before straining the liquid into the glass. Stir time is typically at least about 20 to 30 seconds.

Dry shaking
Dry shaking means to shake without ice. This technique is used to emulsify eggs to create a fluffy texture, before adding ice and shaking again to dilute and chill. Some bartenders advocate a reverse dry shake, where the drink is shaken with ice first, strained, and shaken again without ice. Removing the coil from a Hawthorne strainer and adding it to the shaker can also increase aeration.

Swizzling
Swizzling is a technique used for many Tiki cocktails and it gets its name from the tool used to do it: the swizzle stick. To swizzle a drink, fill the glass one-half to two-thirds with crushed ice and then add the ingredients. Then plunge the stick into the drink and vigorously roll it between the palms of your hands, moving it up and down. If you do not have a swizzle stick, churn the drink instead with a barspoon or chopstick. The goal is to rapidly chill and integrate all the ingredients. The glass should be frosted when you finish swizzling.

Rinsing
Drinks that call for a "rinse" use a very small amount of a spirit or liqueur—often absinthe—to add just a hint of flavoring. Simply add a few dashes of the specified ingredient, then swirl to coat the inside of the glass. Discard any excess liquid.

Muddling
Muddling releases the oils in herbs, such as mint, and juices in fruit or berries. Do not muddle too aggressively, as this can result in a bitter flavor and/or bruise the produce too much.

### Blending

When blending drinks, the amount of ice needed can vary dramatically, depending on the blender and the type of ice used. In general, start with less and add more ice as needed to obtain the desired consistency. You can buy pebble ice for blending, or crush your own ice by placing larger ice in a clean bag and using a mallet, or even using your blender pre-crush before making cocktails. If you opt for the latter technique, do it in batches, a handful of ice cubes at a time.

### Simple Syrup

Many recipes call for simple syrup as a sweetening agent. This ingredient, as the name suggests, is quite simply sugar mixed with water. It is made by combining equal amounts—typically one cup (200 grams) granulated sugar with 8 oz (240 ml) water—heated in a small saucepan over low heat, stirred occasionally, until the sugar is completely dissolved (about 5 minutes). Allow to cool completely before using. Store in an airtight container for up to 10 days in the refrigerator. In this book, where other syrups are needed, specific instructions are given.

### Demerara Syrup

An equal parts syrup made with Demerara (light brown) sugar. Prepare as you would a simple syrup.

### Rich Syrup

Also known as "2:1" syrup. This means there is twice as much sugar as water in the syrup, otherwise prepared using the same instructions as simple syrup.

### Oleo

Also known as "oleo saccharum," this is a sweet, aromatic citrus extract. It is made by covering a mound of fresh citrus peels (typically lemon) with granulated sugar in a nonreactive bowl. When left uncovered at room temperature for a couple of hours, the sugar naturally absorbs the oils from the peels and dissolves, forming a golden brown, thick (and rather delicious) syrupy paste. Oleo is a common ingredient in classic punches. Some recipes call for the whole peels to be discarded before use and use only the extract; others use the entire, now candied, peel.

# INDEX

## BY ALCOHOL TYPE & INGREDIENTS

## BY COCKTAIL NAME

## BY BAR

# BIBLIOGRAPHY

Ankrah, Douglas, *Shaken and Stirred*. Kyle Books, 2004.

Arazo, Maria Angeles, *Valencia, Noche*. Plaza & Janes, 1978.

Baker Jr., Charles H., *The South American Gentleman's Companion*. 1951.

Baker Jr., Charles H., *The Gentleman's Companion: Being an Exotic Drinking Book*. 1939.

Berry, Jeff, *Beachbum Berry's Potions of the Caribbean*. Cocktail Kingdom, 2013.

Berry, Jeff, *Beachbum Berry's Intoxica!*. SLG Publishing, 2003.

Berry, Jeff, *Beachbum Berry's Sippin' Safari* (10th Anniversary Edition). Cocktail Kingdom, 2017.

Bodenheimer, Neil and Timberlake, Emily, *Cure: New Orleans Drinks and How to Mix 'Em*. Abrams, 2022.

Boothby, William, *The World's Drinks and How to Mix Them*.

Boothby, William, *Cocktail Boothby's American Bartender*. 1891.

Bradsell, Dick, *Dicktales or Thank Yous and Sluggings*. Mixellany, 2022.

Brown, Jared and Miller, Anistatia, *The Deans of Drink*. Mixellany, 2013

Brown, Jared and Miller, Anistatia, *Spirit of the Cane*. Mixellany, 2017.

Brown, Jared and Miller, Anistatia, *Champagne Cocktails*. Mixellany, 2010. (original 1998)

Brown, Jared and Miller, Anistatia, *Spirituous Journey: A History of Drink*. Mixellany, 2009.

Brown, Jared and Miller, Anistatia, *Spirituous Journey: A History of Drink (Book Two)*. Mixellany, 2009.

Bullock, Tom, *The Ideal Bartender*. 1917.

Caiafa, Frank, *The Waldorf Astoria Bar Book*. Penguin, 2015.

Cipriani, Harry, *The Harry's Bar Cookbook*. Bantam, 1991.

Clisby Arthur, Stanley, *Famous New Orleans Drinks & How to Mix 'Em*. Pelican, 1977.

Craddock, Harry, *The Savoy Cocktail Book*. 1930.

Crockett, Albert Stevens, *Old Waldorf-Astoria Bar Book*. 1935.

Crockett, Albert Stevens, *Old Waldorf Bar Days*. 1931.

David, Natasha, *Drink Lightly*. Penguin Random House, 2022.

deBary, John, *Drink What You Want*. Clarkson Potter, 2020.

DeGroff, Dale, *The New Craft of the Cocktail*. Berkley, 2021 (original 2002).

Dickens, Cedric, *Drinking with Dickens*. 1980.

Duffy, Patrick Gavin, *The Official Mixer's Manual*. 1934.

Engel, Leo, *American and Other Drinks*. 1880.

Ensslin, Hugo, *Recipes for Mixed Drinks*.

Harrington, Paul and Moorhead, Laura, *Cocktail: The Drinks Bible for the 21st Century*. Viking, 1998.

*Iron Gate of Jack & Charlie's '21', The*. Jack Kriendler Memorial Foundation, Inc. 1950.

Johnson, Harry, *New and Improved Bartender's Manual*. 1882.

MacElhone, Harry, *Harry of Ciro's ABC of Mixing Drinks*. 1923.

MacElhone, Harry, *Harry's ABC of Mixing Cocktails*. 1930.

MacElhone, Harry, *Barflies and Cocktails*. 1927.

Maeda, Yonekichi, *Kokuteeru*. 1924; Mixellany, 2022.

Meehan, Jim, *The PDT Cocktail Book*. Sterling, 2012.

Meier, Frank, *The Artistry of Mixing Drinks*. 1934.

Momosé, Julia and Janzen, Emma, *The Way of the Cocktail*. Penguin Random House, 2021.

Mustipher, Shannon, *Tiki: Modern Tropical Cocktails*. Universe Publishing, 2019.

North, Sterling and Kroch, Carl, *So Red the Nose, or Breath in the Afternoon*. 1935

Poister, John, *The New American Bartender's Guide*. New American Library, 2002.

Saucier, Ted, *Ted Saucier's Bottoms Up*. Greystone Press, 1951.

Schmidt, William, *The Flowing Bowl: When and What to Drink*. Franklin Classics, 2018.

Sipsmith, *Sip: 100 Gin Cocktails With Only 3 Ingredients*. Mitchell Beazley, 2019.

Slater, Jerry and Camp Milam, Sara, *The Southern Foodways Alliance Guide to Cocktails*. University of Georgia Press, 2017.

*Sloppy Joe's Cocktail Manual*. 1936.

Smith, David and Rivers, Keli, *Negroni: More than 30 Classic and Modern Recipes for Italy's Iconic Cocktail*. Ryland, Peters & Small, 2021.

Stillman, Adrienne, *Spirited: Cocktails from Around the World*. Phaidon, 2020.

Tarling, W. J., *Café Royal Cocktail Book*. 1937.

Thomas, Jerry, *Jerry Thomas' Bartender's Guide: How to Mix Drinks, or the Bon-Vivant's Companion*. 1862.

Urushido, Masahiro and Anstendig, Michael, *The Japanese Art of the Cocktail*. HarperCollins, 2021.

Vermeire, Robert, *Cocktails: How to Mix Them*. 1922.

Volk, Andrew and Briana, *Northern Hospitality with the Portland Hunt + Alpine Club*. Voyageur Press, 2018.

Wondrich, David, *The Oxford Companion to Spirits & Cocktails*. Oxford University Press, 2021.

Wondrich, David, *Esquire Drinks: An Opiniated and Irreverent Guide to Drinking*. Sterling, 2003.

Woon, Basil, *When It's Cocktail Time in Cuba*. 1928.

www.cheekykitchen.com
www.liquor.com
www.diffordsguide.com
www.diffordsguide.com
www.forbes.com
www.gardenandgun.com
www.kqed.org
www.punchdrink.com
www.robertsimonson.substack.com
www.spiritshunters.com
www.talesofthecocktail.org

# RECIPE NOTES

RECIPE NOTES

• Both metric and imperial measurements are used in this book. Follow one set of measurements throughout, not a mixture, as they are not interchangeable.

• The measure that has been used in all the recipes is based on a bar jigger, which is 1 oz (30 ml). If preferred, a different volume can be used providing the proportions are kept constant within a drink and suitable adjustments are made to spoon measurements, where they occur.

• All tablespoon and teaspoon measurements are level, unless otherwise stated. 1 teaspoon = 5 ml; 1 tablespoon = 15 ml. Australian standard tablespoons are 20 ml, so Australian readers are advised to use 3 teaspoons in place of 1 tablespoon when measuring small quantities.

• Fruit juice is always freshly squeezed, unless otherwise specified.

• All herbs are fresh, unless otherwise specified.

• Ensure all flowers used for garnish are edible.

• Sugar is always granulated white, unless otherwise specified.

• Eggs are medium (UK small), unless otherwise specified.

• Some recipes include raw egg whites. These should be avoided by the elderly, pregnant women, nursing mothers, convalescents, and anyone with an impaired immune system.

• Always chill glassware in the freezer before serving, unless serving warm drinks in heatproof mugs.

• When using a lighter or long match to ignite alcohol or flame citrus peel, always ensure that all liquor bottles are sealed and placed far away.

• Always drink responsibly.

## ACKNOWLEDGMENTS

This book is dedicated to the generations of bar professionals, and those adjacent, who poured their creativity into the public consciousness.

Many thanks to Phaidon Press for providing me with the opportunity to work on this astounding project, and to Adrienne Stillman for recommending me. Special thanks to my parents, Carlotta and David Schuster, the ultimate gourmands, for their continued love and support of my unconventional career choices. I am very grateful to all the professional consultants who lent their time and expertise in the quest for signature recipes from around the globe—Robert Simonson, Camper English, Emma Janzen, Vivian Pei, and especially my dear friends Anistatia Miller and Jared Brown, who went above and beyond. Thanks to David Wondrich and Frank Caiafa for the ongoing advice, research notes, and friendship. Thank you to all the talented bartenders past and present who inspired us with so many creative concoctions, and to those still behind the bar who generously shared their recipes from near and far. Thanks to friends and fellow patrons of the cocktail arts who are always there for me: John Hedigan, Jason Bylan, Stephanie Moreno, Keli Rivers, Ruth Cole, Garth Ennis, Mike Vacheresse, Francine Cohen, Dennis Shinners, Nick Elezovic, Josh Powell, Colleen Newvine Tebeau, and John Tebeau. Jasper Schuster for the snuggles. And finally, Duran Duran for the much-needed midway point Vegas reset.

## ABOUT THE AUTHOR

Amanda Schuster is a freelance writer and hospitality consultant living in Brooklyn, New York. She is the author of *New York Cocktails* and *Drink Like a Local New York* (both Cider Mill Press). After spending several years as a retail wine and spirits buyer, she has written about wine, spirits, cocktails, and travel for numerous publications, including Forbes, Bloomberg News, Imbibe, SevenFifty, Distiller.com, Bevvy, and is the former Senior Editor-in-Chief of Alcohol Professor. She has served on the tasting panel for Ultimate Spirits Challenge and the John Barleycorn Spirit Awards and is a media judge and Timeless Committee member for the Tales of the Cocktail Spirited Awards. She's coming around to the idea of Dirty Martinis, but please don't ever offer her a pickleback.

## ABOUT THE CONTRIBUTORS

**Jared Brown** and **Anistatia Miller** are the directors of Mixellany Limited, a consultancy and publishing company that specializes in spirits and mixed drinks. They have contributed to numerous publications and are the authors of several books on cocktail culture.

**Camper English** is a cocktails and spirits writer, and the creator of the Alcademics website. He is a lecturer and consultant and the author of several books.

**Emma Janzen** is a drinks journalist, photographer, and author.

**Vivien Pei** is a food writer and consultant, and co-founded the Singapore Cocktail Bar Association.

**Robert Simonson** is a drinks writer for the *New York Times*, author of several books, and the creator and author of the Substack newsletter The Mix With Robert Simonson.

Phaidon Press Limited
2 Cooperage Yard
Stratford
London E15 2QR

Phaidon Press Inc.
65 Bleecker Street
New York NY 10012

phaidon.com

First published 2023
© 2023 Phaidon Press Limited

ISBN 978 1 83866 755 9

A CIP catalogue record for this book is
available from the British Library and
the Library of Congress.

Commissioning Editor: Emilia Terragni
Project Editor: Rachel Malig
Production Controller: Andie Trainer
Photography: Andy Sewell
Typesetting: Ana Teodoro, Cantina

Design: Julia Hasting

Printed in China

The publisher would like to thank Roy
Barone and Barbaro Inan at Silk Stockings
Bar (Dalston), Theresa Bebbington, Vanessa
Bird, Shawn Kelley at Cocktail Kingdom,
João Mota, Elizabeth O'Rourke, Ellie Smith,
Tracey Smith, and Phoebe Stephenson for
their contributions to the book.

phaidon.com

978 1 83866 755 9